CRITICAL ACCLAIM FOR
The Best Travel Writing Series

"Travelers' Tales has thrived by seizing on our perpetual fascination for armchair traveling, including this annual roundup of delightful (and sometimes dreadful) wayfaring adventures from all corners of the globe." —*The Washington Post*

"Here are intimate revelations, mind-changing pilgrimages, and body-challenging peregrinations. And there's enough to keep one happily reading until the next edition."
—*San Francisco Chronicle*

"*The Best Travel Writing* is a globetrotter's dream. Some tales are inspiring, some disturbing or disheartening; many sobering. But at the heart of each one lies the most crucial element—a cracking good story told with style, wit, and grace."
—*WorldTrekker*

"There is no danger of tourist brochure writing in this collection. The story subjects themselves are refreshingly odd. . . . For any budding writer looking for good models or any experienced writer looking for ideas on where the form can go, *The Best Travel Writing* is an inspiration." —*Transitions Abroad*

"Travelers' Tales, a publisher which has taken the travel piece back into the public mind as a serious category, has a volume out titled *The Best Travel Writing* which wipes out its best-of competitors completely." —*The Courier-Gazette*

"*The Best Travelers' Tales 2004* will grace my bedside for years to come. For this volume now formally joins the pantheon: one of a series of good books by good people, valid and valuable for far longer than its authors and editors ever imagined. It is, specifically, an ideal antidote to the gloom with which other writers, and the daily and nightly news, have tried hard to persuade us the world is truly invested.... This book is a vivid and delightful testament to just why the world is in essence a wondrously pleasing place, how its people are an inseparable part of its countless pleasures, and how travel is not so much hard work as wondrous *fun*." —Simon Winchester

Travelers' Tales Books

T R A V E L E R S '   T A L E S

THE
BEST
TRAVEL
WRITING
2010

TRUE STORIES
FROM AROUND THE WORLD

TRAVELERS' TALES

THE BEST
TRAVEL WRITING
2010

TRUE STORIES
FROM AROUND THE WORLD

Edited by

JAMES O'REILLY, LARRY HABEGGER,
AND SEAN O'REILLY

Travelers' Tales
an imprint of Solas House, Inc.
Palo Alto

Travelers' Tales and Travelers' Tales Guides are trademarks of
Solas House, Inc.

Credits and copyright notices for the individual articles in this
collection are given starting on page 345.

Art direction: Stefan Gutermuth
Page layout, photo selection and editing: Cynthia Lamb using the
    fonts Granjon and Nicholas Cochin
Interior design: Melanie Haage
Production Director: Christy Quinto

ISBN 1-932361-73-1
ISSN 1548-0224

First Edition
Printed in the United States
10 9 8 7 6 5 4 3 2 1

*Behold, I have set before you an open door
and no man can shut it.*

— REVELATION

Table of Contents

Publisher's Preface

A Meander through Books and the Journeys of Others

My favorite mountaineering book is *The Mountains of My Life*, by legendary Italian climber Walter Bonatti. While I love being in the mountains—it's a rare day I don't daydream about the Alps or the Himalayas—I am not a climber. It isn't so much Bonatti's exploits that inspire me as his attitude towards life, the preeminence he gives to the expression of his deepest instincts (which in his case is represented by a risky ongoing encounter with the natural world). "Courage," he says, "makes a man master of his own fate. It is a civilized, responsible determination not to succumb to impending moral collapse."

This attitude is reflected throughout this year's Best Travel Writing volume, by the many contributors who, like renowned traveler and writer William Dalrymple (whose Introduction follows), are life-long, hardcore travelers. Whether they are explorers (Cameron Smith), expat gourmands (Richard Sterling), modern Don Quixotes (Brad Newsham), cultural bloodhounds (David Peters), or old-fashioned pilgrims (Amy Carlson), they have woven over the years a cloak of experience for others to wear, a kind of divine raiment to protect those who would follow them.

We need such protection, because travel can be hard, despite obvious rewards. It takes time, energy, and at least modest funds. It is natural to want the benefits of travel without the suffering that can accompany it—illness, heartbreak, accidents, loneliness, banditry, simply being worn down by touts and bad buses. But special places do indeed call many of us from the first time we look at a globe, and we should listen, eighteen or eighty, yet be ever mindful of heart and health.

One of my favorite ways to think about travel is jihad, a concept that has become associated, unfortunately, with suicide bombings and IEDs, that is to say the desperate expression of the brainwashed. But *true* jihad has always been a struggle with oneself, against one's worst tendencies, inertia, self-deception, cupidity, laziness, falsehood. It is the struggle to become a better human being. "Discipline is remembering what you want," one saying goes, which might be another way of looking at jihad, and the whole point of jihad, which is character formation—the thrust of Bonatti's alpinism, and something that travel is very, very good for.

Another of my favorite books is *The Meaning of Culture* by John Cowper Powys, in which he makes the claim that reading creates a different kind of human being. Travel does much the same, as you can see through the eyes of the contributors to this book. I hope some of them, and their stories, come to haunt you, just as do some people whom you meet on the road, even briefly, and who then go on to become the shades of your "memory palace." I recall a teenage monk I met in the cold recesses of the Potala Palace in Lhasa in 1988, who told me his plans to escape over the Himalayas to freedom. I recall a spiritually lost Dutch man in Bangkok, drunk with too many beautiful women and drugs; I think of the wide bewildered eyes of a young woman in Kagbeni, Nepal, who'd just seen death close hand during unseasonable late monsoon storms and avalanches. I think of marvelous, generous people in Zimbabwe with improbable names such as Reward and Never. I think of the Egyptian who whispered to me, as though it were a dark secret, near the dusty desert battleground and cemeteries of El Alamein, "I love grass." Where are they now? They have forever enriched my inner landscape, and I bless them in thoughts and prayers.

Recently I've become somewhat obsessed with Rome as I read yet another classic, *A Traveller in Rome* by H. V. Morton.

This is a book which fills me with dismay that I will ever grasp enough history, but which also fills me with awe at the tidal wash of centuries upon Roman stones. No doubt my obsession also has something to do with growing up in a Catholic family, with attending a beloved uncle, a Franciscan priest, as he died in view of St. Peter's, and indeed with my first visit to Rome as a teenager, en route to what I didn't know would be the last time I'd see a close friend. But what does it matter, for I know Rome is calling again, and so are Cairo, Havana, Jerusalem, Kailas, Venice, and Kathmandu, and I shall heed the call.

So onward! in clear-eyed jihad, towards foreign shores, and home again, with stories that bind, as Bonatti's ideal alpinism does, not only "aesthetics, history and ethics," but the mountains of your own life and the love that brought you here, keeps you here, and animates all you do and dream.

"Herein is the way of perfection, to live out each day as one's last, with no fever, no torpor and no acting a part."

—Marcus Aurelius, quoted by H. V. Morton in
A Traveller in Rome

JAMES O'REILLY
PALO ALTO, CALIFORNIA

Introduction

WILLIAM DALRYMPLE

Not long ago, on a visit to the Mani in the Peloponnese, I went to visit the headland where the great travel writer Bruce Chatwin had asked for his ashes to be scattered.

The hillside chapel where Chatwin's widow, Elizabeth, brought his urn, lies in rocky fields near the village of Exchori, high above the bay of Kardamyli. It has a domed, red-tiled roof and round arcaded windows built from stone the color of haloumi cheese. Inside are faded and flaking Byzantine frescoes of mounted warrior saints, lances held aloft.

The sun was slowly sinking over the Taygetus at the end of a hot day, and there was a warm smell of wild rosemary and cypress resin in the air. From the higher slopes, the distant peal of goat bells cut through the drowsy whirr of cicadas. It was, I thought, a perfect, beautiful, peaceful place for anyone to rest at the end of their travels.

My companion for the visit was Chatwin's great friend and sometime mentor, Patrick Leigh Fermor, who for me at least was Chatwin's only real rival as the greatest prose stylist of modern travel writing. Paddy's two sublime masterpieces, *A Time to Keep Silence* and *A Time of Gifts*, are among the most beautifully written books of travel of any period, and it was really he who created the persona of the bookish wanderer, later adopted by Chatwin: the footloose scholar in the wilds, scrambling through remote mountains, a knapsack full of good books on his shoulder.

Inevitably, it was a melancholy visit. Not only were we there to honor the memory of the dead friend who had introduced us, Paddy himself was not in great shape. At dinner that night, it was clear that the great writer and war hero, now in his mid-nineties, was in very poor health:

"I'm deaf," he told me as we sat eating in the moonlight, looking out through the arches of Paddy's cloister to the olive groves beyond. "That's the awful truth. That's why I'm leaning towards you in this rather eerie fashion. I do have a hearing aid, but when I go swimming I always forget about it until I'm two strokes out, and then it starts singing at me. I get out and suck it, and with luck all is well. But both of them have gone now."

From below came the crash of the sea on the pebbles of the foreshore of the bay. "Glasses too," he added, taking a swig of retsina. "Running out of those very quickly. Occasionally the one that is lost is found, but their numbers slowly diminish…" He trailed off: "The amount that can go wrong at this age—you've no idea. My memory—anything like a date or a proper name just takes wing, and quite often never comes back. Even Winston Churchill—couldn't remember his name last week. Terrific nuisance."

Over dinner we talked about how travel writing seemed to have faded from view since its great moment of acclaim in the late 1970s and 80s, when both Paddy and Bruce had made their names and their reputations. It wasn't just that publishers were not as receptive as they had once been to the genre, nor that stores like Waterstone's and Borders had contracted their literary travel writing sections from prominent shelves at the storefront to a little annex at the back, usually lost under a great phalanx of Lonely Planet guidebooks. More seriously, and certainly more irreversibly, the great travel writers who I grew up reading were all dying.

The best of them had certainly had a good innings. Wilfred Thesiger (born 1910), who was in many ways the last of the great Victorian explorers, produced no less than four remarkable books in his final decade before departing on his final trek in 2003, at the age of ninety-three. More remarkable still, Norman Lewis was heading for his centenary when he published *The Happy Ant-Heap* in 1998, a characteristically bleak collection of pieces about trips to places so obscure, so uncomfortable and often so horrible, that they would tax anyone, never mind a man in his early nineties who should by rights have been shuffling around in carpet slippers with his colostomy bag, not planning trips to visit the smoked ancestral corpses of the highlands of Irian Jaya, or the torture chambers of Nicaragua, or any other of the grisly diversions Lewis settles upon to bring "some stimulation and variety" to his old age.

One typical adventure of the nonagenarian Lewis took place on a trip to Kos. On reading a story in the local paper about a police investigation into rumors that "women on the small island of Anirini were disposing of unwanted husbands by throwing them down dry wells," Lewis merrily set off on a boat with three sponge fishermen and a prostitute they had picked up on the Piraeus waterfront ("they spent the crossing sleeping, eating and making love—the last on a strict rota") in search of this barren island populated by homicidal widows. Before long Lewis, then aged ninety-two, had hopped ashore, rented a room from one of the chief suspects, and was soon cheerfully peering down well-heads in search of rotting cadavers.

Since then, however, the world of literary travel writing, once associated with the drumbeat of hooves across some distant steppe, has begun echoing instead with the slow tread of the undertaker's muffled footfall. Within the last few years, as well as Thesiger and Lewis, Ryszard Kapuscinski and Eric Newby have both followed Bruce Chatwin on their last journey. Others—notably Jan Morris—have put down their pens or busied themselves with a final bout of anthologizing.

All this is a long way from the optimism of the scene twenty years ago, in 1989, when I published my first travel book, *In Xanadu*. At that time, the travel writing boom was one of the most important developments in publishing. The success of Paul Theroux's *The Great Railway Bazaar*, with its sales of 1.5 million copies, had dramatically breathed new life into the sort of travel memoir that had flourished in an earlier age, but which had languished since the European empires imploded after the second world war. Its success inspired Chatwin to give up his job on *The Sunday Times Magazine* and to go off to South America. The result—*In Patagonia*—was published in 1977, the same year Leigh Fermor produced *A Time of Gifts*. The final breakthrough came in 1984 with the publication of the celebrated Travel Writing issue of *Granta*: "Travel writing is undergoing a revival," wrote Bill Buford, *Granta*'s editor, "evident not only in the busy reprinting of the travel classics, but in the staggering number of new travel writers emerging. Not since the 1930s has travel writing been so popular or so important..."

Travel writing was suddenly where the action was, and it remained so for nearly ten years. Among writers the form became popular for it re-emerged at a time of disenchantment with the novel, and seemed to present a serious alternative to fiction. A writer could still use the techniques of the novel—develop characters, select and tailor experience into a series of scenes and set pieces, arrange the action so as to give the narrative shape and momentum—yet what was being written about was all true; moreover, unlike most literary fiction, it sold.

Two decades later, however, the climate in the more elitist literary circles has long changed from enthusiasm to one of mild boredom. Academics have begun accusing travel writers of orientalism and cultural imperialism, while Theroux was himself one of the first to express his dislike of the publishing Leviathan he had helped create: in his most recent travel book, *Ghost Train to the Eastern Star*, he writes that the travel book is: "Little better than a license to bore...the lowest form of literary self-indulgence: dishonest complaining, creative mendacity, pointless heroics, and chronic posturing."

This seems to me to be a deeply myopic and mistaken way of looking at what is, after all, one of the world's oldest and most universal forms of literature: along with heroic poetry, the quest takes us right back to man's deepest literary roots, to the *Epic of Gilgamesh*, the wanderings of Abraham in the Old Testament, and the journeyings of the Pandava brothers in the *Mahabharata*. Over time, like poetry, but unlike the novel, the travel book has appeared in almost all the world's cultures, from the wanderings of Li Po in Japan, through to the medieval topographies of Marco Polo, Hiuen Tsang, Ibn Jubayr, and Ibn Battuta. Moroever, as Colin Thubron has pointed out, it is ridiculously simplistic to see all attempts at studying, observing, and empathizing with another culture necessarily "as an act of domination—rather than of understanding, respect or even catharsis... If even the attempt to understand is seen as aggression or appropriation, then all human contact declines into paranoia."

It is also true that travelers tend often by their very natures to be rebels and outcasts and misfits: far from being an act of cultural imperialism, setting out alone and vulnerable on the road is often an expression of rejection of home and an embrace of the other: the history of travel is full of individuals who have fallen in love with other cultures and other parts of the world in this way. As the great French traveler, Nicolas Bouvier wrote in *The Way of the World,* the experience of being on the road, "deprived of one's usual setting, the customary routine stripped away like so much wrapping paper" reduces you, yet makes you at the same time more "open to curiosity, to intuition, to love at first sight... Traveling outgrows its motives. It soon proves sufficient in itself. You think you are making a trip, but soon it is making you—or unmaking you."

The question is often asked, however, whether travel writing now has a future: the tales of medieval travelers such as

Marco Polo, or the explorations of "Bukhara Burnes" may have contained valuable empirical information impossible to harvest elsewhere; but is there really any point to the genre in the age of the internet, when you can instantly gather reliable knowledge about anywhere in the globe at the click of a mouse? Why bother with someone else's subjective opinions, when hard information about the world is now so easily available? Why read a travel book when you can just go on Google Earth and look for yourself?

These are all issues I have been pondering as I have been writing *Nine Lives: In Search of the Sacred in Modern India,* my first travel book after fifteen years away writing history, which looks at how India's diverse religious and mystical traditions have been caught and transformed in a vortex of rapid change that has engulfed South Asia in recent years. Much, of course, has been written about how India is moving forward and transforming itself at the most incredible rate—the economy has been predicted to overtake that of the U.S. by 2050—but so far little has been said about the way these huge earthquakes have affected traditional religion in India.

Nine Lives explores this process through nine personal stories—a Sufi, a possession dancer, a Buddhist monk, a Jain nun, a tantric and so on, each story aiming to show how faith and ritual are clinging on in the face of India's commercial boom. Each life represents a different religious path. The idea is to find out what it means to be a holy man, a mystical musician, or a tantric minstrel seeking salvation on the roads of modern India as the Tata trucks thunder past. Researching the book has brought home to me just how quickly and strangely the world is changing.

Two years ago, for example, I managed to track down a celebrated tantric at a cremation ground near Birbhum in West Bengal. Tapan Goswami was a feeder of skulls. Twenty years ago he had been interviewed by an American professor of comparative religion, who went on to write a scholarly essay on Tapan's practice of spirit-summoning and spell-casting, using the cured skulls of dead virgins and restless suicides. It sounded rich material, albeit of a rather sinister nature, so I spent the best part of a day touring the various cremation grounds of Birbhum before finally finding Tapan sitting outside his small Kali temple on the edge of the town, preparing a sacrifice for the goddess.

The sun was sinking, and the light was beginning to fade; a funeral pyre was still smoking eerily in front of the temple. Tapan and I talked of tantra, and he confirmed that in his youth, when the professor had interviewed him, he had indeed been an enthusiastic skull-feeder. Yes, he said, all that had been written about him was true, and yes, he did occasionally still cure skulls, and summon their dead owners, so as to use their power. But sadly, he said, he could not talk to me about the details. Why was that? I asked. Because, he said, his two sons were now successful ophthalmologists in New Jersey. They had firmly forbidden him from giving any more interviews about what he did in case rumors of the family dabbling in Black Magic damaged their profitable East Coast practice. Now he thought he might even give away his skulls, and go and join them in the States.

It has been in the course of conversations such as this that I have come to realize what a major role there still is for the travel writer in a fast changing world. As the desperation of the Western world to comprehend events in the Middle East and Central Asia since 9/11 has shown so clearly, the sensation we have of knowing the world today is largely an illusion: in reality we simply don't know nearly as much about the world as we thought. The sense of information omnipotence that we have had through the internet and Google Earth has proved horribly illusory, and we now realize that there are in fact huge areas of the world about which we know absolutely nothing. As print media shrinks, and television becomes ever more obsessed with celebrity, travel writing stands out as one place where the individual can really assess another culture in some depth, without using academic jargon or disappearing down a well of academic over-specialization.

For the travel book remains a vessel into which a wonderfully varied cocktail of ingredients can be poured: politics, archaeology, history, philosophy, art, or magic. You can cross-fertilize the genre with other literary forms: biography, or anthropological writing; or, more perhaps interesting still, following in Chatwin's footsteps and muddying the boundaries of fiction and non-fiction by crossing the travel book with some of the wilder forms of the novel.

Certainly, if nineteenth-century travel writing was principally about place—about filling in the blanks of the map and describing remote places that few had seen—the best twenty-first-century travel writing is almost always about people: exploring the extraordinary diversity that still exists in the world beneath the veneer of globalization.

Rory Stewart, perhaps the most highly regarded of the younger generation of travel writers, believes passionately that travel books allow writers to explore other cultures in a slow and unhurried way that is impossible with most other forms of non-fiction. Stewart is quite clear that travel writing has a more important role than ever: "Just look what gets written about Afghanistan," he says. "In an age when journalism is becoming more and more etiolated, when articles are becoming shorter and shorter, usually lacking all historical context, travel writing is one of the few venues to write with some complexity about an alien culture. An Obama speech, a foreign policy paper, or a counterinsurgency briefing minimizes differences, and the same phrases like 'failed states' are used to link countries which are actually very different such as Yemen, Afghanistan or Pakistan.

"But the best sort of travel book with its imaginative empathy and depiction of individuals inhabiting a landscape helps the reader to live through and understand the possibility of cultural difference. You can deploy paradox and incongruity, and use encounters with individuals to suggest complex problems within foreign societies. Above all you can leave things unexplained, and admit ignorance and uncertainty, and stress the fundamental problems of communication in a way that is almost never seen in policy documents or journalism. What kills so many briefing documents and newspaper reports, apart from their tendency to exaggerate fears and aggrandize ambitions, is their aspiration towards omniscience, and their impatience with everything that is intractable or mysterious. Travel writing provides a space for all these things."

Stewart is also sure that the kind of travel writing which is showing particular durability is that where an informed observer roots and immerses himself in one place, committing time to get to know a place and its languages. Many of the greatest of the travel books of the late twentieth century were about epic journeys, often by young men, conveying the raw intoxication of travel during a moment in life when time is endless, and deadlines and commitments are nonexistent; when experience is all you hope to achieve and when the world is laid out before you like a map: think of the exhilaration of Eric Newby's *A Short Walk in the Hindu Kush* or Robert Byron's *The Road to Oxiana*.

Today, however, some of the most interesting travel books are by individuals who have made extended stays in places, getting to know them intimately: books like Iain Sinclair's circling of the capital in *London Orbital* or Sam Miller's *Delhi: Adventures in a Megacity*. There is also Amitav Ghosh in his Egyptian village in *In an Antique Land*, or Chris de Bellaigue's magnificent recent study, *Rebel Land*, which examines the way that the ghosts of the Armenian genocide and Kurdish nationalism haunt a single remote town in eastern Turkey. As the travel writer, novelist, and critic Pankaj Mishra puts it, in a more globalized post-colonial world the traveler "needs to train his eye in the way an ethnographer does...to remain relevant and stimulating, travel writing has to take on board some of the sophisticated knowledge available about these complex societies, about their religions, history, economy, and politics."

Colin Thubron, perhaps the most revered of all the travel writers of the eighties still at work, is also clear that travel writing is now more needed than ever: "Great swathes of the world are hardly visited and remain much misunderstood—think of Iran. It's no accident that the mess inflicted on the world by the last U.S. administration was done by a group of men who had hardly traveled, and relied for information on policy documents and the reports of journalists sitting interviewing middle class contacts in capital cities. The sympathetic traveler who takes time to immerse himself in a country may gain not only factual knowledge but also a sensuous and emotional understanding, and convey a people's psychology and their response to things in a way that can never be accessed by studying in a library. A good travel writer can give you the warp and weft of everyday life, the generalities of people's existence that is rarely reflected in academic writing or journalism, and hardly touched upon by any other discipline. Despite the internet and the revolution in communications, there is still no substitute for a good piece of travel writing."

Certainly, there seems to be a remarkable amount of good travel writing going on, such as Suketu Mehta's Bombay book, *Maximum City*, one of the greatest city books ever written, in my opinion, while Alice Albinia's wonderful *Empires of the Indus* is a breathtaking debut by an author who writes enviably cadent and beautiful prose, but has nerves of steel and the pluck of a twenty-first-century Freya Stark. I hugely admire Pankaj Mishra's *Temptations of the West: How to Be Modern in India, Pakistan and Beyond,* am currently reading Christopher de Bellaigue's extraordinary book on eastern Turkey, *Rebel Land: Among Turkey's Forgotten Peoples*. Then there is Geoff Dyer's playful novel-cum-travel book *Jeff in Venice, Death in Varanasi* and the work of Rory Stewart, *The Prince of the Marshes* and *The Places in Between,* the latter a particular favorite of mine.

To these names can be added the remarkable crop of new writers collected by James O'Reilly, Larry Habegger, and Sean O'Reilly in the latest installment of their annual Best Travel Writing series. The 2010 volume truly encompasses the globe from Viking feasts and rotting meat in Iceland through sex in Skyros to hot dogs in Saigon; from Pico Iyer's characteristically subtle thoughts on the Japanese mind while wandering around old Kyoto to Martin Mitchinson's old fashioned adventure story of nearly dying in a Darien dugout. The sheer range of writing on show here, from yarns of traveling machismo, through art historical detective work to strippers and bored Japanese housewives shows just how varied and lively and energetic the travel writing scene is today.

This wonderful anthology shows that Paul Theroux's obituary to travel writing is long premature. Perhaps it should be his close friend Jonathan Raban who is given the last word of retort: "Old travelers grumpily complain that travel is now dead and that the world is a suburb. They are quite wrong. Lulled by familiar resemblances between all the unimportant things, they meet the brute differences in everything of importance."

≫﹩ ≫﹩ ≫﹩

William Dalrymple was born in Scotland and brought up on the shores of the Firth of Forth. He wrote the highly-acclaimed best-seller In Xanadu *when he was twenty-two. In 1989, Dalrymple moved to Delhi where he lived for six years researching his second book,* City of Djinns, *which won the 1994 Thomas Cook Travel Book Award.* From the Holy Mountain, *his acclaimed study of the demise of Christianity in its Middle Eastern homeland, was awarded the Scottish Arts Council Autumn Book Award for 1997. In 2002, he was awarded the Mungo Park Medal by the Royal Scottish Geographical Society for his "outstanding contribution to travel literature."* White Mughals *won the Wolfson Prize for History 2003 and the Scottish Book of the Year Prize. A collection of his writings about India,* The Age of Kali, *won the French Prix D'Astrolabe in 2005. In 2007,* The Last Moghal *won the Duff Cooper Prize for History and Biography. His most recent book,* Nine Lives: In Search of the Sacred in Modern India, *is published by Knopf. Dalrymple is a Fellow of the Royal Society of Literature and of the Royal Asiatic Society, and is the founder and co-director of the Jaipur Literature Festival. He is married to the artist Olivia Fraser, and they have three children. They live on a farm outside Delhi.*

꼭 꼭 꼭

Saigon Trio

An expatriate war vet tastes many things,
and finds them worthy.

I. SIX DEGREES

WELL, JUNK FOOD HAS COME TO VIETNAM. I KNEW IT
would. It started with fast food. Colonel Sanders came to
town a few years ago and has become firmly rooted. And it's a
mark of higher status here to dine with the Colonel. Yes, you
read that right. In a country whose annual per capita income
is less than a thousand dollars, it's a feather in your cap to have
your birthday party at, or catered by, "KFC Food Shop." The
Korean-owned Lotteria burger chain came at about the same
time. BK and McD are expected soon.

But it's gone beyond fast food. Bud and (sigh) Bud Light
appeared a few months ago, and with a marketing budget
equal to the GDP of a small country. We've also got mi-
crowave popcorn, all kinds of chips and dips, every kind of

soda pop you've ever heard of and many you haven't, Indian sweets, Japanese crisps, Chinese things that go crunch in your mouth, all of those menacing munchables that have salt, sugar, fat, and ill health as common denominators. And hot dogs. Locally made hot dogs, in fact!

Now, I never eat fast food. And I rarely do more than nibble a chip, sniff at a dip, or politely refuse the others. But a hot dog, now, that's a different breed of cat, to me. Yeah, yeah, I know, nitrates and sodium, cow's lips and pig's ears. And sure, you don't want to see the things being made. But as far back as I can remember going to the movies, I can remember the snack bar where hot dogs were rolling on that tubular grill. Picnic equaled hot dog, ball game equaled hot dog, hot dog equaled childhood bliss. I live in one of the culinary centers of the earth. I dine, and have always dined, in some of the best restaurants anywhere, serving some of the finest chow you could ever ask for. But when I want a dog, I gotta have me a dog. Mustard, kraut, maybe some relish or a pickle spear. Chopped onions are good, too. And while beer is my nectar, I like an ice-cold Pepsi with a dog. *Mmmmm.* And I can tell you that I had me a dog just before I sat down to write you this letter. It got my juices going, see?

So to get down to my story, I found out that Charlie Wong was selling hot dogs from a little old pushcart stand down on De Tham Street, in the backpacker district here in Saigon. "He's just outside the little convenience store that sells junk food, deodorant, and toilet paper to tourists," the report went.

I didn't know Charlie at the time, though I knew who he was. They call him the "King of Hot Dogs." Expats here are often aware of each other even though they haven't met. Charlie is an educated man, of Chinese extraction via Malaysia and the U.K., and owner of a proper sit-down restaurant somewhere in the city. And he supplies hot dogs to all the big movie houses in town. He set up his hot dog stand on De Tham as a hobby. He likes the street life, as I do. He likes to press the flesh with his customers. And he likes hot dogs.

I was down in the district last week, teaching yet another bartender how to make a proper drink. It's easy to teach the ingredients and procedure. It's teaching them that pouring short is not in their long-term interest. They might skim a few pennies per drink that way, but they'll gain more in tips when regulars know that they can expect an honest, or even a generous, pour. This operating philosophy is repeatedly borne out in my regular watering holes where I have to ask for extra tonic in my gin and tonic. So I was pressing this point at the Cyclo bar on Pham Ngu Lao Street when a dire dog deficiency struck. Hadda have a dog! I remembered the reports of Charlie Wong. I headed for De Tham Street.

And there he was, the King himself, tending to a three-foot by four-foot pushcart. The top half was glass, and held the dogs in a steam box, just like at the county fair or the amusement park. The bottom half was emblazoned with the proud logo: Red Hot Saigon.

"You're Charlie Wong," I said. "I've heard about you."

"I know you, too," he said. "I've seen your picture. Hot dog?"

"Yeah. Regular size. Mustard and kraut."

He plucked one from the box. He deftly slipped it into a bun, slathered it with yellow mustard, and dressed it with pungent kraut. He expertly wrapped half its length in white paper and handed me the finished product. I bit into that puppy and the juice burst in my mouth, and the mustard sang on my tongue while the kraut crunched between my teeth and gave up its tangy goodness. I tell you, I was lost in Dog Heaven for a few bites. I was about to tell Charlie how good it was when he said, "I read one of your books."

"Oh? Which one?"

"*The Fire Never Dies*."

"Like it?" I inquired between bites.

"Parts. Especially interested in the story about your romance with the woman named Fatima at Penang, Malaysia. You even wrote about the oxtail soup you had at the E&O Hotel."

Ahhh, Fatima and Chef Lim's oxtail soup. In fact, a painting of Fatima graces the cover of the book Charlie had read. It was my first doomed romance, back in the early '70s. She was a Muslim Malay and I was a G.I. And nothing could go wrong with that affair but the ending, which was completely beyond her control and mine, and was preordained the moment we met. Long story short about Charlie's reference, in the course of the affair, there was a dinner at the grand old E&O Hotel, a holdover of the British Empire and oozing history and romance. It was also my first oxtail soup. Callow country bumpkin that I was, I had never had anything quite so expertly and professionally prepared. I think I had never had anything so delicious. And this in the midst of an affair never so intense or exotic.

I still had a mouthful of hot dog when Charlie mentioned Fatima, and Lim's oxtail soup. Memories long dormant flooded into my mind, into my heart, and into my mouth. I could suddenly see Fatima standing beside me, wearing her signature red sarong, long black hair cascading down her shoulders. And despite the mustard, kraut, and all else, I was tasting the oxtail soup. And I was tasting memory. And I was tasting love. I was tasting all that's good in life.

I swallowed what was still in my mouth, then began to wrap up the remnants in the white paper. When you're tasting memory, it's best not to taste anything else. Charlie, seeing this, asked if there was a problem with the dog.

"No," I said. "And no disrespect to your dog. But I'm thinking about that oxtail soup, and all that went with it. I'm still remembering that soup thirty-five years after the fact. If I'm alive thirty-five years from now, I doubt I'll remember this dog, but I'll still remember that soup."

"Yeah," he said. "I remember the soup, too."

"How's 'at?" I said in confusion. Charlie didn't seem old enough to remember a soup served at the E&O in the early '70s.

"My dad made that soup for you."

"Say what?"

"Chef Wong Lim. He was executive chef at the E&O at that time. And that was his secret recipe. He developed it over some years until it was perfect. I remembered it as I read your story."

"Say what?"

"Six months before you arrived in Penang, Queen Elizabeth and Prince Phillip stayed at the E&O and my dad served them that same oxtail soup. From his reports, I'd say they liked it almost as much as you did. Of course they didn't have the seasoning of a star-crossed romance."

Suddenly, the remnants of my hot dog seemed awfully humble, and yet important. I had been brought to a living connection with one of the most beautiful nights of my life by a cheap sausage. By a hunk of junk food. I didn't know whether to throw it to the curb or freeze-dry and frame it. So I took it home. And I ate it. But despite the mustard and the kraut, all I tasted was oxtail soup, love, and excitement. It's a bad pun, but a link was a link this time.

Charlie gave me a very rich gift after that dog on De Tham Street. He sent me his late father's secret recipe for oxtail soup, the same as enjoyed by Elizabeth and Phillip, me, and many others. I now send it on to you.

Chef Wong Lim's Oxtail Soup

2 oxtails, cut into 2-inch rounds
5 large onions, roughly chopped
5 cloves of garlic, minced
300 grams of ginger, peeled and sliced
2 or 3 *pandan* leaves
5 star anise pods (*bung lawang*)
One 2-inch cinnamon stick
5 tbsp meat curry powder
5 tbsp flour
Salt and pepper
1 tbsp brown sugar
Minced spring onions (for garnish)
Minced celery (for garnish)
5 liters water

Method

1. Blanch oxtail rounds in a pot of boiling water, then drain well.
2. Heat up a saucepan, pour in some oil, fry the onions, garlic, and ginger till fragrant or light brown.
3. Stir in the *pandan* leaves, star anise, cinnamon, curry powder, and flour, and stir-fry till brown (do not burn).
4. Pour in the water. Bring to a boil and stir to make sure all ingredients are well mixed and dissolved in the water.
5. Add the oxtail rounds, reduce the heat, and simmer gently until soup is thick and oxtail is tender, 2 to 3 hours.
6. Stir in the brown sugar and salt and pepper to taste.
7. Garnish the soup with the spring onions and celery.
8. Pour the soup into an empty coconut (cut a slit in the top of the coconut to empty it).
9. Wrap the whole coconut in foil.
10. Steam the whole thing for at least 8 to 10 hours.
11. Bring it out and serve.

II. A DOLLAR AND A DIME

You've always got to have "small money" in your pocket. In Vietnam or any other "Third World" country, any poor country, you need small money. There are too many people who simply can't or won't break a five. Or a six, as the case may be. Here in Vietnam, for example, we have the 50,000-dong note. A laughably big number for a sum that amounts to a three-dollar bill. Years ago I asked a beggar here, when he pressed me for alms, for change of a 50,000-dong note. More the fool I. The poor old sod had maybe one one-hundredth of that in his krinkly, wrinkled hands. Then there was the time in Mexico when I was pulled over by a traffic cop. I earnestly tried to convince him that the stop sign was hidden by the tree (so providently placed), and so I couldn't see it. He politely responded, "It's not much money, señor." The smallest I had was a tenner. I asked him if he had change. He might have had a pocket full of ones and fives, but the answer was, of course, a smiling "Sorry, señor." I ponied up the ten-spot. Lesson learned. Carry small money. Always, carry small money.

I need small money every day. Even at home in apartment 608 in "suburban" Saigon. I tip the beer delivery guy sixty cents. Bills don't come in the mail; somebody rings your doorbell and collects. Water, electricity, and internet are not big but not small. But the guy who sweeps the halls collects twenty-five cents per apartment per month. The elevators operate as a concession: buck and a quarter per head per month. In the event of a power outage (which happens about once a month) we are dunned a few pennies for the emergency generator that keeps the elevator concession operating. That's another ring of the bell and the need for small money. Processing the receipts I require can cost more than the fees collected, so they write them out by hand on scraps of note paper that has already been used on the other side.

Out on the town it's the beggars, the street vendors who offer sandwiches at thirty cents apiece, candy money for neighborhood kids, a dime's worth of dong for the newspaper girl, an errand run by someone with no other useful labor to perform, and the motorbike taxi drivers. They are known as *xe om* drivers and they usually drive a small 100cc bike. I need these guys every day. They are quicker than a taxi, as they can split lanes, and they tend to know the streets better. You often have to wait for a taxi, but on any busy intersection a clutch of *xe om* drivers are sitting astride (or sometimes napping on) their idle bikes waiting patiently (or resignedly) for a fare. And they are cheaper than a taxi. They zip me across town for 20,000 dong, about a dollar and a dime. Small money.

Most of the *xe om* drivers are poor men driving second-hand bikes. Many are sixty-year-old veterans of the losing side of the war. Others might be farmers from the delta who went bust. Still others might be skilled or unskilled laborers when the work is available. On a good day the *xe om* might net five dollars. He'll put in ten hours a day, but gas isn't cheap. His local Vietnamese patrons pay less than I do. And he has to render unto Caesar in the forms of both local police and local mafia. Whether he makes any money or not. If he wants to keep his bike, which may be a loaner or a rental. And on his meager income he must support himself and maybe a family.

Of course not all are poor. Some are "middle class" young men trying to while away their free time and earn a little folding money. The poor guys hate them, for obvious reasons. But, hey, everyone's out for a buck. Right? Some, like my regular daytime guy "Joe," are entrepreneurs. He gathers a posse of less enterprising drivers, and then establishes a relationship with guys like me. His drivers have the prospect of a few fares a day and I have a driver waiting at the door who already knows where I want to go and how to get there. I don't know what cut of the small money Joe gets or how many guys he has, but he's doing well by the local measure. His bike is one of the better models. Joe protects his turf, too.

One time a threadbare outsider in need of a shave and a hair-cut tried to pick me up at the front door on a beat-up old bike. Joe came at him screaming like a banshee and threatening to bean the guy with his brand new fancy helmet. A loud discussion ensued. Joe grabbed me by the arm and tried to drag me to his side. I threw off his grip and told the both of them to go to hell. I stomped off and found a neutral set of wheels to get me to where I was going. I punished Joe with a boycott for considering me his personal resource. But I relented after two days. He's just too handy. And small money, too!

Well, I had a tiff with the landlady the other day, and it was about money somewhat bigger than small. A simple mix-up with the internet bill. "Make trouble for MEEEEEEE!" she wailed, and looked daggers at me. Hells bells, it wasn't even my fault. It was the one-eyed internet bill collector who mixed up the mix-up. But her highness had only one person's troubles in mind: MEEEEEE! "Now I have to talk to the man," she complained. Which meant she would have to put on a pair of her Imelda Marcos shoes and walk across the street. And then who would be left to sit idly on the stoop and collect the rents of a dozen or more properties while sipping tea and munching melon seeds? One thing for sure, it wasn't going to be MEEEEEEE!

In order to sort out the mess I had to zip across town to the internet people to make sure they know that it is I, the foreigner, who lives at 608 and not some local guy with a similar address. Joe's posse were all out on various runs. But before a nefarious interloper with patched pants and broken teeth could scoop me up on a battered old bike, Joe roared up between us and I hopped on his ride. I was in a hurry. I had no patience for the competition. If the competition isn't Johnny on the spot, then it's Joey on the spot for me, thought I. I'm willing to help a poor guy out now and then, but dammit, he's got to be quick.

We caromed across town at top speed until I was deposited

at the requisite offices of the august operators of the www. I told Joe not to wait, not knowing how long this would take. Turns out it wasn't long. They had got their money from the other guy. Having got theirs, they were satisfied. So I came out of the office and saw that I had a choice of half a dozen drivers all vying for my custom. I recognized a broken-down old guy I call Sam. I'd used him a couple of times before. He knew the way home. Joe gives him the stink-eye when he comes around, but I don't like to get involved in their disputes. I summoned him. He putted up to me on what must have been at least a ten-year-old bike. Doesn't even have an electric starter like virtually all the newer ones have nowadays. And it needs a bit of upkeep. So does he.

So when he pulled up he lifted a piece of white terry cloth from the rear seat of his bike. Keeps the tropical sun off the black leatherette, making it much cooler for sitting on. Nice touch, Sam. On the way home we had to stop at traffic lights. He made a point of pulling up short in order to pause under the trees that line the main roads of the city, for a bit of cooling shade. Nice touches, I think. Too bad he doesn't have a posse. I figured maybe I'd talk to Joe about him. Give the old guy a break.

And then we arrived back at 608, Chung Cu, Ngo Tat To Street. I dismounted. I removed the helmet that he is legally required to provide for my safety. I reached into my pocket for the dollar and a dime that he had earned. And all I had was big money. It is my habit, whenever going out the door, to check the contents of my money pocket for both the total amount as well as the presence of small money. But I had been in such a hurry, and been distracted. And now I was going to pay the price. I could just hear that Mexican traffic cop snickering and saying, "It's not much money, señor." Well that's not the point, is it? I don't like being taken for a ride after being taken for a ride. And if they know you've paid too much once, they'll make up reasons for you to pay too much in the future.

Knowing the answer, I handed him the smallest I had, a "three-dollar bill," and asked if he had change. "No," he said, with eyes downcast in acceptable humility. I shoved it toward him in a gesture that said, "Well then take it, you son-of-a-bitch." With a certain delicacy he accepted the 50,000-dong note, switched off his bike and dismounted. Without saying anything, his little half helmet still on his head, he padded over to a nearby sidewalk café and asked for change of the big money. They shooed him away for a barefoot beggar. I figured they would. They usually do. Two more cafés yielded him one dismissive gesture and one shout to go away. He was standing in the street with the big money in his hand and no-where to go. He looked my way and saw that I was standing in the midday tropic sun and sweating bullets, my patience wearing thin. I was about to give him the finger and retreat into the air-con comfort of 608 where a cold beer and a hot female companion were waiting for me. Lunch, too.

He padded back to where I stood. He handed me back the big money. Using one of about a dozen words in his English lexicon he said, "Tomorrow." In my hot and distracted state I didn't quite grasp the import of what he was saying. I was even a little irritated, as I wouldn't be in town tomorrow. "Tomorrow no good," I said. It was Monday, but he didn't know how to say Wednesday, so he said, "Next tomorrow." Then it sank in, that this man who probably lived in a single room and dined on broken rice and tasted beer or whiskey only on feast days was going to lend me the not insignificant sum of a dollar and a dime.

Consider: I could easily stiff this guy for a dollar and a dime, and he knew it. What could be his remedy, after all? Call a cop? People here gladly pay money not to deal with the cops. And who would the cop believe? The one who could pay him to believe. Yell at me when he sees me and badmouth me to his fellows? I could just avoid his corner. Come to 608 and try something bold? I could sic Joe on him. Or maybe take me to court? Yeah, right. Small claims court, right? It doesn't even exist here. Even though, for him, it's no small claim. A dollar and a dime is a meal his family doesn't eat. It's half a tank of gas he can't buy. It's tribute he can't render unto Caesar, whether he makes a buck or not.

What he could do is rightfully claim that he couldn't make change, and that it was my fault for not carrying small money like any other resident of the city. But he didn't. Instead, he decided to trust me. Man to man he was going to trust me for two days for 20 to 25 percent of his daily bread.

He nodded to me and once again said, "Next tomorrow." And then the little shoeless man who had the heart to lend me a dollar and a dime mounted his rusty steed and rode away. I tell you, a lesson in humility can be a bitter pill to swallow. But under this day's mad-dog noonday sun, it came with one cool, sweet drink of water.

III. GOOD TATERS
The south-facing balcony is my favorite feature of apartment 608 here on "No Tattoo Street." It's at the perfect height to observe both street life below, and such things as New Year's fireworks above. And it provides me a front row seat for the fireworks of the magnificent lightning and thunder shows of the rainy season, now underway. When that starts, I drop whatever I'm doing, pour a glass of wine and settle in to watch the pas de deux of Zeus and Thor in Asian skies.

Now, on calm and sunny days I often stand out there and dreamily watch the waters of the nearby canal empty into the Saigon River. The Saigon is one of the many branches of the mighty Mekong River as it splits into the several arms of the delta. I navigated that river in wartime. Many powerful memories still lurk in its eddies and swirls and its brown water rushes. There was a time when gazing at it from 608 might have sometimes given me the fever, or the need of a strong drink. But those days are gone. I've worked through those things, for the most part. The river rolls over

them. Sure, sometimes I have a moment of sadness, but with
the river's current it passes. The moment floats by. But the
thought that has been coming to me these last few months,
as I watch the river, has been of my old G.I. buddy Charlie
Motz. He plied these same waters during the war. If I climb
to the top of my building on a clear day I can just see his old
station, to the east.

Charlie came home from the war with his mind and soul
full of screaming demons. They never let him have a night's
sleep. He tried to drown them with booze. They drank it
up. He tried to kill them with drugs. They ate them for
breakfast and then screamed in his ears for more. He tried
to push them out of his body by overeating. They belched
contentedly. He thought about blowing his head off, just to
spite the evil things.

And then he met a man who taught him how to meditate.
It wasn't a Buddhist or Hindu-transcendental sort of meditation. It came from a Sufi tradition. Now the Sufi are Persian/
Iranian. That's Muslim. I don't know how that works. I don't
know how any kind of meditation works, frankly. I plead
total ignorance. But it gave Charlie some degree of peace. He
could get a night's sleep. He still chain-smoked and overate,
but he could sleep. And he could laugh again.

The guy who taught Charlie how to meditate was a pretty
serious sort of Sufi guy. I'm not sure what that means, but
some things are not there for me to be sure of. He told Charlie
that to be a better Sufi meditator, he should take a Sufi name.
Charlie thought that was fair enough. So the guy gave Charlie
the Sufi name Sherdyl. "Rhymes with 'sure deal'," the newly
named Sherdyl always said. I've always been skeptical of foreign religions and strange names, at least for us Americans.
But if it gave Sherdyl sleep and laughter, if not complete
peace, I'll just thank the Sufi guy.

Sherdyl and I became participants in a writing program for
war vets organized by the writer Maxine Hong Kingston. She
had been my creative writing teacher in college, so she asked

me to be her assistant. Sherdyl, like the other vets, was there to learn how to turn some of his war experience into literature. We wrote a lot of good stuff together. The best of it was compiled into a book called *Veterans of War, Veterans of Peace*.

The project ran for about three years. During that time we had a few social occasions. I remember one time we had a potluck lunch. I had brought a dish of potatoes, diced and cooked in a sauce of coconut cream, ground nuts, chile, and curry spices. It was something I just threw together with what I had on hand. My kitchen is a place of continuous improvisation or, as Alice Waters says, "edible jazz." There are few dishes that I prepare the same way every time. I refer to them collectively as "The Canon."

Anyway, the dish was enjoyed by many that day, but especially by my buddy Sherdyl. He liked the lingering and savory slow burn that the chile and curry spices left behind. Later that day I entered a room where he was sitting with some others. He looked up at me, gave me a smile and said simply, "Good taters." I smiled in return and said, "Good taters to you, too." And that was it. Just a short, smiling exchange between friends. The rest of that day is lost to my memory. I look for it, I listen for it, but there is nothing there. Nothing but that one warm moment with an old friend. It resonates in my memory like the last long note of a steel guitar that has just played some old, sentimental song.

Sherdyl died a few years ago. I think he was fifty-five. Being far away at the time I was unable to make it to his bedside. But I'm told that death carried him away gently. And I know that, finally, my friend is at peace.

I never made the "good taters" again. It was just one riff in the never-ending jazz session that takes place in the kitchen. That is, until a few days ago. Constance and I entertain frequently. Indeed, our place has become the focus of our social circle, so I'm always in the kitchen concocting new concoctions and mixing new mixes and trying not to repeat myself.

But without my really thinking of it, those very same good taters issued forth from my kitchen. Those very same ingredients were on hand at the same time, and I must have been in the same frame of mind as I was those years ago. I set the dish alongside the several others and our guests enjoyed them all.

The good taters were the general favorite, especially among the vegetarians. Someone asked me for the recipe. Another asked me what the dish is called. I smiled and opened my mouth to say "Good Taters." But my mouth did not obey me. Some gentle force rose up from that place where memory, mind, and heart sometimes lurk and conspire, and it moved my mouth to say, "Potatoes Sherdyl." I was surprised when I heard those words, as I didn't plan to say them. But immediately I heard them, I knew they were true and correct. Potatoes Sherdyl. So the dish will be known, forever and aye. Potatoes Sherdyl has entered The Canon. Potatoes Sherdyl.

I look out upon the Saigon River from my balcony, and I know he likes the idea. I can see him smiling and waving at me from the other side, and he is young again and free of demons. And though I cannot hear him, he is mouthing the words, "Good taters."

And that's the news from 608, No Tattoo Street.

≈ ≈ ≈

Richard Sterling is the author and editor of many books, including a travel memoir The Fire Never Dies, *the Lowell Thomas award-winning anthology* Food: A Taste of the Road, How to Eat Around the World, *and numerous Lonely Planet guides. He served in the United States Navy for seven years during the Vietnam War, and now lives in Saigon.*

✖ ✖ ✖

Stuck in Bulawayo

There are some things the dictator can't steal,
beat, or kill.

BUS PASSENGERS WARNED, "DO NOT TRUST ANYONE in Bulawayo. Be wary of what surrounds you." I assured them my stay would be too short for trouble. The bus dropped me in Bulawayo, southwestern Zimbabwe, and I walked to the train station. My overnight train to Victoria Falls left in a couple hours, and I approached the ticket counter. The agent said, "Oh, you don't know? That train wrecked two days ago. It's not in service."

I panicked and asked if there was alternative transport. "The bus leaves tomorrow morning. You must overnight in the city," he said. I sighed and left the train station. The conductor shouted after me, "Do be careful. This area is not safe for your people."

I hadn't done my normal research: I didn't know anyone, I hadn't made any friends on the bus, and I didn't consult

Lonely Planet. Bulawayo did not host many tourists. I was tired and scared. What was I going to do?

I trudged to a nearby internet and phone shop. I'd come from a rural village in southern Zimbabwe. A family there had invited me to stay with them, and they'd adopted me as their American daughter. I remembered that my "sister" in the family, Sara, had given me a list of Zimbabwean contacts spread throughout the country. She'd said, "Just tell them who you are and what you need, and my family will always take care of you."

I thumbed through my journal to see if she'd provided any in Bulawayo. Yes, there was a cousin named Mark, and a phone number scribbled next to "Bulawayo." I paid for a phone call and hesitantly dialed. Sara remained in the village without cell phone service, so Mark would not expect my call. The phone began to ring.

He answered the phone before I thought of what to say, "Hello?"

"Um, hello, greetings, my name is Laura Lee, and Sara, um, Rafuro, gave me your number to help me." He yelled something in Shona, the principal language of Zimbabwe. I did not understand, "What?"

He said, "I was talking to my friend. Where are you? We will come to collect you." I told him I was near the train station, at the phone shop next door. He said, "Five minutes. Goodbye."

Thirty minutes later, a small black car pulled up outside the shop. Besides the owner, I was the only person in the shop. A dark-skinned young man, probably my age and height, got out of the car and came inside. He saw me but continued looking around. Confused, he seemed to search for someone else. I said, "Are you looking for me? I am Laura. Are you Mark?"

My voice startled him. "Oh," he said, "Um, yes, then. Let us go. Mark is in the car. You called my phone, but I called

Mark, and we are, um, here to help you." He hesitantly picked up my backpack and threw it in the car. I followed him, climbing into the passenger seat.

The driver, who I supposed was Mark, also looked confused. He asked his friend something in Shona, and his friend shrugged his shoulders and replied. I could not understand. I greeted him and fastened my seatbelt. We screeched down the street, saying nothing. Finally Mark told me, "We have business to do. We must deliver the petrol. Then we will feed you."

I thought the itinerary sounded strange. There was a girl, also in her early twenties, in the back seat along with two young men. We dropped her off in front of a library. She waved goodbye. We hadn't said anything to one another.

We drove for twenty minutes and stopped in what seemed an affluent neighborhood. Mark stayed with me in the car, and he instructed the men in the back seat to get out. They grabbed something from the trunk—two large tanks, it turned out—and knocked on the door of a house. A well-dressed man opened it. The man stuffed a wad of cash into their hands. They all walked to the garage. They poured the liquid in their tanks into the man's canisters. I asked Mark if it was petrol.

Mark said, "Yes. In Zimbabwe, we have resource shortages, little petrol. So I drive big fuel trucks to Botswana and fill up with petrol. Then distribute it privately to make money."

I didn't remember Lonely Planet suggesting what to do in this situation: gallivanting with private petrol distributors on the black market. I didn't know where I was or who I was with, but I guessed it wasn't something a white tourist should do in Zimbabwe. I silently prepared my testament to use in court if arrested.

I nodded. "That sounds like a lucrative gig," I said. He nodded.

We sat in silence until the guys returned. They gave Mark the cash. We went to the next stop. The process repeated.

Mark always looked in the rearview mirror, observing everything around his car. He seemed nervous. I wondered if "petrol" was code.

On the third stop, I pulled out the groundnuts that Auntie Mae had given me. Auntie Mae was my "second mother" in my adopted family from the rural district, and she gave me a bag of this peanut-like snack. I offered some to Mark. He seemed excited. I said, "Here, would you like to see pictures of your family?" I pulled out my camera and showed him a picture of me and Sara.

Mark was stunned. "How do you know Zaka?" he said. Zaka was the rural district.

I explained that I'd met Sara on a bus in Mozambique and that her family adopted me. I flipped through pictures on my digital camera. His mouth hung open. I told him the groundnuts were from Auntie Mae and that Sara gave me his number in case I needed assistance.

He stroked his chin and said, "Oh. God. I had no idea how you got my number. You called my friend who had my cell phone, and he told me you were a coloured girl from Botswana we met on the train. Then you were the only one in the shop, so we picked you up. I didn't know who you were, but I knew somebody had given you my mobile to help you. So that's what we did."

Now I was stunned. He blindly accepted responsibility for me. He knew that I needed help and someone offered his assistance but nothing else. We laughed about the misunderstanding and finished the groundnuts.

We made one more stop and dropped the young men off at their house. I relaxed on the final delivery. Mark took me to get pizza in town. "Will you drink a beer with me?" he asked. I rarely drank in Africa. It was a social taboo for African women to drink in public, and most who did were prostitutes. But I trusted Mark, and he seemed Western-minded in this regard. I accepted a beer—a "clear" one called Lions. He insisted on paying for everything, since I was "his" visitor. We drank and ate my pizza in his car.

We listened to a cassette of Thomas Mapfumo, a famous musician exiled from Zimbabwe now living in America. His lyrics criticized Mugabe's government using coded language, calling them "big fish." Mapfumo's music is still banned in Zimbabwe.

Mark said, "You know, just three years ago we could not sit together in this car. White people are for the opposition parties. We could not be seen with white people or else Mugabe could shoot us. But now, it is different. It is much better." Just as he finished this statement, a car pulled up behind us. Mark whispered, "Ooopppaaa! Quiet." He studied who was inside the car. "Oh, O.K., they are fine." Apparently the improvements in civil liberties did not include freedom of speech.

Mark did not travel to Zaka during elections because Bulawayo was the center of the opposition movement. Mugabe followed people traveling from Bulawayo to rural areas. He was afraid they would educate and sway the rural electorate. He violently confronted them.

Mark said, "I supported the willing buyer-willing seller philosophy. It was not right to repossess the land of whites without giving them proper compensation for the developments they made to the land." I agreed.

Mark also mentioned the "Dead" newspaper, a liberal outlet published by the opposition. The paper earned its nickname "The Dead" because "you'd be dead if you were caught reading it," Mark said. I asked Mark if he voted for the opposition, and he said he didn't vote.

He said, "Mugabe told the people on farms, the rural electorate, that there were cameras in the voting booths. That anyone voting for opposition would be persecuted, even killed." I wondered if my democratic appreciation would withstand these rigorous threats. Probably not.

I finished my pizza, and Mark said that we would go to a

lodge where I could stay the night. Pulling up to the lodge, Mark said, "They know me well here. You should get a good rate."

An employee met us in the driveway and immediately recognized Mark. Mark asked how much a room cost. The employee looked at me, then looked at Mark. He shook Mark's hand and said, "You know we'd never charge you for the hour."

Mark quickly explained that I, *alone*, needed a room for the night, and he would return in the morning to take me to the bus. The abashed employee, Willard, showed me to my room. His mistake earned me a great discount.

I returned to Mark's car, and we went to a local joint to eat *braai* and get another beer. "*Braai*" is an Afrikaans word for "barbeque" and centers around a social gathering in southern African countries. They grilled our meat over wood and newspapers, and it was the closest I'd come to good American Southern barbeque in Africa.

We sipped beers waiting for our roast, until Mark whispered, "Quickly, get in the car. I see the police. We cannot drink outside."

I wondered how drinking in a car was more legal, but I did not question it. I got in the car, and we finished our beers in the comforts of our transport. I asked him what would happen if we got caught drinking outside.

Mark said, "For me, not much. I just give the police 300 Zim dollars or something. For you, being white, it would be much more expensive to avoid arrest."

I wondered how much, and he was unsure. I did not want to find out. Three hundred Zim dollars at the time was about fifty cents, and the fine coincidentally equaled the cost of a beer.

Mark went to pick up our *braai*. I told him the story of my first experience eating roasted beetles on the way to Zaka. He laughed until tears streamed down his face. He wondered why I didn't try the mice. Mark said, "I knew this white guy—an Afrikaner—whew! He ate mice like it was nobody's business!"

Mark recommended that I return to the region during rainy season. I asked why. "Oh," he said, "that's when the big toads come out after the hard rains. You boil them and then prepare them nicely. You would like them." He took a bite of his *braai* and continued with a full mouth, "But you always, always, have to remember to put a big heavy rock on top of the pot when you boil them so that the toad won't jump out when the water heats up. Otherwise, you lose your lunch."

Hmmm, I thought, *I'd probably lose my lunch anyway.*

I told Mark, "If the toad escaped, then it would give new meaning for a meal 'to go.'" He said nothing, but he gave me the signature African look, to mean, "That must be white people humor." I did not explain the concept and chuckled to myself.

We finished our *braai* and beer, and Mark dropped me off at my lodge. He said that he'd collect me in the morning. My bus left at 6 A.M., so I declined his offer and requested a cab. Mark shook his head and said, "You are my guest. I will collect you at 5 A.M."

It was midnight, so the night would be short for both of us. Saying good night, Mark mentioned, "If only you could stay for another day. I want to show you where Cecil Rhodes is buried. You would like it very much." I told him that I would have to visit again, and I skipped off to my room to rest.

The next morning, we traveled to the bus station. He exchanged money for me (at a better rate than the current black market) and bought me a banana for breakfast. He pulled over to buy a telephone card from a vendor in the street.

I wondered what he was doing, and he told me, "You said that you did not tell your parents you came to Zimbabwe.

You will call them and tell them that you are safe. You will use my phone."

Mark's generosity and thoughtfulness touched me. But I was concerned at how my parents would react. I hadn't mentioned that I was going through Zimbabwe; I just said I was on my way to Victoria Falls. Mark shoved his phone in my face and told me to dial. I did, and I anxiously listened to the ringing. I almost hung up after two and said that my parents weren't home, but my mom and dad answered at the same time, "Hello?" They sounded sleepy but nervous.

"Oh! Hi Mom, Hi Dad! Did I wake you?" I asked.

They said, "Yes, dear, it's midnight. Is everything all right?"

"Oh, sorry. Yes, everything is fine. Just wanted to say that I killed a chicken on a farm in Zimbabwe and ate some beetles. Everyone is so nice here. I also delivered some petrol. I am safe and almost at Vic Falls."

I expected an onslaught of expletives criticizing my decision to enter Zimbabwe. I feared my mom would say, "If you're not on the next plane home…" I braced myself. My parents calmly stated in unison, "That's great, honey. Can you call us later?"

I'd timed it perfectly! They were tired, vulnerable, not really understanding what I said. I could say anything right now, that *I* was the one who broke the lamp in middle school. But I didn't push my luck. I told them I loved them and wished them good night. They said, "Good to hear from you. Love you too. Call us later."

I imagined they both woke up the next morning and, at breakfast, my mom would say, "Can you pass the butter? DID LAURA LEE SAY SHE WAS IN ZIMBABWE??" I would not be there to hear about it, so I thanked Mark for use of his phone. It was good to speak with my parents, and I felt better.

Mark took his phone and said, "Good. Your parents will

not worry now." He said he would call his friend Hamilton, who lived in Victoria Falls town. I questioned whether Mark should call at 5:45 in the morning, and he said, "Hamilton is lazy. He should be woken up."

Mark told Hamilton that he was sending a white friend to him, and that he should take care of me. Mark said that he would call him later to ensure I had arrived safely.

I entered Zimbabwe without one contact. I would leave with a notebook full of Zimbabwean friends and family. Mark walked me to my bus and told the conductor to be careful with me, that I was family. Leaving the parking lot, I shot Mark a thumbs-up with tears in my eyes.

I was finally on my way to Victoria Falls. My intentions had been to speed through Zimbabwe, to get out of the place riddled with danger and political corruption. Now I wished for more time in this beautiful country, with the best people in the world.

❧ ❧ ❧

Laura Lee P. Huttenbach is a tall, blond American. She likes to travel where these attributes are not common. In 2006, at age twenty-four, she independently backpacked the East Coast of Africa using public transport. Currently, she is writing the biography of an eighty-eight-year-old Kenyan independence leader known as "The General." You can learn more about the organization that she founded to preserve oral and cultural histories at www.TheGeneralHistoryProject.com.

✒ ✒ ✒

A Dugout Canoe in the Darien Gap

Rot, fear, danger, enlightenment—it's all here
in the jungle.

THE EMBERÁ AND WOUNAAN PEOPLE LIVING IN
Panama's Darien Province are often collectively referred
to as the Chocó. They are riverine people, formerly living as
nomadic families with their homes built along the river's edge,
usually around a curve and out of sight of the next family.

Their *piraguas*, the dugout canoes they carve from single
logs, have the lines and graceful curves of a slender woman's
body. A Wounaan man tells me that the bow point is the
piragua's ass. The inner V lining the ass is the vagina. The
dugout's flat bottom is its lower back, the sides are the rib
cage, and the stern point where the man steers is the boat's
nose. Both ends of the hull taper to a rounded point in the
water, but the topsides widen and flatten out to form a curled

platform at bow and stern. Even tied off to the bank, a *piragua* looks as though it's running fast through the water.

Only ten years ago it was common to paddle and pole a dugout between the headwater village of Manené near the Colombian border and Darien's provincial capital at La Palma. It took two or three days each way. Now there are only a couple of families in the village who still make the trip without an outboard motor. They're considered to be poor and unfortunate rather than purists.

When Ortega's wife hears about my plan to paddle from Manené, she tells me that I can't go alone. Her neighbor says that the *piragua* I bought is made for rivers, and that I shouldn't try the final stretch across the Gulf to La Palma. He says that I need a bigger boat and an outboard motor.

One-armed Geronimo looks worried, but he doesn't try to stop me.

"Can you swim?" he asks.

"Like a fish," I lie to him.

He nods his head.

Jesús, a young Emberá, offers to give me a paddling lesson before I head out on my own. In the morning, we meet at the riverbank. A large group of villagers has already gathered, and although they pretend to be washing clothes or inspecting their dugouts, I can tell that they've come to watch.

Emberá and Wounaan men prefer to stand in a dugout when they paddle, even in the smallest canoes that are as stable as a ten-foot log stripped smooth of its branches. They say that it's easier on their back and knees, and they can see shallow rocks more clearly this way. At the river's edge, I try to copy their style, but the dugout floor has a slick film of wet algae. Even braced against the sides with a wide stance, I can't stop my feet from sliding.

"Maybe I'll try kneeling until we get going," I say over my shoulder to Jesús. But he doesn't hear me. Or it doesn't register. It wouldn't make any sense to him for a man to want to kneel in a *piragua*. As I turn around to repeat my suggestion, he pushes the boat out of the eddy and into the current. The river grabs the bow and we bank hard to the right. Jesús is expecting this to happen. He's done this since he first learned to walk. My feet slip out and fly into the air, and I crash down on the floor. I drop the pole overboard, but recover it before it floats away.

This happens again and again. I fall twice in the boat and four times into the river. I spend less time poling than I do swimming in the rapids. Each time when I look up, Jesús is standing in the stern. He smiles, but he doesn't laugh out loud.

On our return downriver he puts me in the stern to assess my steering skills. I immediately run the canoe onto a shallow boulder where the current shoves the bow up high and swings the dugout around so that we're racing backwards through whitewater. I dig my paddle in and try again and again to pivot the boat, but nothing works. As we slide sideways over a shallow bar of gravel, I hear Jesús laughing out loud. From behind, I can see his body shaking. I don't fully recover control until we enter the deeper section at Manené.

"You'll be fine," he says when we tie off at the village.

The riverbank is lined with spectators. Village women are whispering back and forth amongst themselves. They do this a lot.

"No problem," I assure them as I walk by, water dripping from my hair and down my glasses. "Jesús says I'll be fine."

My shorts and t-shirt are soaked through. Ortega's son takes my paddle and we walk together up the pathway to his house.

Late in the morning on the first day of my trip, my stomach begins churning. I try to ignore it, but later I can feel the first flush of a fever. By the afternoon my burps taste like sulphur and I realize that I have some sort of stomach parasite.

I also finally realize that the Chocó are right about standing in a *piragua*. It is the most comfortable way to travel. Or it would be if my paddle wasn't so short. By the time I reach a Wounaan village in the late afternoon, my back and arms ache.

At Chuletí, *Dirigente* (the village representative) Santos insists on calling a village meeting so that I can be formally presented. He uses a piece of rusty rebar to bang on a suspended steel rim. Old women climb down from their homes, and men hike in on the trails. While he waits, Santos puts the finishing touches on a new yellow-pine paddle. By the third call, twenty minutes later, the room is almost full.

I chose the small tributary to Chuletí because I was sick and needed a safe place to sleep. I'm just starting to realize that they expect me to announce a plan for a development project. No foreigner comes to Chuletí to sightsee. They're sure that I must be launching a study of animals or presenting a proposal for a health project, or a potable water system, a cooperative venture or something like that. They have no experience with travelers arriving here for pleasure.

Santos turns to me and says, "O.K., Martin, everyone is here. Tell them why you are in Chuletí."

Imagine if this happened every time you felt like going for a drive. You're on a short vacation and you stop for a meal or a room. When you go into a shop to buy ice cream, someone rings the church bell and the entire town gathers to hear your intentions for the weekend.

My fever is rising and my stomach is churning and gurgling. Perspiration rolls down my chest and back, soaking my shirt and pants. I must look desperate. I clench up my loose bowels and I say something about the tourism project I've been discussing with Emberá in Manené, but that only makes things worse.

"Always Emberá!" the *dirigente* complains. "They run the Emberá/Wounaan Land Reserve. They get all the projects."

"And our weaving and carving is better than their work. They learn from us!" a woman shouts.

She's right. *Dirigente* Santos is probably right too. I don't really care. I just need to lie down and fall asleep. I have nothing to offer the people of Chuletí. The discussion and the debate go nowhere. I buy a woven *bejuco* basket to carry thirty mangoes and two pineapples, and I buy the paddle from Santos. It's over six feet long. It feels good in my hands.

I collapse in a hammock at Santos's house, and I eat their rice and fish.

Santos's wife tells me that her family still paddles to La Palma if they don't have money for gas or if the motor is broken. I think that Chocó women see more clearly than the men what a family sacrifices for the convenience and speed of a motor. I don't want to use an outboard because I like to hear birds singing. I like to surprise a caiman or a peccary or a capybara at the water's edge, but to a Chocó male, a motor is essential. It is a necessary tool and a symbol of his strength and ability. A man will work for years and save every penny that could go toward so many other things. His children might have to move to Panama City to find work and send money home. A father will split up his family to buy an outboard motor. Afterwards, the cost of fuel and maintenance will take up what is needed for flour and oil and clothing and school supplies. But a man feels as though he is a failure if he can't provide his own outboard.

A woman understands all of this.

After sunset, Chuletí becomes a nightmare of mosquitoes. They pile thick on the surface of my tent screen. As soon as I lie down, my stomach churns again. Four times that night I have to tear open the zipper and run through the dark to squat in the bushes.

Bats dart and flit in front of my face. I wrap my head in a

shirt and leave my ass out to get chewed. Even worse, I partially soil myself.

Then again, there really isn't anything partial about shitting your pants. Either you did or you didn't.

Near the end of the following day, I see a clearing ahead on the riverbank, and I can hear a man shouting in the distance.

"¡Carajo!"

Aldo's shack looks black with the paint peeled off the moldy walls and porch. He lives there alone beside an abandoned sawmill in the Darien jungle. When he has company, Aldo never talks. Instead he shouts everything, and it's always driven home with an exclamation mark. I can hear his voice from almost a mile upriver.

"¡Carajo!"

Again. It's the only word I can make out from the distance. It's like a beacon to me now, drawing me forward as the sun begins to slip behind the horizon.

I'm sick with dysentery. I've been shivering and sweating for two days, and hanging my ass over the edge of the dugout canoe every time my stomach gurgles so that my bowels are completely empty. If I can reach La Palma I'll buy medicine to kill the parasites, but it's still a two-day paddle away. A safe night's sleep in Aldo's shack is the only thing in my world right now that gives me any hope.

¡Carajo!

It's like "Damn!" or "Hell!" Or like "Crikey!" if we still used that...but with an edgier feel to it, depending on your delivery.

By the time I reach Aldo's muddy landing, the daylight is fading and I can barely lift my paddle. My fingers fumble with the bow-line when I tie off to a boulder. A Latino visitor has also stopped by to wait for the tide current to change and carry him farther upriver to Camogantí. I can hear them talking on the lopsided porch where Aldo spends his days watching the río Balsas.

A month earlier, while I was traveling with a group of Emberá, I stayed at Aldo's home. That night he told me he was holding out for his last paycheck from the sawmill owner. Aldo showed me his notebook with the dollar amounts owed to him since the company declared bankruptcy. He knows that if he leaves he'll never get the final payment. He's the only worker to have stayed behind. At night he drives off thieves with his shotgun. In the day, he calculates his hours spent guarding tools, hoping that the future owners will reward his commitment, and at the very least pay him his final two-week check. He has been waiting for two years now, and he's starting to get frustrated.

When I offer the bag of food and provisions to Aldo, he first looks into the bag and then back at me.

"…¿y eso?" he asks, handling the bag of rice, the cooking oil, sugar, coffee, onions, garlic, and canned sauce.

"It's for you," I say, "to replace the food you cooked for us last month."

For a moment it looks like he might start to cry. He bows his head and turns, taking the food into his shack where a diesel candle smokes and glows a dirty yellow. He cooks two cups of rice, three *huakúko* fish, and boiled plantains, but when he serves it I can barely manage the bony fish. I have no appetite and the rice gets stuck in my throat. I'd choke if I tried the plantains.

The Latino visitor is in his late forties. His two sons are with him, and he's telling his machismo stories.

"That girlfriend was beautiful," the man tells Aldo. "I was crazy about her. I put her through high school and bought her a house in La Palma."

"¡Carajo!" says Aldo. "*Bien preparada, ella.*" She's well looked after.

"Yea, but she treated me badly, and she left me in the end."

I'm sagging in my chair with the plate of food on my lap. I can barely lift my head. The visitor from Camogantí describes one woman, then another. Apparently they're all very beautiful.

"I explained to my wife that she doesn't have to worry about this *calentura*—this fever of mine. I might fuck around, but I'd never leave her," he says. "I'll always have enough money for our sons and for her..."

I have no energy. I want to tell him that nobody cares. That he's just a lonely, aging, middleweight searching for validation.

His two sons sit silently in the dark while he drones on until the tide finally turns and begins to flood the river again. I can see the beam of his flashlight as they walk down the path to his boat. I hear the outboard start, and then they disappear in the night.

"You haven't eaten anything," Aldo says as he takes my plate. He's loud and animated, but I like the sound of his voice. "And you'll never get across the Gulf to La Palma. Your canoe is made for rivers. And not with a paddle. You won't make it."

"I'll leave around 2:30 in the morning," I tell him. "I'll go out with the tide current."

"No. We'll get some gas," he says. "And I'll fix this motor."

Aldo has an old Evinrude in a hundred pieces. I remember it from the last visit. It looks like it's been dismantled for twenty-five years.

"You can leave your *piragua* here. I'll get someone to tow it down."

I might be tempted to change my plan if I thought there was any possibility that he could assemble the antique motor, resurrect his leaky boat, and conjure up five gallons of gasoline. But I know that it won't happen. I tell him that my mind is set on paddling.

In a book I once read about the Sahara, Swedish writer Sven Lindqvist describes a number of eccentric characters who have wandered across or died in the desert. Lindqvist wrote that travel and expedition decisions are often carried out under very different conditions from those in which they were made. By poring over maps, drawing lines and creating schedules, the journey can take on a life of its own. It pushes the traveler forward. Long after the original notion and reason have been forgotten, the traveler continues onward only because sometime earlier in Paris, or wherever the dream was hatched, he told himself that was what he would do. Something seemed important then. Out here, in the jungle or desert, it often makes no sense at all.

When I think about the last month on the Balsas River, that passage comes to mind. I can recall a lot of physical details—the long hikes, stories around campfires, cutting my foot with a machete—but I can't clearly remember how the idea started. What was it that seemed so important about paddling alone on a Darien river through the rainforest...the feel of the paddle in my hands...slowing the pace of life? I think I said something about wanting to fish more...or hear bird songs as I traveled...or ask questions and sleep on the floor with the host families in native villages? Maybe there wasn't ever such a clear reason.

At Aldo's swampy home-site, with my net set up on his porch, at least I'm safe from mosquitoes. Rain drums and hammers hard and beautiful on the zinc roof. I have a fever again, and I lie naked on the floor, feeling bouts of sweat come and go and soak the clothes I use for a mattress.

Aldo lies down on his bed in the shack just before midnight. I try to sleep, but twenty minutes later I hear him fumbling in the kitchen.

"Do you want some coffee?" he asks.

"No thanks," I answer. "I think I'll just sleep for a while," I say from the tent.

We go through the same routine at 1 A.M.

"There's no moon," he says. I don't answer.

A long pause.

"You'd be crazy to go out in this rain at night."

And then silence again.

I wish I wasn't sick. I just want to sit up and drink coffee and talk all night with Aldo. This Colombian transplant. This survivor, woodcutter, mechanic, sharp shooter, and rain-forest raconteur.

He doesn't go back to bed. At 1:30 I accept his third offer of coffee. I crawl out to feed the mosquitoes, and we sit on his porch.

This is the first time in my experience that Aldo isn't shouting.

"I have a girlfriend in La Palma," he says quietly.

Silence. We sip our coffee from enamelled tin mugs.

"She was supposed to move out here, but someone said that she's burning me."

Silence. Coffee. I can hear the river slowing.

"They say that she's living with Luis…the guy who fishes off Punta Bruja. He stops by here sometimes and gives me fish."

Mostly I just listen.

"It's still a long trip to La Palma," he says.

This shack on the river might be a good place for a writer. I think about that while we sit on his porch. Most of Darien is a heavy rainforest that closes in on you, strangling your thoughts and suffocating your imagination, but Aldo's shack is on a wide and open section of the river. In the daytime, there's plenty of space and light, and you can see storms rolling towards you across the hills. And Aldo has at least thirty mango trees. I love mangoes. They might be my favorite fruit.

I could probably write here. I think about that while we sit drinking coffee.

At the river's edge, I slip while I'm bailing out the *piragua* and loading my basket and bags. I can't see anything in this blackness. I can't see the river or the trees, and I can't see Aldo, but I know that he's standing beside me. He explains how to use a fat balsa pole to shove into a crocodile's mouth if I'm attacked.

"They'll try to knock you out of the dugout," he warns me. And then he tells me to hug the shore. And that I should spend tomorrow night at the town of Chepigana. He shares a few other gems of wisdom, but both of us know that the tide has peaked and the river is turning around to flow towards the Pacific.

The rain has tapered off, but it hasn't stopped. It still comes in shifting mists and light showers so that my clothes are already soaked through. I feel mud squeezing up between my toes at the landing. I'll have to paddle hard at first to warm my body.

Aldo fills my mug with a sugary coffee that mixes with rainwater as I head out in the current towards the Gulf.

For almost a week, I stay at the home of a Wounaan family near the town of La Palma. They feed me rice, root vegetables, and soups made with iguana and mountain-pig broth. After the fever breaks and I feel my strength begin to return, I load the baskets of food into the *piragua* again.

I paddle a short stretch of the Tuira River in the morning, eating lunch and resting at the ruins of a Spanish fort until the noon hour when the Pacific ebb tide turns. I launch the dugout and let the tidal current carry me as ocean water floods into the Tuira Basin pushing me upriver and towards the heart of Darien's jungle.

I feel more comfortable now paddling Chocó style, standing in the dugout through the afternoon, my bare feet planted on the wood floor and my toes curled up the sides. Fish break the surface. Sunshine bakes my arms and legs. I drink water from coconuts and eat guavas that I picked near the ruins.

I wish I could be traveling with my younger brother, Paul, on this river. I've been thinking so much about him this afternoon that I start talking to him while I'm paddling.

"Over there. A blue Morpho butterfly," I say. Or, "Wow, listen to those monkeys." Simple things like that.

Whenever I speak out loud to him, I'm surprised that he doesn't answer. I wish he could hear the parrots, or watch a keel-billed toucan sprint across a mangrove channel.

I become hypnotized by the rhythm of the paddle, hardly noticing the hours slip away, until early evening arrives and I still have nowhere to land. The lower Tuira isn't like the river headwaters. The shores here are swampy banks and mangrove channels populated by caimans and crocodiles. I haven't seen any high banks with dry ground where it would be safe to camp for the night.

The hills to the east are turning pink as the sun begins to slip behind the horizon. The flooding tide is about to turn around again. It still feels as though Paul is in my dugout, so I'm embarrassed at having planned so poorly. I've done this to him so many times before, yet for some reason he still trusts me. He doesn't know that I'm unsure of what to do, that I'm frightened of the night coming on.

I say, "You should spread the tarp and rest for a while on the floor."

Paul doesn't answer. I look and he's not there.

The sky is still clear overhead but I can see rain falling in the mountains. I watch the towering cumulus clouds anvilling off on top, and the lightning-strikes walking across the hills toward me. After the flood tide peaks, it barely pauses before turning around to empty back to the sea.

I don't remember when it was that I first traced my finger along a map of Darien's Tuira River, but now I'm sitting in a moment of intense beauty. A brief moment that will slip away and be gone, and I have no one to share it with.

The morning after.

I sit in the dugout canoe, holding onto a tree root protruding from the riverbank. I have no strength left in my body. My clothes are soaked. My back and shoulders ache. A white ibis stands on one leg and floats by on the back of a driftwood log. He passes so close to my boat that I can see the texture of his pink leg and mud stains on his feathers. He pretends I don't frighten him, but if I moved at all he would fly away.

I look into the ibis's eye, and the ibis looks right back.

Last night I tied off to a submerged tree in the river as the day ended and the tide peaked. If I had been traveling with Autemio or Manuel or anyone who knew anything about Darien's jungle and rivers, they would have told me I was making a mistake.

On the lower Tuira, the Pacific tide floods in and out twice each day. For six hours it pushes inland, swelling the basin and holding back the river's outflow. When the tide turns around, the river lets go and drops as much as twenty feet in the same amount of time. In both directions the current usually moves slowly for the first hour. It picks up power during the second hour. The third and fourth have the strongest flow, followed by a gradual easing over the next two hours before stalling at slack tide and reversing direction again.

But last night was different. It was raining in the mountains, and the rivers must have flooded. There wasn't the usual slack period between tides. One minute we were still creeping upriver. A moment later the current was in a hurry to empty the flooded basin.

I opened a jar of beans as the sun set. I sliced a fresh tomato, and the sky went dark. As I tore off a piece of bread, I thought of how Paul would appreciate this picnic menu. By the time I finished eating, drift logs were bumping and then hammering into the dugout. I couldn't see them coming in the dark. I tied the packs and baskets to the thwarts and I cinched the strap on my glasses so that the frame pressed into my face.

I should have done even more. I should have untied the bowline right then, but I didn't want to lose the distance I'd paddled that afternoon. I thought that I could survive the worst of it if I stayed low in the boat. By the time I fully understood my mistake, the river was racing out and the current began dragging the dugout from one side to the other. After little more than an hour, I'd already lost control. Uprooted trees hooked onto the bow and then let go with a shudder, and the low branch I'd used to tie the bowline was already too high to reach.

Dragging a machete beside me, I began inching forward on my belly to cut the rope. As my weight shifted to the left or right it sent the dugout shooting off in one direction and then correcting hard to the other side. When I was still a few feet from the bow, I felt the dugout veer hard to the right, then tip even farther, and then farther still as the river grabbed the gunwale and water flooded over the bow.

The current washed me back until my feet hit a thwart. For a split second we were under completely. I gripped the sides and waited. Fully submerged, I thought of my brother again. I thought of the loose paddle and the glasses strapped to my face. And then we leveled off. The boat was filled to the top, the current racing and washing over the gunwales whenever we dipped to one side even slightly.

Sometimes in a moment of crisis, when it's something real that you can see and touch and taste, you can force yourself to focus only on the tiny steps ahead. You don't let the overwhelming entirety destroy you. And just by moving forward, tiny step by tiny step, you find a strength and confidence that might be far beyond what you have any right to feel.

I still had my glasses. I felt the spare paddle strapped to a thwart. I carefully moved one hand behind to find the half-gallon can tied to a string. Balancing the full canoe, I began bailing bit by bit while logs with tangled roots and branches lumbered past at chest height. Maybe it took a half-hour, an hour, or maybe it was more. I just moved and didn't think of anything else until the canoe was empty.

Again I went down on my belly. This time I came within a machete blade's length from the bow. I cut the line with one swing, and the tail shot off and was gone. In that same second, as the current swept us away, the world went calm. I stopped fighting nature's forces. The dugout washed downriver with the current while I paddled steady strokes away from the bank until we ran aground on a sandbar. The tide would be emptying for hours. I heard thunder in the hills, and then the sky opened overhead and rain poured down. I wrapped a tarp around my body and drifted in and out of sleep so that I never noticed when we floated free on the next flood tide.

This morning, sitting exhausted in the dugout, everything is soaked from the river and rain. I know I have to throw my soggy bundles onshore before the tide turns around again, but I don't have the strength to move. I tell my body to lift, and it responds without me. I crawl onto the bank, but I'm not really here at all. I sit on the ground and I watch another bird float by on a balsa log. An egret this time. Black legs and a yellow beak.

I don't do anything else for those first minutes.

When the sun edges over the trees, I take off my shirt to feel the warmth.

I take off all my clothes and I sit on a log.

Then butterflies arrive in twos and threes. They land on my hands and back, and they stroke my skin and tickle me with their antennae. I wonder what they want. I shake my arms and brush them aside, but they fly back and start again, so I leave them to their work. They're my only companions. It's the most intimate touch I've felt in a long time.

Just before noon I see a storm in the distance, but it looks as though it will miss us. My shirts and socks and plastic bags flutter on the clothesline

"The tide will be flooding again in a few hours," I say out loud. "We won't have much time to get upriver to Mercadeo before dark."

And Paul answers, "Let's camp here for the night, brother."

He feels safe because I'm here. That's how it seems. He doesn't know how frightened I am sometimes.

"O.K.," I say. I just sit there, naked in the sun, butterflies stroking my arms and back.

The next day I make steady progress upriver, but again have trouble finding a place to camp along the river lined with mangrove forest. After tying the dugout to a mangrove root on shore, I take off my clothes. I drag myself and a small pack up the riverbank using broken branches and tree roots to keep from sinking into the mud.

The highest patch of ground is soggy, but it looks as though it will stay a few inches above the high tide mark tonight so that I can sleep. That's the plan, but barely five minutes later, three black men approach in a fiberglass fishing boat. *Colombianos*. They must have been watching me from the far side of the river. They arrive just as I'm sorting out my bag of food.

"Awwooo!" the driver calls out, as he turns off the motor.

I respond the same.

He gestures with his hand, the palm turning upward, fingers spread. The *what-the-hell-are-you-doing-here?* gesture.

I respond with the same hand movement, and I point at his boat with my lips, as if it's strange for me to come upon a fishing boat in these waters.

"*¿A donde va?*" he asks. Where are you going?

"*Aqui no más.*" Just here, no farther, I answer.

"And you?" I ask. "Where are you going?"

He seems a little taken aback at the implied equal status.

"We're fishing," he answers, nodding his head toward the coolers and fishnets.

The other two men are either uninterested or they're fugitives. They keep their heads bowed. I never see their faces, only their hat brims and ragged clothes.

"*Que tenga suerte,*" I say, wishing them luck with the fishing.

They motor off against the current.

I avoided answering their questions, but when they leave, I lose my only possible ride to the next village. My gut tells me I shouldn't have anything to do with these three. They feel like trouble, but it's less than an hour before dark and I have nowhere to turn or run, and now they know where I am. I spent the entire day without meeting another boat on the river until this final moment when I really want to be invisible and forgotten.

Last night before leaving the Emberá village, *Dirigente* Cachoro said, "There are Colombians in the Laguna Lirial. They'll see you, and they'll think you have money. They'll try to rob you and kill you."

There was only one candle burning. I couldn't see Cachoro's face clearly.

He also said, "And no matter what happens, don't try to sleep in your *piragua*. A *lagarto* (a caiman or alligator) or a crocodile will tip it over and eat you. Get some long poles and sharpen them..."

He stopped.

"You don't carry...?" He squeezed an imaginary trigger with his finger.

I shook my head from side to side.

"O.K., get some long, strong poles, and use a machete to sharpen them. *Bueno*," he said.

Good. It was settled.

In one of the few Panamanian books written about Darien, a former schoolteacher/author writes that you have to drive the spear right into that soft spot in the *lagarto's* armpit.

Bueno.

In a mangrove swamp at night, it's all those things that I can't touch or see that frighten me most. Fear of everything I don't know. Things that might or might not be waiting for me in the shadows. Fear of death. Fear of the dark. Fear of noises I can't identify.

Fear hobbles me on this trip. It's fueled by all the warnings I've heard and read to stay far away from Darien province—reports of kidnapping, violence, Colombian guerrillas, *narcotraficantes*, and the jungle itself. It's trapped in my head now, so that every tiny noise develops a life of its own. I can taste fear in my mouth tonight. It's causing this kink in my neck, a dull ache that keeps me awake.

By midnight I'm sweating and soaked through in my nylon tent. The air is thick and wet and black so that I can hardly breathe. I can't see anything. I wish that a breeze would rustle the trees and drown out these unknowable water noises. These clicks and pops. Branches snapping. The sound of voices. Whose voices? I'm far from any village or any pathway, so why do I hear machetes and rifles scraping over a mangrove root?

I'm on the highest patch of the mud flat, but the water is still rising, inching higher and higher, until it's lapping at the doorway of the tent. This is just how an alligator or a crocodile wants his supper. He'll charge out with his jaws open, chomp down on the tent with his jagged teeth and crush my body, grinding back and forth while dragging me into the water.

This isn't like swamping a dugout canoe in a racing flood current at night. I don't have anything to confront. No wild animal, no thieves in the night, or a Colombian guerrilla. There's only my fear, and my unbridled imagination.

Now I hear boots trampling the ground outside. I can't get this madness under control. I fall apart in the tent, trembling and weeping. I can't find my glasses or even my shirt. I pull on my pants. I've lost the flashlight, but I grab my machete. I tear open the tent zipper and burst through the doorway into the mud and shallow water. Mosquitoes cover my body and face. I raise my machete overhead to attack, to cut someone down, anyone, anything.

I try to roar. I let go with everything I have left, but it gets caught in my throat and warbles. I try a second time to roar like a beast. Still nothing. And nothing answers. Only the mosquitoes in my ears. My heart pounding in my head. Mangroves clicking, more water noises. Everything the same as before.

I fall to my knees in the mud. My tent is full of insects.

I've heard that alligators and crocodiles prefer to wait for their prey to enter the water before attacking. I remember the sharp pole I have in my dugout, but I'd never be able to find a reptile's armpit in the dark. It seems impossible to me, and I wonder if Cachoro and the Panamanian writer were serious, or if it's just a joke that Darien natives play on gringos. I think about that while I'm still kneeling in the mud.

I'm so damn tired of being afraid. I don't know what beast I was trying to imitate. Is there some sorry animal that tries to protect itself that way? At first crying and curling into a ball, and then suddenly rearing up and shouting? Is there such a freak?

And FARC guerrillas, and those so-called *maleantes*—bad people—what would they think of my roar? How would they respond to a gringo warrior exploding from his tent, waving a machete overhead, tears streaming down his cheeks? What would they think?

I really want to go home. I've felt that way for twenty years. I want a good night's sleep. I want a hot bath and a family Christmas. But I was hoping that I would sail home. I wanted to return someday from an epic journey. Not crying like a baby and helplessly weeping in the mud. Desperate for not writing. No well-told story. No lines of poetry. No art. No passion. No battle between good and evil, with scenes so horrible that they mark me with a sadness that never fully leaves my eyes.

I think every traveler wants a version of that. From there, we believe, with the wisdom that comes from hardship, maybe we'll finally be able to work our way home again.

❧ ❧ ❧

Martin Douglas Mitchinson lives in a cabin on the coast of British Columbia. His varied work life has spanned the extremes of harsh winters on oilfield and diamond-drilling rigs in northern Canada, to writing and photography projects while sailing through Latin America aboard his 36-foot ketch Ishmael. *Most recently, he spent eighteen months traveling by foot and dugout canoe throughout Darien's roadless jungle region. This story was excerpted from his first book,* The Darien Gap: Travels in the Rainforest of Panama.

PETER WORTSMAN

❦ ❦ ❦

Epiphany of a Middle-Aged Pilgrim in Tea-Stained Pajamas

"In every way, then, such prisoners would recognize as reality nothing but the shadows of those artificial objects."
—Plato, *The Republic*

ONVALESCING FROM RECENT ILLNESS, COMFORTABLY ensconced in a black leather easy chair at home, I sit perfectly still, the paper spread open on my lap, careful not to spill the steaming contents of the teacup resting on the crook of my knee or stain my fingers on the ink of distant unrest. Sickness seals you in that way with a callous disregard for the world beyond your four walls. Unmoved by the big news of the day: the usual potpourri of war, famine, and scandal, I am about to nod off with a long drawn-out yawn when a

45

minor news item catches my eye, an article concerning the whereabouts of a missing painting by the seventeenth-century Italian master of dramatic effect, Caravaggio, an artist I once admired. And suddenly, altogether unexpectedly, a caption identifying a black-and-white photograph of the painting in question as a Nativity stolen from a church in Sicily in 1969 strikes like a bolt of chiaroscuro lightning, disturbing my tender balance, splattering me with tea and memory.

At middle age, revelation is a messy business.

According to the report, Marino Mannoia, a Mafia snitch and self-styled authority on stolen art, the State's key witness at the corruption trial of former Italian Prime Minister Giulio Andreotti, then in its second year, broke the monotony of the interminable legal proceedings with the revelation that it was he who, twenty-seven years ago, snatched the *Nativity with Saints Francesco and Lorenzo* from the Church of San Lorenzo in Palermo—snatched it right out from under my eyes, altering, if ever so obliquely, the course of my life!

Cut to Italy, summer of '69. A seventeen-year-old aesthete, I am on a quest to track down every Caravaggio canvas in Italy from Florence to Palermo. Having interned in my senior year of high school at The Metropolitan Museum of Art and briefly flirted with the idea of becoming an art historian, my compulsion looks strictly legit to my parents, who are relieved that my raging hormones should find such a salutary "cultural" outlet.

The truth, of course, has little to do with culture as such. I am stirred by the filthy feet of Caravaggio's virgins and the jarring blend of tenderness and violence in every brush stroke. Other artists make you stand in awe before their handiwork, Caravaggio sucks you in. At the Uffizi in Florence, Isaac squirming under Abraham's knife mirrors my own malaise ("So when are you gonna get a haircut already!") and Medusa reminds me of my mother. At the Galleria Borghese in Rome,

I try David's destiny on for size, clutching Goliath's head in his hand, trembling with the knowledge that but for a well-aimed pebble, Goliath would have been clutching his.

The New Testament tableaux move me too. Six years of Hebrew School training notwithstanding, I am morbidly fixated on martyrdoms. And in the Church of Pio Monte della Misericordia in Naples, amidst the angel flutter of *Le Sette Opere di Misericordia*, I leer at a young woman brazenly baring her breast for an old man to suck while a nobleman's lackey strips the clothes off a corpse.

Which brings me to Palermo in search of a tame Nativity, having run out of crucifixions and beheadings.

It is 4 P.M. or thereabouts and this sprawling ancient slum is devoid of its hibernating hordes. The only soul in sight, a balding apostle with leathery skin and a loose-lipped smile assures me he can show me the way for a few hundred lire. Having shaken me down for the price of a drink, he leads me to the wrong church and leaves me with a shrug: "*Mi dispiace, signore!* They must have changed the street signs." By this time Palermo is squirming with life. And though every man could have modeled for Matthew, Peter, or Paul, every woman for the Madonna, every child for an angel or Christ, nobody seems to know where the church is. These are the same streets Caravaggio traipsed between commissions, duels, and vendettas, I tell myself to assuage my mounting frustration. When finally I do stumble on the battered façade of San Lorenzo, its heavy metal portal is locked and I collapse like a beggar on the steps, cursing Caravaggio for ever having ventured south of Rome before I notice a cat slipping in through a side door.

"Where is the Nativity please?" I ask an old man slumped over on a bench inside, who may or may not be the sacristan.

"*Nella capella!* In the chapel!" He points to a parcel of darkness to my left.

Twice I circle the church, peeking into every sacrosanct alcove, nook and cranny, but there is no sign of it.

"The Nativity!" I insist, gently shaking the old man, who has since drifted off to sleep.

He looks up with a scowl and limply points in the same direction.

"Show me, please! *Per piacere!*" I gesture, holding out a 1,000-lire note, which magically awakens his interest.

The sacristan perks up. We take the same direction he previously indicated, stopping before a chapel recessed in a curl in the wall. "*Ecco li, signore!* Here it is!" he points, crossing himself.

"*Dove?* Where?" I scour the vacant wall.

The old man strikes a match. Grumbling unintelligibly, he shoves me to the altar, atop which a small black-and-white photograph hangs askew crudely affixed with strips of yellowing tape to the bare wall. It is, I realize on closer inspection, a snapshot of the painting. "*Ma questo e una fotografia!*" I protest.

"'LA NATIVITA CON I SANTI FRANCESCO E LORENZO,' *si!*" the old man insists, reading the caption, firmly clasping the 1,000-lire note lest I try to retrieve it.

Perhaps it's my faulty Italian. "*Non capisco!* I don't get it! *Dove é l originale?*"

"*Ah si!*" he nods, finally fathoming the source of my confusion. "*E stato rubato!* Stolen!" he shrugs matter-of-factly, as if relating an unfortunate fact of life.

It's a bad joke. Unable to believe my eyes, I don't know whether to laugh or to cry. I've traveled the length of Italy's boot to see a painting that isn't there, a phantom masterpiece which this old man has watched over much of his adult life; yet to him, nothing's missing. Three centuries ago a man of talent mixed his pigments on a palette and applied them to cloth capturing the image of a couple of local vagrants disguised as saints, an urchin masquerading as an angel and a cow looking on as a *signorina* makes ready to suckle a reclining infant. Seeing is believing. The image draped with the halo of sanctity engraved itself on the sacristan's consciousness. The painting's subsequent disappearance is beside the point, the canvas itself a disposable negative in the photo-optic chemistry of faith.

Not that I am quite capable of reasoning things out at the time, but I understand in some wordless way that I've been on the wrong track, hunting down illusions instead of going after the real thing.

Cut to the present. More than a quarter-century's gone by, the snapshot having long since fallen off the wall of the church, possibly replaced by another, the old sacristan having carried his image of the Nativity to the grave, and yours truly, the disappointed pilgrim, sedentary now, having grown up and forgotten the fever of his teens—when suddenly, out of nowhere leaps an Italian Rumpelstiltskin, Marino Mannoia, a messenger from the past whose name evokes an unsavory onomatopoeiac mix of mania and ennui.

How often do we encounter one of the many invisible agents of that hodgepodge of chance and choice called destiny, an individual who, unbeknownst to him, and by an act of no immediate concern to us alters the ground rules of the game?

And now with a final brush stroke worthy of the master, this unlikely angel straight out of Caravaggio's dubious circle of friends completes a tableau I've never seen but which has moved me profoundly, thus resolving the mystery of the missing canvas—a mystery obliquely linking the late sacristan of the Church of San Lorenzo in Palermo, a painter, a thief, a seventeen-year-old aesthete, and a convalescent middle-aged pilgrim in tea-stained pajamas, rekindling the latter's faith in miracles.

❧ ❧ ❧

New York-born nomad Peter Wortsman has peddled his impressions of elsewhere to numerous newspapers, magazines, and websites.

His text "Holy Land Blues" was published in Encounters with the Middle East, *and again in* The Best Travel Writing 2008. *Another text, "Confessions of a Born-Again Cowboy in France," that originally ran on the popular website World Hum, was republished in* The Best Travel Writing 2009. *His column* Rx for Travel *appears in* P&S, *the journal of the Columbia University College of Physicians and Surgeons. He is the author of a book of short fiction,* A Modern Way to Die, *and two plays,* The Tattooed Man Tells All *and* Burning Words, *and also a translator from the German, most recently of* Selected Prose of Heinrich von Kleist. *A past recipient of the Beard's Fund Short Story Award and fellowships from the Fulbright and Thomas J. Watson Foundations, he was the Holtzbrinck Fellow at the American Academy in Berlin in spring 2010.*

CAMERON M. SMITH

~✺~ ~✺~ ~✺~

A Viking Repast

The relentlessly terrible history of Iceland
in three courses.

FOLLOW THE WIND EAST OF REYKJAVIK — EAST PAST
the basalt pillars of Thingvellir, the chieftain's gathering
place, east past booming mount Hekla, east past Helgrindur,
the Peaks of Hell, east over acres of slush and black quick-
sand and east almost to the edge of the mighty Vatnajokull
ice cap—and you will find two wooden huts lying low in a
treeless, hilly vastness of dark volcanic cinders. They are hard
to spot; from far off their red roofs look like drops of blood
soaking into the porous ground. Air is always on the move
here, and low-blowing clouds often slide across the bare hill-
tops like a great lid. The Icelanders call this place of two huts
Jokulheimar: glacier-home.

A number of decisions, delusions, accidents, and wild
fortunes funneled me toward Iceland, and then toward
Jokulheimar. More precisely, life stood me, one February

night, on the porch of the smaller of the two huts. I drank in the sterile, supercooled air that flowed off the blunt toe of the ice cap, just a few miles away. Above were the familiar planets, galaxies, stars, and star clusters that had guided me in the wilderness for years. Below, the brightest of them were caught in the ice of a frozen stream.

I huffed into my mitts and headed for the larger hut. There were people in there, Icelanders who'd invited me to join them in Thorablott, Thor's Feast, an ancient winter rite. I'd always found Icelanders to be rather reserved, but these folk had discovered me dragging a sled in the wilderness and either through pity or bemusement they had invited me to the feast.

On the way to the hut I stopped for a moment to examine the Icelanders' snow vehicles. They were giant contraptions with chest-high tires, sprouting radio and GPS antennae. Banks of floodlights, big as soup bowls, were mounted on the roofs, protected by wire cages. Equipment trunks and tools were strapped to the roofs and hoods, bumpers protruded feet ahead and behind, and each truck was equipped with a winch and a spool of cable mounted on the front; some also had one on the back. The trucks had miniature ladders to get in and out because the floor was at waist level.

These were working vehicles, cobbled together in the most utilitarian way. The Spartan forms turned my mind to the stout, simple lines of Viking ships. Years ago, a farmer named Hordur had shown me a picture of such a vessel, a full-scale replica he'd built in the mid-1990s and sailed across the North Atlantic with a small crew. The undecked, forty-foot boat had rolled and banged and wallowed, but they'd made it to New York City. The original Iron Age design was a product of minds that revered utility, and the 1990s replica was a product of minds that equally revered history—minds that still drove Icelanders into the wilds for ancient winter rites, like Thorablott.

A history of utility...it was the story of the Icelanders. Although a thousand years separated this evening's feasters from the first Norse to land in Iceland, an ethos of severe pragmatism bound them like a chain.

That chain stretched back to primal Iceland, to a time and place of nameless ice caps, restless volcanoes, and snow-blown moors; a time and place of nameless exploding seas, cracking crags and moaning caverns, forests of cold-stunted birch, snapping river-ice, and gurgling streams.

Millions of years passed before the island was visited by its first animals: beetles and birds came with the wind, foxes and polar bears stranded on Greenlandic ice floes, fishes swam into fjords. In Europe, the Neanderthals came and went. Eons later, farming spread from the Balkans to Scandinavia. Millennia after that, Rome rose from dust, flourished, and collapsed, five centuries after Christ. All this time, the little storm-lashed island was unknown to humankind.

But one blustery day (we can safely presume it was blustery) a sail appeared off the north coast. The first arrivals were not Norse, they were not Vikings: they were Irish monks, Christian *hermitae* who'd set out to find new land in which to worship in peace, and the farther from Dark Age Europe, the better. They arrived some time after A.D. 750, and for just over a hundred years, they farmed in what must have been unique isolation.

Their isolation didn't last. By the 790s, clever and cunning Scandinavian chiefs had devised tactics—and built warships—for the express purpose of ransacking mainland Europe and Britain, both still anemic, dazed by the collapse of Rome centuries before. These chieftains and their people—collectively called the Vikings—struck out from Scandinavia to test their way of making a living. They descended on their first target, the English monastery of Lindisfarne, in 793. Of the rout, Simeon of Durham wrote:

...the pagans...robbed, tore and slaughtered not only
beasts of burden, sheep and oxen, but even priests and
deacons, and companies of monks and nuns. And they
came to the church of Lindisfarne, laid everything
waste with grievous plundering, trampled the holy
places with polluted steps, dug up the altars and seized
all the treasures of the holy church. They killed some
of the brothers, took some away with them in fetters,
many they drove out, naked and loaded with insults,
some they drowned in the sea...

Centuries later, Christianity would use the same tactics on
"heathens" worldwide, but for the moment, early medieval
Europe—where the borders of modern Europe were just
being sketched out, and organized armies were only a memory of Rome—was stunned by the Viking assault. Only one
thing united Europeans at this time, a commonly-muttered
prayer: "*From the fury of the northmen, deliver us, O Lord.*"

The Vikings took full advantage of the disarray, ranging
east as far as Kiev, rowing up the Seine to raid Paris, and
barging into the Mediterranean and North Africa. But in
some of those places there was stiff resistance, so they also explored the little-known west, voyaging on the north Atlantic
in open wooden longboats equipped with square sails. They
discovered the Faroes, the Shetlands, and Orkney, and in 894
they made their first permanent settlement in Iceland.

They arrived in a warm period, when the sea was relatively free of icebergs, and the land was thick with dwarf
birches, willow, mats of sedges and grasses, and expansive
moors that made good pasture. There's little mention of the
Irish hermits after the Vikings arrived. Some say they chose
to leave, not wishing to live beside pagans, but I doubt they
had much choice.

Reykjavik ("smoke bay," named for the hot springs) was
settled, and word spread that life could be good there. Within

twenty years so many Norse had arrived that most of the farmable land was in ownership, and newcomers had to buy land rather than simply claim it. They came anyway, settling grassy plains near springs and building modest crofts composed of a semi-subterranean turf house and a few outbuildings enclosed by a low stone wall. Sheep and cattle grazed on the moors in summer, but, like the people, spent winters in the little turf bunkers, protected from the savage cold. Families of a wife and husband, several children, and perhaps a slave or two (many slaves were Irish, handily snatched up on the way to Iceland) tended to the animals, growing hay in the summer to store as winter fodder. Crofts were normally a few miles from one another, and an ethos of independence began to crystallize as one of the Icelanders' most striking characteristics.

That characteristic can't be bottled or bought, and it's best described by Bjartur, the principal character of Halldor Laxnaess's Nobel-prize-winning epic of Icelandic life, tellingly titled *Independent People*: "…freedom is of more account than the height of a roof beam," Bjartur declared, "…the man who lives on his own land is an independent man. He is his own master. If I can keep my sheep alive through the winter and can pay what has been stipulated from year to year—then I pay what has been stipulated; and I have kept my sheep alive… He who keeps his sheep alive through the winter lives in a palace."

Mere survival, then, became a palace in the Icelandic psyche. That survival was based on the same utilitarian philosophy that had built the monstrous snow machines I stood before just outside the main Jokulheimar hut. I could hear the festivities inside, and, sure that it was going to be a special night, I paused just before ascending the steps up to the hut door. It was always good to come in from the cold, and I savored the transition.

But I knew it wasn't smart to linger. An old Icelandic legend describes the folly of wandering outdoors during a Winter Feast. Centuries ago a fellow named Thidrandi went out into the cold moonlight during a Thorablot. He was waylaid by eighteen ghosts: nine swordswomen in white, nine swordswomen in black. It's said that Icelandic ghosts aren't mere specters; they can kill you. Poor Thidrandi wasn't heard from again, but everyone knows what happened to him—he was simply and swiftly hacked to pieces.

I tramped into the hut's fore-room with all the puffing and flapping of arms and clunking of boots on wood that is now so familiar and satisfying to me. Taking a moment to revel in the wholly sweet feeling of coming in from a cold wilderness is one of the treasures of winter travel.

I opened the door. The party was loud and nobody saw me.

"Evening," I ventured, awkwardly fiddling with my hat. Finally someone noticed me and I was seated at the end of the thirty-foot-long wooden table.

These were not supermen or superwomen, but they were a people touched by the weather, their cheeks colored by icy wind, the men's hands scarred here and there by frostbite, chipped here and there by contact with cold metal. They wore thick wool of muted colors: ivory, deep blue, rich blood-red. Rows of their boots stood in the fore-room, but here, wool socks padded on the wooden floor. Some of the Icelanders were Nordic blondes, others were short, stout, and raven-haired. There were occasional chuckles but, perhaps because I was there, they seemed guarded, precise, almost dour. And at times there was a dark cast to their mannerisms, as if culturally they carried an ancient memory best left alone. There was also, though, a sort of subdued collective satisfaction, a genuine contentment rooted in the fact of cleverly-devised survival. Iceland is hard, but they and their ancestors thrived in it. They and their ancestors were harder than Iceland's stone and ice itself, and they all knew it.

In the long, narrow wooden hut, with the big oil stove softly rumbling and the scene lit by flickering candles, I imagined myself in a Viking longhouse. Perhaps, here in enchanted Iceland, I'd wandered through some warlock's time-portal, right back to the thirteenth century. Looking into their faces—intelligent, brusque, stoic, revealing little—I wondered if these Icelanders were magical beings.

As I took my seat, the Icelanders quieted and looked at me as one man spoke.

"Hvill you start vit a goodie?" he asked politely. His words were English, but somehow their cadence and delivery had an ancient resonance. I had indeed wandered back into the thirteenth century.

A goodie. *What the hell.* "Sure," I said.

A plate supporting a ramshackle pyramid of small, gray, meaty cubes was set before me. The blocks, about the size of sugar cubes, were slightly off-white, and they reeked. My eyes swam.

"Shark flesh," the man said gravely, "Ve let it...er... ROT...before ve eat it."

The putrid little cubes had all the appeal of a urinal cake, but I popped one in my mouth. Before I could even chew, the whole crew of Icelanders was screaming with laughter. Some were banging their fists on the table. Chewing hard, I grimaced at my audience and crushed the urge to vomit. Shreds of rotten shark flesh slid down my throat. My mind scrambled for analogies. Filthy gym socks? Ammonia?

I swallowed. I didn't throw up. I was doing well. I smiled. Everyone smiled. I was approved to stay. Perhaps I'd even broken the ice.

The hilarity subsided like a tide, but then a reserved cheer rose again; reserved because who could say what calamity was poised to descend on ghost-crowded Iceland? At any moment, Ymir, the Frost Giants of the Icelandic mythos, might just bluster up over the horizon and smash the huts to splinters. But until that inevitable disaster, some merriment was allowed. *After all*, I imagined my friend Halldor, barking with a wolfish grin and a cavalier wave of his hand, *the whole island could just blow up or sink tonight, so why not try to drag your sled across the ice cap alone in winter, or any other damned thing you please? It's all the same, in the end, if you look like a hero or a fool for a day.*

Conversations picked up again, but, kindly, the Vikings didn't resume singing, which would have made me feel profoundly useless. And they didn't ask the usual barrage of questions, which was also kind. They were going to let me eat, first. It was the hospitable practicality of Icelanders, the same shown by the looming, quiet, welcoming Hordur, who also took me in from the cold, four years ago, on my first visit to Iceland.

A smorgasbord was laid out on the long wooden table. Piles of meats, blocks of cheese, bricks of butter, and hunks of bread; a colander of boiled potatoes and a pile of salt on a big plate that everyone dipped into. Everyone was drinking Gull beer, an Icelandic standard, from tall cans. Before long, I was working on a plate of sliced meat, heavily-buttered bread, and potatoes. Gull washed it down and the nip of alcohol tilted me into pleasant contentment. It was a simple and wonderful meal.

Later, it was time to talk.

"So, American, you hvill vok all de vay across de ice cap?"

"Yes. I pull my sled-hut. It contains my supplies, and it opens so I can sleep inside."

"But hvill it hold in de storm?"

I took a breath. "I think so. I hope so."

"You have radio?"

"Iridium." Iceland is high-tech, and everyone knew this satellite phone. There were approving nods.

"And how did you come here?"

"With my friend Halldor," I said. "Halldor Kvaran? From Reykjavik?"

Although Halldor seemed to know every one of the quarter-million Icelanders, it was like asking if anyone knew "Joe" from New York.

"Just one truck?" The man was not hiding his incredulity too well.

"Yes, just one."

"Dis is crazy," he said, touching the table with his index finger at each syllable. "Hvee never do dis. Hvee never do dis." He was right, it had been crazy. I remembered Halldor bellowing gleefully as he gunned his truck across an expanse of deep slush: *If we get stuck here, they won't get us out until spring!*

"There are risks," I nodded, "but this is my fourth attempt to cross the Vatnajökull. I have to make it." It was a weak defense, but perhaps they reasoned that it had worked, and that was enough...further Icelandic pragmatism.

"You need help?"

"Well, I have a repair to make on the sled-hut." Everyone loved this. Now I was speaking their language; the Icelanders loved the repairing of things. As I described the repair I had to make, people talked earnestly of baling wire, crescent wrenches, and the benefits and merits of various classes of low-temperature bolt lubricants.

The big oil stove rumbled; guttering candles wavered darkly; festivities calmed. The food piles dwindled from the large metal platters. The Icelanders leaned back in their chairs, some humming, some stroking their lovers' arms, some staring at the ceiling or the space beyond. A jar of toothpicks was passed around. Then the women cleared away plates and platters and brought in new ones, heavy with more food, and two men went into the fore-room and came back in with cardboard cases of Gull.

As the cold cans were passed around I noticed the clan leader looking at me intently. He looked back at his plate when I saw him.

Again the evening seemed to wind down, but then again there came more platters bearing piles of meats. These were strange meats, stranger-looking than even the shark-flesh cubes. I squinted at them and the clan leader looked at me again. Suddenly all eyes were, again, on me.

"You like dis?" asked one man, presenting me, like the finest waiter, a platter holding stacks of meaty gray-white discs, the size of pepperoni slices, but thicker and more ir-regular. They swam in a cold gray broth. I was determined to ingest everything that came at me that night, so I cavalierly stabbed two with my fork. The man settled in his seat as I cut a slice and started chewing.

"*Hrutspungar*," he declared, rolling his R's like a Panzer tank, "Rrram's testicles!"

I chewed, looking straight into his eyes and sagely nodding my head, as if I'd known it all along.

"Ram's testicles, soaked in de milk acid," he said proudly.

Milk acid? What the hell is milk acid? I kept chewing. Not bad, really. Stinging, like over-salted meat, and a little fleshy—but not entirely bad. Tolerable. But the anatomy gave me a shiver. I was eating some ram's balls. *Poor bastard!*

I started working on the second slice. It took a little effort. I like to think I'm not squeamish, but I shivered at least once as I gulped down the chunks of cold, wet, pulpy meat.

Finally, the clan leader spoke, his black eyes locked on mine from halfway down the table.

"You see, de meats are vrom de old days," he said sternly, "De *harrrd* days." Then he softened, and spoke almost defensively. It was quiet in the hut and I could hear the fluttering of candle flames.

"In de old days, ve had to survive de vinter," he said, patiently searching my eyes. "Dere vas notting else ve could do."

I was an intruder who had to be educated, like someone who's discovered a band of cannibalistic mountain survivors.

"In de old days it was colder and life voss *harrrder*," he repeated, "Dere voss notting else ve could do. Ve had to eat *every*ting. Dis is vy ve eat de vinter meats, to remind us off de old days, de harrrd days."

He rested his fists on either side of his plate; case closed.

I hadn't tried to survive as a crofter in Iceland in the "harrrd days," but I'd learned more than a little about desperation in Iceland's diabolically damp, stabbing, bone-splitting cold. I took a swig of Gull and nodded, thinking on the history of the Icelandic people, the history that led right up to tonight's Thorablott like an ancient, winding path. It was a path that passed through terrible darkness.

Not long after the Vikings arrived and established their independent ethos, and the habits of keeping their sheep alive and farming in the northernmost brink of the farmable world, the climate began to change. By the 900s, things began to go dark, and cold. The four seasons were collapsed into two, summer from May to October, the rest winter. By 974, the winter was so harsh that it was written: "Men ate ravens then and foxes, and many abominable things were eaten which ought not to be eaten, and some had the old and helpless killed and thrown over the cliffs."

Such acts were the herald of what demographer R.F. Thomasson titled *A Millennium of Misery*.

The climate continued to deteriorate in the following centuries, but even a sharp downturn in the 1200s failed to dislodge the Icelanders. In 1057, and again in 1118—and seemingly forever after, at odd intervals—there was famine. The ice sheets surged outward, grinding crofts to splinters and rubble. Volcanic eruptions draped the island with choking ash and melted enormous quantities of snow, liberating devastating floods that carried away sheep, horses, cattle, people, entire farmsteads. The Abbot of Arngrimur wrote of one such fourteenth-century glacial melt: "From under these mountains at times falls a torrential stream, its volume enormous and its stench foul enough to kill birds in the air and men or beasts on the ground." In the wave of hydrogen sulfide that poured forth with the reeking rivers, vegetation withered, and metal blackened.

Calamities visited Iceland like devilish clockwork, and through the ages they didn't just leave the proverbial "indelible stamp" on the Icelandic psyche: they shaped it from first principles.

In 1400 the Black Plague arrived by ship, killing two-thirds of the 120,000 Icelanders; their numbers didn't recover substantially for four centuries. The volcanoes also continued to reshape the land, blasting the very moss from the moors, withering idyllic dales into moonscapes. In 1783 the Earth opened at a place called Laki, initiating "...the most violent, extensive and prolonged volcanic episode which has occurred in the northern hemisphere in the modern era." The eruption blasted ash all the way to Europe, where clouds of grit blocked out the sun from Edinburgh to Naples. Plants shriveled, the sky bulged with thunderclouds, and trees were stripped of leaves overnight.

Iceland was nearly annihilated; it was brought to its knees. Reverend Jon Steingrimsson wrote:

> This said week, and the two prior to it, more poison
> fell from the sky than words can describe: ash, volcanic
> hairs, rain full of sulfur and salt peter, all of it mixed
> with sand. The snouts, nostrils, and feet of livestock...

turned bright yellow and raw. All water went tepid
and light blue in color...All the earth's plants burned,
withered and turned gray, one after another, as the fire
increased and neared the settlements.

The eruption continued for six months, draping the island
with ash, wiping out most summer pasture, sheep, and horses,
and half the cattle. In the famine that followed, 9,000 Icelanders
(a fifth of the population) starved to death. Complete evacua-
tion of the country was seriously considered.

All in all, the population declined by 50 percent between
the years 1100 and 1800.

You simply have to ask, what kind of people are these
Icelanders? Do they eat rocks for breakfast? Are they *made*
of rock? Or perhaps they're sustained by deep religious con-
victions?

You can't find the answers, or the essence of the Icelanders,
in ornate architectural monuments: even today the president
inhabits a red-and-white structure that looks like nothing
more than a large farmhouse. Nor is it found in complex
statecraft or the colonization of other nations: Iceland has
never been in a shooting war with anyone. No, to find their
story you have to look into their collective monument, their
literature.

When Iceland was converted to Christianity in 1000, the
Icelanders began to record their history in what even I—a
lover of history—can only call excruciating detail. The earliest written works are the twelfth-century *Islendingabok*
("Icelanders-book") and the *Landnambok* (the "land-taking-
book"), which recorded the names, places of origin, ancestors,
and descendants of the colonists. There are also the famous
sagas and Eddas, for generations told as stories, and only
first written down in the 1300s. In today's print they consist
of five hefty volumes totaling about two thousand pages.
They recount the deeds of heroes, common folk, adventurers,
outlaws, and—occasionally, seemingly grudgingly—gods.

Icelanders have the most complete historical record of any Europeans.

Their literary treasure trove reveals a people who came to Iceland largely from Norway and other Scandinavian countries, with a healthy percentage of Irish as well: in fact, modern Icelandic blood groups are more Irish than Norse. The Scandinavians arrived as pagans, driving out the Christian Irish hermits and building temples to the Norse gods. Norway was only six days' sailing away, and though Iceland was isolated, it was never wholly ignorant of doings on the continent.

Through travelers' tales, word-of-mouth, and the arrival of a few Christian Norse, the Icelanders became aware of a great change sweeping Europe, and even Scandinavia itself: the spread of Christianity. The first missionaries arrived in the 930s, but they had little effect for two reasons. First, the Althing—the Icelandic parliament, composed of regional representatives who refused any single ruler—made proselytizing a punishable crime. One such punishment was levied against Hjalti Skeggjason, a Christian who composed an obscene stanza against the Norse goddess Freya: for trying to push his religious views he was banished from Iceland for three years. And second, many of the Icelanders were godhlaus, the "godless," atheists who rejected not only Christ, but also the whole violent pantheon of Norse gods. The godhlaus revered only survival and independence. The evangelists moved on.

Even so, Iceland watched as all Scandinavia eventually capitulated to the new religion. Finally, Christian King Tryggavsson of Norway threatened to invade and slaughter every last Icelander if they did not convert, and the Althing accepted the new religion in 1000. The Icelanders were just then experiencing the earliest effects of the climatic downturn, and likely had other things on their minds than attempting to resist a religious, economic, and cultural juggernaut that had overrun all Europe. And though the history of Iceland is known largely from church documents, dogmatic religion never seems to have deeply structured the Icelandic mind: one church manuscript, written on tough, heavy parchment, was torn apart before the pages were sewn back together as a sheet which was then perforated and used as a sieve. It is a perfect example of the Icelanders' stark, no-nonsense ways, and today it's proudly displayed in a museum.

Since conversion, the hardly-religious Icelanders—it's proudly said that only four people have ever died for their religion in Iceland—have continued to tend their farms, keep their sheep alive, and pay their debts.

It has not been easy. When you read that from 1270 to 1390 there were "bad years," you can't help but nervously chuckle at your own morbid fascination.

As early as the 1200s, the old human habits of overgrazing the land and cutting too much forest were radically reshaping the land. Without proper stands of dwarf-birches in which to shelter sheep, a single, particularly cold night could so devastate a croft's flock that it would take years to recover. Trees were never particularly plentiful, and soon they were all but gone, cut as firewood and building materials. Rootless soil blew away, and fortunes were fluid. The resulting land grabs, disputes, and turmoil are depressingly predictable.

In 1262, Norway learned that all-but-treeless Iceland could no longer build its own ships, and demanded total economic and political submission as the price for lumber. This initiated over five centuries of profound misery, as the Icelanders toiled like slaves for their Scandinavian overlords.

The 1400s brought the Black Death, described in one folk tale as an inescapable vapor that crept across the countryside. By this time, Icelandic farming had little to offer Europe in trade, and Icelanders were forced into nearly full-time fishing, which was done absurdly, and heroically, in small open boats on the north Atlantic.

In 1530 there was perhaps a spark of hope, the arrival of a fantastic new invention, the printing press. But this spark was snuffed out. The Icelanders still labored for other countries—Denmark now effectively held title over the entire Icelandic population—and they couldn't possibly realize the potential of the press. Most printed works remained chained up in church libraries, of little use to the common farmer.

The following generations brought strange new horrors. In 1627 Algerian pirates enslaved 200 Icelanders and took them off to Africa. In 1684 came a dry directive from Copenhagen: all Icelandic exports were to be devalued, and all import prices increased. It seems that Denmark simply wanted to exterminate the Icelanders, and they almost did. By 1703, 11 percent of the 50,000 Icelanders were listed as "parish paupers," surviving on rations distributed by regional churches. The year 1707 brought smallpox, killing 18,000.

Forty years later, the apparent program to kill off the Icelanders by the cruelest means possible was drawn to a point when the Horkraemmer Corporation of Copenhagen sent moldy meal to Iceland. By 1750, 9,000 or 10,000 were dead. Then in 1761, 300,000 sickly sheep had to be slaughtered. It was like draining off half the country's blood, and so enfeebled, the Icelanders faced their next catastrophe, the cataclysmic 1783 eruption of Mount Hekla.

The devastation was so widespread that Denmark made an unexpected—to use the term lightly—concession, offering to take everyone off the island. But only one-fifth of the promised disaster relief money reached Iceland, and in 1785 the population was just over 40,000 people, where a century before it had been closer to 60,000.

Eleven years later Hannes Finnsson was compelled to write the cheerfully-titled *Population Decline Resulting from the Bad Years in Iceland*. He concluded that the Icelanders probably wouldn't last more than a few generations; they were going extinct. In 1806, Magnus Stephensen summarized the eighteenth century for Iceland: "During this century, Iceland experienced 43 years of distress due to cold winters, ice floes, failures of fisheries, shipwrecks, inundations, volcanic eruptions, earthquakes, epidemics, and contagious diseases among men and animals..."

Around this time, those who survived the various forces arrayed against life did not survive for long. Life expectancy was roughly 31 years for men, and 37 for women, each more than 20 years less than in Norway. It's been estimated that of the 2 million people born in Iceland since colonization, less than half survived to the age of 16 until the late 1800s.

Considering this litany of misfortune, it's not surprising that the Icelandic psyche orbits the core concept of self-sufficiency. Poverty as a way of life; survival a palace. The legacy of existing on the edge led another character in Halldor Laxnaess's *Independent People* to wryly comment that peasants "...simply can't afford to be born."

Then a great change in 1786: fickle Denmark granted Iceland self-government, ending 524 years of crushing exploitation. Maybe they reasoned that the Icelanders simply could not be exterminated. Things had begun to flow *into* Iceland—potatoes were introduced in 1759, reindeer in 1771—and soon, centuries of effective excommunication ended when the first regular postage vessels sailed. In 1874, the Icelanders' self-regulating, kingless government, the Althing, was re-established. Greenhouses were erected in 1923, taking advantage of geothermal heat sources.

The modern era, since the global transformations of the world wars, is still reshaping Iceland and Icelanders. What they have done with independent rule is concern themselves with the building up of Iceland, rather than concern themselves with the rest of the world. There is a new affluence, partly derived from decades of fishing with improved equipment, partly from the rise of the post-World War II tourism industry. And despite a near-total economic meltdown in recent years—the kind of catastrophe that has split other countries, driven people to suicide, and entrenched entire cultures in new forms of religious belief—the Icelanders remain among the least dogmatically religious people in the world.

In my experience, the Icelanders continued to tell their tales and keep their sheep alive and remain as independent from one another as possible, even as modern urbanites— over half live in Reykjavik. The one exception to this small-group solidarity and independence is expressed in their communally-minded ethos of hospitality and generosity, and their distaste for stinginess. Time and again I was welcomed into the homes of complete strangers, fed and assisted as if I were family. I can't help but think that such hospitality is rooted in the fact that, here, mere survival is a palace, and that without much interference from government or state religion, there's simply less to be uptight about. Share and share alike; you never know when Ymir will blast your croft to matchwood and send you scurrying to your neighbors.

In the warmth of the Jokulheimar hut, Ymir seemed a quaint idea…until I looked out the window at the space-black night. It reminded me that our little feast was only a spark, a fragile, glowing gem set in a vast and frigid wilderness.

Some time later, when the evening was pleasantly fogged with beer, one of the Icelanders presented me with the crowning horror of the feast. It was a platter of alarmingly unfamiliar bony meats, again presented to me like the finest caviar.

"Can I interest you in de sheep's face?" the man asked politely.

I nodded and he pushed one of the sheep's faces off the mound. It splashed in the gray testicle broth on my plate. The sheep's face was about the size of a football, but chopped in half long ways, laid on the flat side. I rotated the plate, and the anatomy made sense. It was, as advertised, a sheep's face. There was no hair, but all the skin and muscle remained.

It didn't look cooked, but mummified. Like many of the Icelandic winter meats, it had probably hung in a cold barn for months. A cloudy eye squinted up at me. The lips were shriveled to retracted strips, like the dried worms you see on the sidewalk after a rain. The teeth were clean and sharp: a youngster.

I dug in to the *svid*. My plastic knife bent and then snapped, and the man beside me motioned for me to just pick up the face and gnaw. I tore through the cheek muscle, and moved on to the eyelid. I looked at everyone else, at my can of Gull, at the oil stove, out the window. Everyone approved, and I even gestured for more *hrutspungar*.

Finally the *brennevin* was passed around in shot glasses. Like most things in Iceland, it had several alternative names, all forbidding. Some called it "Burn Wine," others, "Black Death." Whatever its right name, it was an earthy potato-liquor, spiced with caraway, similar to vodka but with more severe effects on both gut and mind. It burned, and I tilted.

After the Black Death the table was cleared again, and the serious drinking commenced. The time for food had passed. I needed an early start on my sled-hut repairs, so I reluctantly stood and made my way down the table, thanking everyone for taking me in, feeling unworthy, apologetic, and deeply grateful.

As everyone turned to say a last good-night, and to toast my luck, the clan leader reminded me of the invisible chain linking the Icelanders, ancient and modern, living and ghost:

"Icelandic vinter meats! *Dere vas notting else ve could do!*"

❦ ❦ ❦

Cameron M. Smith's writings have appeared in The Best Travel Writing *(2008 and 2009),* They Lived to Tell the Tale: True Stories of Modern Adventure from the Legendary Explorers Club, *and many magazines including* Hang Gliding and

Paragliding, Cultural Survival Quarterly, Scientific American MIND, Playboy, *and* South American Explorer. *He is currently writing three books, including* The Frost Giants, *a wild narrative of his attempts to cross Iceland's Vatnajokull ice cap. An active paraglider pilot and SCUBA diver, he is a member of the Portland, Oregon writing group The Guttery. You can follow his expeditions and writings at www.cameronmsmith.com.*

❦ ❦ ❦

Bored Japanese Housewives

It's tough being a guy.

"HELP WANTED: FOREIGN MEN NEEDED FOR STRIP CLUB."
I am just desperate enough to reply to this ad. I'm
living in Tokyo and I'm broke; I can't get a steady English
teaching gig, or any other form of employment, to save my
life. Unfortunately, the days when a native English speaker
without any qualifications, besides being a native English
speaker, can waltz into town and score a lucrative position are
long gone. I'm learning this now that I'm already here and
running out of money.

Just to be clear, I am not what you would call a "male stripper type." I am hairy. Very hairy, everywhere, except on top of
my head, where I would generously be referred to as balding.
I am overweight. Not a fattie, per se. A former fattie—I've
lost a lot of weight in the last couple of years and this has not
left me with rippling abs, but loose, rippling, residually flabby
skin. Facially, while I'm certainly not handsome, I'm not bad

looking. I'd give myself a six or a seven. Decent for an average guy, but not a male stripper.

I don't mention these particular attributes when I phone Evan, the manager of the club, an American. I focus more on my entertainment experience, never specifically describing what it was I did as an entertainer—comedy, performance art, balloon animals—but he seems impressed by my credentials. As we arrange to meet, I ask Evan what he looks like, before he can ask me.

"I'm hard to miss in Tokyo," he says, "I'm black and six-foot-four."

Two days later, I step off a subway train at our pre-arranged stop and wind my way through a sea of Japanese commuters. Evan was right—he's impossible to miss. At six-foot-four, black and built like a professional linebacker, he's a mutant superhero towering above the Japanese. As I approach him, it appears pretty obvious that he's waiting for a Fabio, not me. He looks around, expectantly, everywhere that I'm not. When he finally realizes that the man who is standing right in front of him is the man he is here to meet, his expectant smile fades. His mouth opens to speak. I quickly jump in.

"Before you say anything, let me just say two words. Novelty...Act."

I plead my case to him, playing up the comedic aspects of my entertainment background. He naturally has his doubts. But he also has a club which faces a lot of stiff competition. He confesses that he's been looking for something to make his club stand out. And maybe, just maybe, a short, balding, flabby man could be his answer.

"All right, I'll let you audition," he says, "but you've got your work cut out for you."

We leave the station, get into his car and drive to the club, chatting along the way. Evan tells me about his life in Tokyo, being stationed there while in the Army and why he decided to stay after his tour was up.

"Japanese women love the brothers," he says, "I'm not kidding. Take a look around. Every time you see a black man, he's got two women on his arm."

I never noticed this before, but now, as we drive through the nightclub/strip club district, I see it so often—black men surrounded by giggling Japanese girls in silver foil hot pants—that I decide it would make an excellent drinking game.

Evan unlocks the front door of the club and I follow him inside. I hear him flip a switch and a blue spotlight illuminates a tiny octagonal stage, which rises a few inches above the floor. It is surrounded on three sides by a dozen tiny, matching, octagonal tables, too small for holding anything except drinks. Evan throws his coat over one of the tables and tells me to get ready. He walks into a side room that appears to be his office. I take my costume out of my backpack: a brown suede Hefneresque smoking jacket and a brown felt jester's hat. I borrowed the jacket from an English teaching acquaintance and the jester's hat, which proudly sprouts three long, firm, turgid cones topped with yellow puffy balls, I bought at a Renaissance festival many years before. I had been traveling with the hat throughout Asia, never knowing exactly why I was letting it take up valuable space in my backpack. Until now.

I am dressed. I am ready. Evan comes out of his office and tells me to begin.

"What?" I ask, "No music?"

"The sound system's off and I don't feel like messing with it. Just do it without music."

I grumble about needing music to get into the mood—I can't strip cold. He's tells me I should try humming something. It's no substitute, but what choice do I have? The only stripper music that comes to mind is the old '40s stripper song, which I believe is called "The Stripper."

Da da DAAA da DA da da

Ba da da dum
Da da DAAA da DAA da da...

I hum, I strut, and I preen. Before long, "The Stripper" becomes the old Noxzema Shaving Cream commercial.

"The more you shave, the more you need Noxzema... Noxzema Medicated Comfort Shave," I sing as I shimmy the smoking jacket off my shoulders and down my back.

When I reveal the thatch of hair covering my chest, back and shoulders, I detect a small wave of revulsion pass over Evan's face. He quickly composes himself, but it's too late. I decide to make the most of it, twirling and twisting my body hair, suggestively plucking out individual hairs on the accented horn blasts of the song:

DA (pluck!) da da da
DA (pluck!) da da da
DA (pluck!)
DA (pluck!)
DA (pluck!)
DA (pluck!)

The moments of pain are but a small price to pay for my inspiration although, if I had thought of this bit ahead of time, I'd have bought some waxing strips to strategically place around my torso.

Evan is chuckling and shaking his head. I've got him where I want him—time to bring out the big guns. I drop my pants to reveal, between my two hairy legs, a fully stuffed, leopard print G-string. (This was also a loaner from my English-teaching friend—she couldn't get me work, but she definitely came in handy in other, less tangible, ways.) I reach deep into the G-string and rummage around. I pull out a long, thin, peach-colored balloon. (I had also been traveling with a stock of balloon animal balloons. You never know when they'll come in handy.) I stretch and pull the balloon as sexily as one can stretch and pull a balloon, loosening it enough blow up. A twist here, a fold there, et voila: a three foot long phallus complete with scrotum, shaft, head, urethra, and a little bit of balloon left over at the end to carry between my legs. (I developed this trick while working adult parties in San Francisco. Like all my balloon animal tricks, it's basically a variation on "The Doggie.") I do a Mick Jagger around the octagon with my inflated manhood and mime a bit of balloon abuse. Working myself up into the proper frenzy, I turn my back on Evan and reach again into my G-string. I pull out a white balloon, blow a small bubble of air into it, insert it into my "urethra" and spin back around for the grand finale:

The Ejaculating Penis Balloon, Ladies and Gentlemen!

I stand there, my arms and legs spread wide, like Liza Minnelli expecting rapturous applause. The balloon drops to the floor.

Evan claps a few times and says, "O.K., I get the idea. Get dressed."

As I change into my civvies, Evan tells me, much to our mutual surprise, that he is interested in hiring me. I must appear a bit overeager because he tells me to calm down, that nothing is settled yet.

"Ordinarily, I do all the hiring. But for something like this, I'm going to have to run it past the owners. You'll probably have to audition again."

This is not a problem at all. I am overjoyed, never thinking I'd even get this far. It was a shot in the dark, a desperate bid just to raise some money. But now it was more than money. It was money possibly being shoved into my G-string, night after night, by bored, Japanese housewives. Maybe even so bored that I might get lucky from time to time.

Three days later, I'm back in the octagon, parading around in my G-string for the owners. I was expecting some poly-ester-shirted, permed-up Japanese Yakuza swinger with a couple of giggling bimbos hanging onto him, but the own-ers—two men, two women—are quite respectable looking, very well-tailored. They're in their early forties and seem a little strait-laced to be in this sort of business. Maybe it's a tax write-off. Or maybe there's more to them than I can see. For all I know, they could be into all sorts of kinky things. Even hairy, flabby white men wearing jester's hats and G-strings.

I work the same act as before, but I'm feeling a little off. I'm not connecting with the audience. Last time, Evan laughed, he got the parts he was supposed to get, but tonight, I'm not getting any real feedback. The men have faces of granite—no twitch, no tic, no change of expression. They're giving me nothing. The women are smiling, but it might only be good manners. At the "big" moments, they merely cover their mouths and giggle slightly. Maybe they find it funny. Maybe they're embarrassed. I haven't lived in Japan long enough to know.

I finish, again with the ejaculating balloon. The owners applaud for what I presume they deem to be an appropriate amount of volume and time. They stand in unison, turn in unison and walk single file into Evan's office. Before closing the door, one of the men says something in Japanese to Evan while gesturing towards me.

"What did he say?" I'm hoping for a clue.

"He said you should put your pants on."

I get dressed and wait with Evan. I ask him how he thinks it went with the owners. He doesn't have any more of a clue than I do and he's been in Japan for nine years. After about fifteen minutes, the door opens. Evan is called inside. The door closes. I wait.

The door eventually opens again and Evan steps out.

"Well?" I ask.

"It was a close vote…" he says.

"And…?"

"Three to one. Three for, one against."

"I got the job!" I jump up.

"Well…no. It has to be unanimous. If one owner has doubts, then they all have doubts."

"No!" I cry, "That's not right! It's majority rules. Everybody knows that."

"Not here. I'm sorry."

"Well, who voted against me? It was one of the men, wasn't it? Let me talk to him. I can get him to change his vote."

"Forget it. It's over. Let me buy you a drink."

Evan walks behind the bar at the rear of the club and brings over two large cans of Sapporo.

"Listen," he says, "for what it's worth, I thought it was a great act."

"Thanks."

We drink as the owners file out of the office. As they pass, each bows politely to me, still with no expression, except for the woman at the end of the line. As she walks out the door, she turns to me, smiles and gives me a thumbs up. She wasn't stuffing money into my G-string, but it made me feel a little better. Then again, it could have meant anything. I return to my beer and ask Evan if the guy who voted against me told him why.

"He didn't give me any specific reasons," Evan says, "but I think he might have gone for it if you were black."

❧ ❧ ❧

Phil Goldman has, over the years, been a jungle guide in Thailand, nude model in Singapore, martial arts instructor and bank spy in Boston, and just missed being a male stripper in Tokyo. He is the creator and host of the award-winning storytelling show Live Bait: True Stories from Real People *because he'd still rather not get a real job.*

❦ ❦ ❦

Kaptein, Span die Seile

In South Africa, the author sails
the seas of humanity.

THEY SAY THE CAPTAIN ALWAYS GOES DOWN WITH THE ship. But what about the crew…are all those on board bound to this same fate?

From Friday to Sunday a group of us had been holding an extended birthday celebration for a friend in Clarens, a small mountain town in the Free State, South Africa. Sunday morning found Pieter and me sitting at a picnic table outside of the hostel drinking coffee, writing poetry, and surveying the wanton destruction of the previous night's party in which anything flammable and not bolted down had found its way into the bonfire. I reflected upon how the word *party* may be the most inclusive verb in the English language. It can be used to denote anything from the most benign revelry to something on par with an orgy with Latvian immigrants all wearing Viking hats. Indeed I had partied last night. Suffice it to say that my overindulgence had led to a drunken belli-cosity that left me with few allies by morning. Luckily, Pieter had himself consumed heroically and passed out early enough to miss my tirades, making him my companion of choice by default. Our friends in this life are not as often those we seek out as those we find ourselves backed into a corner with.

He was one of those South Africans who doesn't often speak English. This is not to say such people are lacking in ability, but rather their Afrikaans heritage monopolizes their cultural identity. He worked for Radio Pretoria, a bastion of apartheid politics. Read: completely racist. I'd found in South Africa that racism was the elephant in the room like booze is for a recovering alcoholic. I often felt while talking to cer-tain people that they were one transition away from a racial tirade. Pieter was one such person. While nothing racist had yet come out of his mouth, I felt certain he was one in the way that at home I'm positive the guy buying Busch Light beer has at least two vehicles in his driveway that don't run. Precedence is an uncanny prophet.

A rule of thumb while traveling abroad is to stay out of local politics. However, outright engagement cannot elimi-nate passive observations. De jure South Africa is sixteen years removed from apartheid. De facto South Africa is one where a black government has failed to deliver the promises of an equal society to all but a few, where one in three people live on $2 a day, where whites drive around in cars and live in gated properties while blacks live in cramped shantytowns without electricity and beg for work on the side of the road, where a large number of blacks, while not locked up during curfew, are desperate enough to kill you in cold blood for a few bucks and a cell phone. In accordance with that traveler's dictum I steered clear of any polemic on racism. It wasn't my country and I didn't know the ins and outs of the topic enough to speak with authority. Yet I couldn't deny that in modern South Africa, equality is still a dream of the future.

At about 10 A.M., the rest of the group turned their bleary eyes on the outside world. Their base pleasantries to Pieter and me may have been due to hangovers but I could sense hesitation to approach our poetry jam. By now we'd moved past coffee and on to beer, which seemed the only logical conclusion in response to the past three days. We would keep this train rolling at the risk of abrupt sobriety derailing us. Pieter and I had singled ourselves out as an odd couple united by disgrace and a love of poetry. At least, I *assumed* he was producing flowing verse on the beauty of nature. After all he was writing in Afrikaans and very well could have been commenting on the Negro's inferior cranial capacity.

The morning slogged on in a fashion typical of post-revelry. We all went for lunch as a final token of celebration. Over greasy fare and several more beers it was decided that I would catch a ride back to Pretoria with Pieter, who lived close to where I was staying. After eating we returned to our quarters to gather our things before departing. From somewhere on the property somebody played a song entitled, "*Kaptein, Span die Seile*" (Captain, span the sails) which in South African vernacular would be described as "zeph" (think white trash). The song is at best a ballad, at worst an assault on music as we know it, but goddamn if it isn't catchy. I parroted the chorus several times and it stuck. It was an appropriate verse to sing while loading my things into the back of Pieter's white Mercedes. I serenaded him with it as he made the final preparations, which seemed to please him. He was my captain, and his stout build and roomy, powerful German auto offered a degree of security.

When I said goodbye to the others they expressed concern over his level of intoxication. I had a brief thought of myself as Ishmael, a wanderer lured in by the mad Ahab promising adventure and reward while really only pursuing his own monomaniacal goals. However, those fears were overshadowed by my rule of thumb that people who drink heavily and drive superior machines are trustworthy. "*Kaptein, span die Seile!*" I announced as a vote of confidence. The eight cylinders roared to life and we were off.

Almost immediately his driving gave me a scare. He showed a tendency to accelerate recklessly and steer toward telephone poles. However, I knew from experience that drunk driving requires reorientation and this faith was rewarded as we merged onto the highway and he gained a steady hand. The Mercedes hugged the long, straight South African highway with precision and I relaxed.

The road out of Clarens was one of expansive views of sky, plains, and mountains. Upon rounding a corner and seeing a particularly fine view we pulled over to write poetry. Even though we'd spent most of the morning together we hadn't spoken much to each other. It wasn't awkward because I knew he was shy about his English and I also felt a silent camaraderie with him which came from a common purpose. We were two men in adoration of nature and poetry. While we were stopped he pulled a bottle of whiskey out of the trunk. "Help yourself," he invited. *Well,* I figured, *better to be drunk with him than to sit here sober.* This became especially true as he revealed a propensity for driving at high speeds. All at once he gunned the car up to 200 km/hr and passed several cars like they were standing still.

"Fuck I love this vehicle," he proclaimed. "I hope you like a bit of speed." It was not a question but an ultimatum. I assured him we were on the same page.

"Yes, *Kaptein!*" I said. "Fuck yes! *Span die Seile!*"

He chortled, but there was a hint of madness in his voice.

The needle passed 200 km/hr, 210, 220. He steered with one hand while the other passed the whiskey bottle to his mouth. The cars in the oncoming lane flashed their lights. 230, 240. He veered back to the left, cutting off a truck and the approaching line of cars whizzed by a bit too close for comfort.

"So, do they have guys like me in America?" he asked.

What, drunken, racist madmen? I thought. "Yes, lots of them." I replied. He seemed a bit disappointed.

"And what about this kind of scenery?" he said.

"Sure, out west," I said, "but not in the northeast, where I'm from." The whiskey had loosened our tongues and we conversed amiably to a backdrop of stunning scenery.

We stopped again for a poem and a piss. In one massive chug he finished the whiskey and threw the bottle into the bushes with a grunt. He then produced another from the trunk. I was all for a little booze to pass the tedium of a long drive, but this was bordering on excessive. As we pulled away he ran through the gears and reached 250 km/hr in about ten seconds, nearly running into the back of a car before swerving around it and then back in front. I gripped the edges of my seat and again thought of Ahab. I recalled the last scene of *Moby Dick* where he is caught by his own harpoon and pulled down into icy depths by the whale. Only now, a member of the crew was entangled with him. I realized with horror that the White Whale was the Mercedes. We were being dragged inevitably to our deaths on the back of the powerful beast. I thought perhaps I should demand he slow down and gain some control, but I didn't want to provoke him. I wondered what my role was in the story. Was I Ishmael, the thoughtful, reflective but non-confrontational survivor or Starbuck, the one who sternly objects to the captain's madness but ends up perishing?

The smaller country highway gave way to the N1, the main vein which runs the length of South Africa from Cape Town in the south to Messina on the Zimbabwean border. The White Whale held the road expertly despite Ahab's loose grip. This automobile was meant for top speed on an open road, which was one of the few points of consolation. As we merged onto the N1 there was a police road block pulling people over at random.

"Oh shit," said Pieter. "I can't afford to be pulled over. This vehicle isn't registered."

Never mind the fact that you're totally shitfaced, I thought. I was, in my own way, unregistered as well. My tourist visa had long ago expired. I wondered what the penalty was for being an illegal alien accomplice to a drunken man with an unregistered vehicle. Perhaps if I turned on the captain they'd show leniency. Yes…mutiny was my only option…

We made it through the blockade and both of us sighed with relief. To celebrate, Pieter took a long swig from the bottle.

"Your car really isn't registered?" I asked, probing for an explanation.

"No. I took the case to court last year and won. I don't support the government. It's my right not to give my money to them," he said.

I took "don't support the government" to mean "hate the blacks."

I pressed ahead tentatively. "So, what political party do you support?" I asked

"Ach!" he exclaimed with disgust. "It's all a bunch of bullshit. Majority rule. It's a pity. The blacks have fucked this country up." As he said this he grew agitated and the White Whale drifted a bit into the next lane.

"A fucking pity," he said and punched the dashboard lightly, further drifting into the adjacent lane.

Here it comes, I thought. *Change the subject. Obviously he can't drive* and *focus on hate for the black man at the same time.*

I switched the conversation to chauvinistic small talk. The thought of degrading women seemed to ease his mind…for now. Still, the specter of a racist outburst and a total descent into madness hung about the car. The White Whale had yet to submerge and take us to our deaths, but I didn't know how long we could stay above the surface.

The White Whale barreled down the center lane, the

Mercedes emblem looking like a periscope to guide the way. Up ahead in the road was a flash of something yellow.

"I'm fucked now!" said Pieter.

In a moment the grim reality dawned on me as well. The yellow was the vest of a traffic cop. We were being pulled over. Surely this was the end of the line. There was no way the driver of this speeding, unregistered vehicle didn't reek of booze. I clumsily shoved the empty bottles under the seat and tried to look casual. The cop approached the window and said something in Afrikaans. I could make out "180" which I knew must be our speed. The limit was 120. I made eye contact with the officer, trying my best to not look like an illegal American. The men carried on in Afrikaans and I imagined it sounded something like this:

OFFICER: License and registration, please.

PIETER: Well, actually, this vehicle is unregistered.

OFFICER: Oh, so you mean to tell me that in addition to smelling like a distillery and driving well over the speed limit this vehicle is illegally on the road?

PIETER: Come on, give me a break, just this once, please, I beg you.

OFFICER: When you're blatantly breaking three laws? Are you serious?

PIETER: Yes, well, it's my right because you goddamn blacks ruined this country.

OFFICER: Well, you deserve it because you treated us like dogs for so many years. You're in my country now, honky.

PIETER: [begins to write down something] What's your name? I'm going to report you to your owner. Mdelgaba...is that with one clicks or two?

OFFICER: Smart guy, huh? We'll see how clever you are when I haul your ass into the station and hand this car over to my friends for scrap.

PIETER: You black son of a bitch.
OFFICER: Cheers, whitey. Have a nice day.

Did that really just happen? Are we really just driving away scot-free?

"Did you see what I've just done there?" Pieter said, laughing.

"What the hell did you say to him?" I asked in disbelief.

"I told him I'm a freelance reporter and that I'm going to write a favorable story about him and his department in the newspaper. Did you see me take his details down? He actually believed me!"

This man is a legend, I thought. *He's some sort of mad, twisted, drunken, smooth-talking genius.* I congratulated him and acknowledged that was too close for comfort. I was tempted to heap praise upon him before realizing it was his fault for getting us into the mess in the first place. Or was it? I was beginning to lose the ability to make sense of things. I felt a strong allegiance to this man for some reason. Perhaps I'd been locked inside the car for too long, or, was his madness rubbing off on me? Was I becoming no more than Ahab's protégé? Laughing, I took a gulp from the bottle and encouraged the captain to give her some gas.

It was nearly 6 P.M., which meant darkness was firmly established on the mid-June evening. I hoped the cover of darkness would provide safe passage but also realized it could bring out the worst in a man. We were less than an hour from home and things had settled down considerably after we'd avoided the grips of law enforcement. The White Whale moved at a steady 150 while Ahab quietly took sips from the bottle. Perhaps the close call had put some sense into him.

Along the side of the road bushfires burned. When I asked Pieter about them he answered, "The bloody blacks. They want to destroy everything the white man has built."

I couldn't connect the dots between burning grass and his racial explanation. But it was clear I'd reignited the captain's madness.

"My friend, I tell you, this country was fuck all before the white man came here. There were no roads, no hospitals, no government, nothing. We turned this into a proper civilized country. Before us it was a country of savages and they want it to be that way again. I tell you, apartheid worked. A lot of people didn't like it but at least there was progress. This country was growing. Now, it's turning into nothing again. I tell you, these bloody blacks are savages, the way they burn things down, kill people for fuck all."

If there was somebody to tell, "I told you so," this would have been the time to say it. The racial tirade that I'd sensed simmering all afternoon had been unleashed.

"Have you ever been the victim of such things?" I asked him.

"Yes. I've had a knife held to my throat. I've been jumped and beaten. People I knew were brutally murdered on farms. I tell you, it's horrible. They're butchers. Trust me. This isn't your country, you don't understand. Peace is not possible with these people. They're animals."

What could I say in response? Surely there was no changing this man's mind. We drove along in silence, the fires burning brightly in the night.

Somewhere on the edges of Johannesburg we exited the N1 and turned onto another highway which led northeast to Pretoria. As we did, a *whump whump* sound began. It was the unmistakable sound of a flat tire. We pulled over to check and confirmed that the back left tire was totally deflated. Cars whizzed by on the highway dangerously close. Pieter got the jack out and we set to lifting up the car. This proved difficult because where we had stopped was on an awkward pitch. Each time I got the car up the jack slipped out. Pieter put the car into neutral and tried to ease back to a flatter spot but the entire section of road was uneven. We'd been at it for over thirty minutes and our tempers were growing short. Just then a taxi van pulled up behind us and a man with a big smile jumped out.

"Is this a hijacking?" asked Pieter, raising his arms.

The man laughed. "No my friend. I'm here to help you," he said. He pulled a beefy hydraulic jack from the back of the van and helped us raise the car. It held steady and we were able to swap the flat for the spare. We both thanked him profusely.

"My friend," said Pieter, "I'm in your debt. This is a symbol of a new South Africa, white and black working together."

The taxi driver smiled and said, "Of course. How could I not? We must help each other."

We shook his hand and he pulled away with a friendly toot of the horn.

Back inside the car I felt certain the uncanny timing of a black man stopping to help two white guys right after the driver had insulted the entire African race was beyond mentionable irony. However, I felt as if I had to say something. "You know, despite all of the terrible things you hear about black on white crime in South Africa I haven't had anything even close to dangerous happen to me since I've been here. If anything, I've found the guys to be really friendly and helpful. Like that taxi driver. No white people stopped to help us and they're the majority of people on the road." I waited for a change of heart, an admission of overreaction. Instead, all I got was:

"One in a thousand of the kaffirs are actually fucking human. I tell you, in almost every break-in, every home murder, it's the maid, the gardener, somebody you trust, who's helped you raise your family or business, they're the ones that fuck you over. They may not kill you or rob you themselves, but they'll let the criminals in."

I thought again of Pieter as Ahab, of the mad captain's

pursuit of the White Whale and what it actually stood for.
The captain of the *Pequod* was driven by rage and revenge.
His tale was a warning against the madness and destruction
inherent to believing in something too much. Melville wrote:

> The White Whale swam before him as the
> monomaniac incarnation of all those malicious
> agencies which some deep men feel eating in them,
> till they are left living on with half a heart and half a
> lung. That intangible malignity which has been from
> the beginning; to whose dominion even the modern
> Christians ascribe one-half of the worlds; which the
> ancient Ophites of the east reverenced in their statue
> devil;—Ahab did not fall down and worship it like
> them; but deliriously transferring its idea to the
> abhorred white whale, he pitted himself, all mutilated,
> against it. All that most maddens and torments; all that
> stirs up the lees of things; all truth with malice in it; all
> that cracks the sinews and cakes the brain; all the subtle
> demonisms of life and thought; all evil, to crazy Ahab,
> were visibly personified, and made practically assailable
> in Moby-Dick. He piled upon the whale's white hump
> the sum of all the general rage and hate felt by his
> whole race from Adam down; and then, as if his chest
> had been a mortar, he burst his hot heart's shell upon it.

I understood the symbolism properly now. The Mercedes
was not the White Whale. Pieter's White Whale was the
black man. In that race of people he'd found a singular object
to direct his rage. To him, they were the cause of all life's ills.
Only the restoration of apartheid or an equally oppressive
system would allow him to feel at peace.

The Mercedes pulled up outside my gate. As I said goodbye
to Pieter I realized that he was a hero of the Shakespearian
mold: bold and charismatic yet possessing the tragic flaw of

hatred. I was very fond of the man and could even understand his racism. It was the essence of the banality of evil. Who's to say I wouldn't feel the same if I or my family or friends had been the target of violent crime? Had I never made a racist joke or reflected upon the vast dissimilarities between people of different skin color and culture? I had many times. Did that make me a racist too? The difference perhaps between being a racist and not isn't the preference of one race over another. Cultural misunderstandings are natural and should be expected. The truth lies in the acknowledgment that, despite differences, equality and unity are possible. A racist is a totalitarian. Their world is bipolar, hateful and cruel. An Ahabian view on race, or anything for that matter, leads to tragedy, destruction and death.

The conclusion of our saga was like an alternate ending to Melville's classic in which Ahab survives the fate of his own mad hatred and is given another chance to pursue reason. And, like the original Moby Dick, there was another survivor. As my feet touched down on solid ground I at last knew my role in the tale. Call me Ishmael.

～ ～ ～

Brian Eckert is a freelance writer. A native of New Hampshire, he has traveled to five continents and lived on four. His work has appeared in The Wanderlust Review *and* Beatdom *magazine. He is a contributor to The Nervous Breakdown (www.thenervousbreakdown.com) and also maintains the blog The Bohemian Experiment (www.thebohemianexperiment.com). You can reach him by email at brian.eckert10@gmail.com.*

KEVIN McCAUGHEY

~ ~ ~

We Wait for Spring, Moldova and Me

A teacher at The Didactic School of Language longs,
without knowing his desire, for renewal.

I T WAS A MISTAKE, FINISHING THAT BOTTLE OF KAGOR. But with no heat and no lights, no TNT all-night movies, there wasn't much to do, except wait for spring.

But that was last night. This morning, outside my apartment block, the bare trees clump with snow and the potholes in the road are filling. It's the end of March.

The country is Moldova, a wishbone of a land scrunched between Romania and Ukraine. The year is 2000, and Moldova has surpassed Albania as Europe's poorest nation. This is—will be—my third spring.

I ride the trolley bus, held upright by fur-coated people who squeeze from all sides. My wallet is in my front pocket.

Stuffed in my shoulder bag are teaching tools and a towel. Down between my shoes, I watch the snow swish by through a hole in the floorboards.

The Didactic School of Language is on Armeneasca Street, four blocks off the main thoroughfare. It could be a village street. Its single-story houses with unstraight walls lean toward the sidewalk, and, as you walk by, you smell the steam of tea escaping beneath doors. The new snow muffles the noise of passing Ladas and makes the cars seem whispery and diffident.

I'm the first to arrive at the school, not from a sense of duty, but because there's no water in my apartment. First I make coffee. Then I remove my shirt. Then I take my towel and the electric tea kettle into the bathroom, add icy tap water, and pour the mix over my head, splashing my armpits and soaping my hair.

I will have six hours of English lessons and then some placement testing, but it's Saturday and in the evening—ah, the evening—we will have the yearly school-sponsored dinner at the restaurant Sanatate.

Most of my classes are downstairs in the windowless Green Room. It has the shape of an uneven triangle, wedged into a corner of the building. The classroom decor is post-communist modern, meaning that the contents have been purchased through a Western philanthropic concern, and while chairs and whiteboards look new, they are falling apart because an administrator has cut corners. The furniture in the newly built home of said administrator is reported to be sturdier.

My twelve students, aged seventeen to forty, sit with their backs to the wall. Coats and fur hats overwhelm the rack in the corner, and occasionally topple it. The air is thick with body odor—no one likes cold-water showers in unheated apartments—but despite this, they *look* fresh, especially the girls, who are made-up and snug into outfits—dresses or skirts or jeans with boots—of which they own just one or two, but wear them bright-eyed, again and again.

Today this level four class is subdued. Perhaps it's the snow—there is no window to see out of. The students steer clear of English, whispering in Russian and Romanian, "R&R" as it is known in our class. The game I have just made up, "Spill the Glove"—using one of my mittens and some torn up shreds of paper with questions on them—is not very good. But still they should *try* in English.

Eventually I start into a guilt-producing speech. *How many hours are you in class with a chance to speak English? Five. How many hours in the rest of the week? One hundred sixty-three?* And blah, blah, blah.

The speech sounds passionate and improvised, but after two years of teaching in the Republic, it is fairly well scripted.

"So you think about that…" I say, then exit the room without another word, ostensibly to quell my anger, but really to brew some more coffee.

In the teachers' office Carolina and Alyona prepare for their lessons. They are like all our Didactic teachers: mid-twenties, pretty, and serious. Because they have lives outside of the school, they take the office to be a place of work.

"I gave my students the speech," I say.

Carolina is shaking her head. "Kevin, *ty zaraza*." Literally, *You're an infection*. It means pain in the ass.

Alyona is cutting up strips of paper and doesn't bother to look up. She is divorced, dating a big jolly bear of a drunk, an ex-military man who brings his alcoholism to office hours. (Years later, he will, astonishingly, become a bigwig in TV production; then, at a family picnic, showing how Russian roulette is played, will shoot his head off.)

"Hey, Alyona, did I ever tell you about Carolina's wedding night?"

"Everybody told me," she says.

For our first school-financed trip, in the spring of '97, we crossed the border to Romania. That first evening, Carolina revealed that she was married; in fact, the ceremony had taken place *that very day*. She did not invite her husband on the trip.

"Carolina wouldn't let me stay in her hotel room with her," I tell Alyona. "I wasn't going to make any moves. But it might've been my only chance at a wedding night."

"Stop, *tupeetsa*," Carolina says. *Imbecile.*

I get my coffee. "Remember girls, tonight's Sanatate!"

Back in the classroom, the students put on sheepish faces. One girl, with bright lipsticky lips and awful teeth, acts as spokesperson: "Kevin, we promise not speak R&R."

I accept this apology. Why not? I've got coffee now and the Sanatate party tonight. The class deserves some fun, so we listen to Petula Clark's "Downtown" too loud, and one of the front desk girls arrives to scold me.

The day is long. Four eighty-minute classes, then testing. During the next lessons, I dash out for coffee, my guitar, some dice, a ball or a stuffed animal—anything that will get me through.

Halfway through the late afternoon class, the last one, just as the caffeine in me is no longer pulling its weight, I catch a break. Olga, who is eighteen, and bundled in a red dress, with a whisper of mustache, announces it is her birthday, and, in this part of the world, she is duty-bound to provide merriment. She brings forth a fluffy Moldavian cake dabbed with ashy-tasting prunes; then, from behind the coat rack, digs out a bag clinking with bottles of wine.

The whole class drinks. A big Romanian business guy, always in a suit, tells a joke in English. The punch line is, "A hat on his head drinking a rose." Everyone laughs. I pretend to. Why not? I've almost made it through the day.

"Kevin, you understand our specific humor?" the joke teller asks.

"Not at all."

"Play '*Cel Mai Mare*,'" a student requests.

I feign reluctance a moment, then pick up my guitar.

"*Cel Mai Mare*" is the only song I have ever composed in (mostly) Romanian, and stretches my knowledge of that language to the brink:

Cel mai mare
Cel mai bun
Cel mai mare
Cel mai bun
Cel mai mare
Cel mai bun
Feed me mamaliga
With a silver spoon

The English translation would go like this:

The biggest
The best
The biggest
The best
The biggest
The best
The biggest
The best
Feed me your traditional national dish made from ground
    hominy
With a silver spoon

One of the Vicas pushes in—the front desk girls are all named Vica—and she says, "You know that placement testing started five minutes ago. You are in the Red Room."

I carry a plastic cup of wine up the steep staircase and into a second-story classroom. There are windows, and the view

from here astonishes me. Sunlight everywhere. In the last
four hours, the temperature outside has risen twenty degrees.
There is no snow in the trees, not a flake. The roofs of the
one-story houses glint with light. There is not a trace of slush
on the roads now, only brown puddles.

Prospective students come into the room, one by one, and
face me. I question them for three minutes, five if they are
girls, more if they are attractive girls. So what? The sun is
warm. Wine lifts my insides. Spring comes running.

And in several hours I will be off to Sanatate for the once-
in-a-year night of cheer paid for by the school.

It is 5:00 P.M., still light, and there is lots of time, so I walk
through the spring-the-pretender weather with Michael. He is
the only other American currently at the Didactic school. He
has a Ph.D. in literature, and a beard and glasses to prove it.

Stumpy the Dog is on the corner of Armeneasca and
Scuisev, hobbling next to a plump woman with felt boots who
sells cigarettes, candy, and detergent packs. Stumpy is homeless, but spends his daylight hours here, with the cigarette
lady. He is dirty, wire-furred, and his right forepaw is gone.
The stump is worn smooth, red and white like a neatly cut
bone at the butchers.

"Two and a half years ago," I say, "when I came to
Moldova, Stumpy's leg was longer. He used to actually walk
on it. And I have honestly seen, I mean visibly, how it sort of
got filed down."

We are both wondering what years in Moldova have done
to us.

We reach Boulevard Stefan Cel Mare (Stefan the Great),
Chisinau's main thoroughfare, where the streetlamps often
work, where cars swarm, where the fashionable find Big
Macs, and the legless wheel themselves on wheeled boards.

Farther down, the boulevard widens. Here are the government buildings, cast back from the main street; they have

the look of mausoleums. We cross a park here, passing the blue-and-white onion-dome church of St. Nicholas—a storage shed in Soviet times—down to a street called The Youths' Prospect, and one kilometer to the restaurant.

Sanatate is a Romanian folk-style restaurant. The staff is Romanian, the clientele Romanian. Old-style wooden tables and benches. Fast Moldavian music with its Turkish and gypsy influences. The Russians of the city prefer white tablecloth places and lip-sync pop divas.

Michael and I drink beer at the bar until the rest of The Didactic School of Language arrives.

This is the big spring dinner, and there are thirteen of us—teachers, staff, and the director. Carolina and Alyona, among others, are no-shows. We're squeezed at one long table in a semi-private room. Waiters in baggy white shirts and sashes jam the table surface with traditional Moldavian fare, everything on a separate plate: first bread, and thick salads soppy with sunflower oil, fresh cucumbers and piles of dill and parsley, tomatoes stuffed with whipped garlic, salty squares of sheep-milk *brinsa*; and later, more plates, overlapping now, chicken and cutlets. And there are ceramic pitchers of wine, as much as we like.

But it's clear that no one really wants a big night. Everyone is tired. Everyone has problems.

I have a problem too.

"This wine," I say to Michael, "I can't even drink it." It is the mustiest thing I've ever tasted. I try to explain to the Romanian waiter, who must listen to my Russian. I don't know how to say musty. So I describe it as old and dirty.

"It all comes from the barrel upstairs," the waiter says. And he insists that I accompany him upstairs to prove it.

Up through a dark stairwell we go, then a dim corridor with chipped aqua walls, into a small room where a metal wine cask is locked behind bars. The waiter keys open a padlock, and clanks upon the barred door.

"Now you will see that I'm not deceiving you," he says.

The waiter turns the spigot and fills me a glass. I drink. "It's disgusting," I tell Michael in English.

"Is it the same?" asks the waiter.

"Yes, it's the same all right."

This is not really the point at all, but the waiter believes the case is solved. He pours himself a glass, and toasts to our health.

It is one of those Moldovan endings, like the punch line "a hat on his head drinking a rose." Or, to take things further, the reason we often have no electricity. The power plants exist only in the east, in a pro-Russian enclave called Transdniester, which has declared itself an independent country. They have their own borders, police, stamps, and money. They get testy on occasion, being poorer than the rest of the poorest country in Europe, and they pull the switch—presto, no electricity. They often do this at night. A student provides the punch line: "If they turn off light in the day people will not use it."

Downstairs a non-electric Moldavian band has started up. A stand-up bass, accordion, *timbu* (like a piano-sized hammer-dulcimer), guitar, and pan flute churn out fast riffs for a few dancers. Only after an hour do they slow things down, and I ask our audio visual girl to dance. Mariana is a sweet *moldavanka* with light skin. Her husband is in business, a blanket term for Mafia employment. Mariana is in tight leather pants, her plump rump not quite buying into the look. We're alone on the dance floor, and I ask a question.

"Why are slow songs so rare in Moldavian music?"

She thinks for a moment as we turn a small-stepped circle. "What do you name people who steal from rich and give to poor?"

"Bandits. Or Robin Hoods."

"Well," she says, "In these songs Robin Hoods sit and drink the wine."

Another unintended puzzle, a Moldova punch line.

But I for one am done with the wine. After the dance, I order ten bottles of beer to our table, hoping to jump-start things.

Just then, the teachers and staff start rising to go. And it's only ten o'clock.

"All right," I say, "you have forced me to be silly." I put a crown of parsley on my head and dill sprigs behind my ear, but their minds are made up, and I only succeed in being an infection.

Michael and I are the last to leave. We take our bottles of Chisinau beer with us out to the sidewalk. The night is coolly pleasant now, the morning's snow like a memory from another season.

"I'm going to walk home," I announce.

Michael suggests that it's too far and unsafe. There are holes in the sidewalks. Police ready for the shakedown. Wild dogs. Robin Hoods. Bandits. Most of us foreigners have been hassled, bitten, beaten, or robbed. Michael has even been pistol-whipped. But unlike our local friends, he doesn't insist.

I walk a long way, a good hour, through the city center, then up toward Telecentre, my region at the edge of the city. Three-quarters of the way home, something comes over me—an infection of sorts, I suppose—and I set off through streets I have never walked before, roads where the streetlamps haven't worked in years, an area that looks like a village—with its thick-tree darkness, streets of mud, and shadowy dogs melting into the blackness.

And then, when I am utterly lost, like a miracle, I break out onto familiar Dacia Street, so close to the group of block buildings where I live. I feel wonderful, fate having guided me homeward. The first building, the tallest, has never been beautiful at all, a ten-story tombstone. But now coming out from the trees, the night so sharp and clean, seeing those rounded balconies on the corners, unlit but visible under the starlight in a faint glow.... So many stars. And everything makes sense for these moments. I feel like I have moved through the universe.

Here I am, in a city—the capital city of a country!—and there are so many stars I can practically feel the Earth moving through them.

Out of one season and into the next.

Spring is definitely coming soon.

Even Moldova deserves spring.

⤞ ⤞ ⤞

In 1996, Kevin McCaughey applied for teaching positions, on a thematic whim, in countries beginning with the letter M. Mongolia and Morocco passed, but a desperate school in Moldova offered him a job. Today Kevin is a wandering teacher trainer who also writes stories and composes music. He has been a Fulbright Fellow in Belarus and has taught in Russia, Yemen, India, Jordan, Tajikistan, and Turkmenistan. His memoir-in-progress is called Beyond the Iron Skirt: Puzzling Adventures with Russian Girls, *and his teaching website is English Teachers Everywhere (www.etseverywhere.com). This story won the Grand Prize Silver Award in the Fourth Annual Solas Awards (www. BestTravelWriting.com).*

❧ ❧ ❧

Submitting to Shasta

Mountains always remind you that
you are not in charge.

Shasta! Oh Mount Shasta!
What secrets do you hide
What dwells within that heart of yours
What Light does there abide?...
What Knowledge do you guard so well
From those who seek too bold?...
—Godfre Ray King (1878-1939)

WE ARE FOUR ON A ROPE ON THE SLOPE.
Said like that there's a certain poetic appeal to
our ordeal. We are four on a rope—without hope? No, no;
we have hope all right, hope born weeks ago when we, eager,
decided to climb the 14,179-foot strato-volcano in California
called Mt. Shasta. But here it comes: the rock the size of a
Chevy Suburban. It rockets off a colossal shale outcrop directly

above us, and with an eerie crack it crashes once, now twice on the steep, snow slope to which we cling for dear life with crampons. A searing flash of fear slices into me and I wonder if perhaps such hope is nothing more than our mistake. Our miserable mistake. Spinning, the boulder picks up sickening speed; it plunges, it charges, it *lunges* now dead ahead toward Camille, who stands frozen as the rock bears down. The advancing hulk seems to have decided: she, yes she, has been chosen its victim—the sacrifice expected for our conceit. Stricken with shock I watch the rock fall and in an instant know: this mountain of terrible beauty, where a dazzle of glacial seductions entice so many climbers to prove their mojo as its match, may allow its slopes to be scaled and its summit won, but in the end? Shasta will not be conquered.

I am no mountaineer. Let Jon Krakauer climb *Into Thin Air* up Everest to taunt death all he wants. Let Simon Yates, broken-boned and bloody, disappear down a crevasse high in the Peruvian Andes; let *him* endure an ordeal arguably worse than death: the four harrowing days he crawled inch-by-inch through fear and pain and desolation to safety. The avalanches on K2, the falls off Denali, the high-altitude cerebral edema enjoyed in the "death zone" above 23,000 feet—no, thank you. Sunny spring skiing at a chi-chi resort like Sun Valley? My speed. Still, when my sister Camille and our friend Mark, both avid climbers, conspired to summit Shasta in a three-day adventure that promised (they promised) terrific hiking, delightful camping, and a wonderful excuse to get out in the wild for fresh air and fun, I would not be left behind. Neither would Camille's sixteen-year-old son, Gabriel. And so we prepped.

Shasta, after all, is hardly Everest. It's only the second highest peak in the Cascade Range, and the fifth tallest in California, and hundreds of ambitious hikers a year scale its eight glaciers without too much to-do, despite the occasional bout of altitude sickness or not-too-serious fall. Crevasses and avalanches and a nose or toes lost to frostbite? This is not the stuff of Shasta. And so it was with excited anticipation I did what all actual mountaineers surely do: I shopped. Gotta gear up properly went Mark's and Camille's counsel. Boots, helmet, ice axe, crampons—these and other accoutrements of climbing, including a harness with which to attach myself to my team via rope, were on the list, as was an amped-up work-out schedule of running and yoga and biking and weights. I mean, if no less a mountain man than John Muir can run into trouble on the mountain the first Spanish explorers of 1808 christened Jesus Maria, I wanted to be sure I wouldn't be calling on either to save me from some unwelcome hell. It was during one of Muir's three Shasta climbs in 1874-75 that he got trapped on the summit by a storm. He survived only by warming himself in the mud of the hot sulfur springs that bubbled near the peak. Lesson learned, Mr. Muir: I was not going to be caught without a proper mountaineering outfit, much less body, so help me Jesus Maria.

> *'Ho, 'ho, yo!*
> *Yo!, 'ho, yo!*

The lyrics of Mark's gansta rap music, such as they are, boom in the car as we pull in to the parking lot at Shasta's base. Rather than climb the popular, easiest and typically crowded Avalanche Gulch route, we plan to summit via the less-publicized and more challenging Hotlum/Boland Ridge route on the mountain's northwestern side—the glacial route, it turns out this late July day, of not one other soul. I gaze up at the glacier that awaits us, sun-sparkled and still. In the dis-tance it looks none too steep and far from foreboding. Surely here there will be no falling into the void like can happen on Annapurna, and with today's flawless azure sky, certainly no lightning strikes are expected to doom us like they do sometimes the climbers of Kilimanjaro. Doable, I decide. That will be *our* Shasta. After much fussing, we shoulder our massive packs and I stagger under the weight of the three-days' worth of four-course meals, six-weeks' stash of survival snacks (what if we get lost?), plus eight changes of clothes I simply have to have, but no matter: we will shuck the tent and all cooking paraphernalia, at least, once we establish base camp. So the crushing burden of mostly frivolous things will slow and cripple me for only a couple of hours. Never mind the sweaty and strenuous six it actually takes to reach the site of our first night's camp: a flat-ish rock plateau 2,700 feet up that's tailor-made for our tent. The hike is so lovely we hardly notice the time. It winds through luscious alpine meadow, pine-scented forest, rising slopes of scree. *'Ho, 'ho, yo,* I intone to myself with each footfall, an odd yet rhythmic mantra that adopts me as I stagger and step, *Yo, 'ho, yo.*

Step after step, higher and higher we rise up Shasta's side. We're climbing! I realize at some fresh vista where the view of the green, leafy lowlands we're leaving is keen and my joy, too, rises. Shasta seems to be coddling us along, its weather perfect, its mountain breeze soft, and its stars now spangle the darkening sky in a splendor so stunning it is almost enough to swerve my worry away from the hike's first fierce bite of surprise. Almost. A short, nearly vertical slope of broken shale suddenly appears between us and the rock plateau.

"Uh-oh," says Camille.

"Whoa," gasps Mark.

"No way," goes Gabriel.

Yo...ho...no! I intone and then stop to behold the specter: a climb certain to test our guts if not our luck. "Yikes, that sure looks steep and (gulp) crumbly."

But we do it. And Shasta helps. We crawl and claw, crab fashion, up the sliding falling wobbly shale, our unwieldy packs threatening at every step to throw us off balance and send us crashing head over heels back down from whence we've come. It is said by legend that Shasta harbors a secret city within its core, a city of jeweled corridors home to a mystical brotherhood descended from mythical Lemuria. I hope the brothers can't hear my panic-tinged yelps as I crawl and claw, and I hope the purity of Lemuria will be none the worse for Mark's curses as he does, too: *Damnyoudamnyoudamnyou*. But Shasta does not pitch us off, neither does it nauseate us with its altitude-gain or conjure a wind so cruel it whips us into regretting our first success. In fact, upon the plateau the wind is kind in which we, too pooped to eat, hurriedly pitch our tent in the quickening dark—so hurriedly that our first night on the mountain is spent sleeping on pillows of sharp rocks and poised at an unnatural angle: Shasta doesn't deign to freeze us as we lie snoring side by side, stuffiness filling our sinuses positioned down-slope from our feet. Instead sweet dreams of Lemuria—is it beautiful? are the brothers handsome and, I don't know, hot?—are borne to me on the night's soft flutter of a breeze.

It's 1:30 A.M. when Camille steps on my head to exit the tent. "Sorry," she whispers. "It's time." In the silence and chill of the dawn yet far off, we knock about blindly to rig ourselves up for summit day. The mountain's peak lies uncountable hours ahead, so dressing in harness, helmet, and headlamp, we rope together, man our ice axes, and head up. Step by slow, deliberate step we make our silent way from scree to snow, climbing ever and ever higher. As I rise up Shasta's side and the slope steepens, a mild concern steals in. Trussed up as I am as part of a team, how will I maneuver the...well, the bathroom breaks? Pull the rope left and my fellow climbers follow. Ducking with discretion behind the right rock? A problem. It will be the least of them.

As we climb, the sky brightens in a brilliant rhapsody of roses and golds, and Shasta continues to beckon us toward its summit. We are lured higher and higher by its lack of difficulty, and we are beguiled ever onward by its apparent promise of a conquest easily achieved. I mean, Camille, Mark,

Gabriel, and I, we all feel great! We step and sweat and greet the rising sun without so much as the slightest high-altitude headache. *'Ho,' 'ho, yo.* Hour upon hour I place my crampon into each clear footprint Camille, ahead of me on the rope, stamps into the soft glacier snow, *yo 'ho yo.*

Ten thousand feet, 11,000, 12,000—at each elevation the volcano dormant since 1786 is proving itself a gentle soul free of cliffs or crags or crevasses; it offers no wretched hazards like ice to avoid. Possibly the New Agers and old legends are right. Possibly Shasta really is a sacred site where a powerful energy vortex calls to believers like those who, in the 1980s, gathered here for a "worldwide harmonic convergence." I am definitely harmonically converging with Shasta's happy absence of killer ice storms like those found on Mt. Ranier; I am blissing over its freedom from the deadly blizzards of Mt. Blanc. This mountain's sweet terrain and sunny-day disposition make our climb feel graced by...here I'll say it: grace. In fact, when we reach the summit—all 14,179 feet of it—I am as elated as any real mountaineer dating back to Otzi the Iceman. While his 5,300-year-old remains were found high in the Alps in 1991, thus making him surely the world's first summit junkie, my very alive body thrills to the view (spectacular), the feat (we did it!) and the fact that Shasta has been so amenable to our success.

"Smile!" says the stranger we ask to snap our official summit photo. And we do, well-pleased with ourselves. We are oblivious.

I wonder if Petrarch, the fourteenth-century Italian poet whose mountaineering exploits endeared him to many as the father of Alpinism, ever met a descent he didn't like. The smallest slip on a chip of ice, the merest misstep on a piece of unsteady scree—these and other tiny climbing mishaps are all it takes to turn a perfect day into a perfect fright. And for Camille, Mark, Gabriel, and me, the fright begins on a soft-snow slope that climbing up seemed benign but stepping down is—strangely—appallingly steep. Down and down it shoots to an insanity of rocks hundreds of feet below. How did we not see these on the way up? Its hold on *our* feet is tenuous. My overworked crampons cling to the slope with as much shaky strength as remains in my legs after our nearly ten-hour ascent. It isn't a lot. We are traversing the slope with prudence for Camille and Mark, experienced, know the downside of climbing foolishness. I am the caboose on the rope—last—and moving with innocent confidence. *'Ho, 'ho, yo,* I step. And slip. My foot slips and I sit. I think nothing of it. *I'll just get up,* goes my thought. But to my surprise I find I can't. Instead, I am sliding. Oh-so-slowly, but picking up speed, I am sliding—sliding with no way to stop, sliding with nothing to grab, sliding then spinning and thinking nothing but, *Oh!* Then: a jerk. The rope at my waist pulls taut and upside down, I stop. A little dazed I look up the slope to see Gabriel with his ice axe dug into the snow and his body flung over it to anchor its hold.

"Way to go, Gabe!" cheers Mark, impressed with the boy's successful climbing arrest. Quickly, I am back on my feet and in the team's single-file line, but with an awakened jittery sense that perhaps we are not as safe as all this time we've supposed. Step by (more careful) step, we zig-zag our way down the slope and then: Just like that, Gabriel is off his feet sliding and I feel my rope pull hard. My face hits the snow and it's the two of us now, tumbling, sliding, spinning, picking up speed. Gabriel cries out but I am too stunned to utter even *oh!* Flailing, I try to grab what I can; there is nothing. I have no clue what to do with my axe because, like I say, I am no mountaineer. We slide, we spin, we pick up speed and it is forever, or maybe mere seconds, but I feel it: the jerk. Suddenly, I stop. Below me I see Gabriel has, too. My heart hammers, my face burns—the fear, the fear—but I glance up the slope and see Mark kneeling as if beseeching Jesus Maria.

He has thrust his axe into the snow beneath him in classic "team arrest" fashion and stopped us all from falling down, down, tragically down to the murderous crags below. Camille hoots wildly in approval.

"You did it! Go you! Oh, my God, that was *great*," she hoots. Mark just kneels, his attitude prayerful; his silence speaks for us all: *Thank you*. Gabriel, shaking, gathers his wits and I do, too, and we reattach crampons come loose, readjust glasses askew, and ease back into single-file on the rope. The confusion of rocks at slope's bottom seems now to issue a dare and the sun-sopped field of snow we have yet to cross feels newly treacherous, a peril for which we are unprepared. Suddenly, our footing is not sure and the slope is fraught with who knows what next? Step by step, each now agonizingly deliberate, we again get moving. *'Ho, 'ho, yo*, I squeak and notice I am intensely, *life-and-deathly* focused on the right here, right now. Shasta is showing me something important, something it would be good to know. Is it that the mountain cannot be trusted? That it is not in the least what it seems? Easy. Neither to know nor to predict, Shasta tells me it's got its secrets, and safety's just another word for something I don't own.

Especially now. "Mom!!" Gabriel screams. "Rock!!" And here it comes. The boulder that shoots off the outcrop above us seems ferocious in its intent. It bears down on Camille, faster and faster it rolls. If she runs right she will pull us all off our feet and into a sure sliding fall. If she stands still the rock will slam into her and drag the rope—with us—to some ill-defined doom that I, right now, am too, too stunned and confused to foresee. My eyes go blurry with fright and then: my sister with a jolt rockets left as Mark yells "Go!!"—her two or three steps fired by something unearthly in its potential for speed. Via angel or adrenaline, I've never seen anyone move as fast as Camille. The rock whizzes past by mere inches and crashes its wretched way down the slope. Its whine carries on the wind; its moan is a heavy thud on the snow. Later she says she felt its breath, the life of Shasta thriving.

Sixteen hours, thirty minutes, and however many seconds it takes to strip off the gear—pack, helmet, harness, rope—and collapse in the tent in a delirium of both achievement and relief becomes the official time of our summit. We four on the rope make it back to base camp safely, sanely, and after the fun of some high-speed glissading that seriously goosed up our moods. Yet even as I dropped to my bottom to slide sled-like and laughing down the glacier's lower slopes, I felt somehow that Shasta was allowing me the thrill only because…well, because. In the mountain's wild caprice, in its willfulness almost wanton, the merry moment might have transformed, just like that, into one altogether not so, with Shasta itself deciding how it would go. A hidden crevasse that yawns open, a seemingly solid rock shelf that gives way, any sudden and unexpected whim can, indeed, catch us unaware, with only Shasta itself in on the understanding.

Still, the satisfaction is sweet for Camille, Mark, Gabriel, and me, snug in the tent our final night on the mountain before we hike out and rejoice in the sight of the car. We did it! We came, we climbed, we…survived. We had tons of fun, in fact. The evening air seems more lusciously scented, with our success, and the stars that shyly show themselves with the setting sun wink especially bright. Is it my pride in our accomplishment that makes Shasta's charms seem so delicious, now that all danger has passed? A breeze rouses itself to whisper *good job* and clouds, just a few, gather to tell us, *you guys are hot*. Happy, sore, and exhausted, I drift off to sleep to the lullaby of the melting glacier snow that rushes bubbling down the mountain in a nearby stream of soothing music. Back to those handsome Lemurians…

It is 10:15 P.M. when the first flash of light ignites the dark and the low rumble of—what?—jolts me bolt upright. "Oh my God," moans Camille. "Oh. My. God." The flashes come fast now and, too, the booms—explosions that shake us from our sleep with a slap of shock. Lightning! Thunder! Yes, thunder and lightning and now, the rain, buckets of it, and hail, hail that hammers the tent and drowns our gear and our clothes outside. The bitter wind joins in with its ire—all arrived out of nowhere.

"Camille?" I croak from deep within the cocoon of my sleeping bag, now pulled over my head to hide me from the truth of our predicament. "Is this tent waterproof?" Gabriel croaks his own, *oh, great*, from the depths of his bag. "No," she says in a tone so bleak I swear we're in for it now. *No.* And the soul of Shasta opens to us, the enigma we take home.

≈≈ ≈≈ ≈≈

Colette O'Connor lives and works around the Monterey Bay area of California. Her lifestyle features and travel essays have appeared in many publications including the Los Angeles Times, France magazine, *Travelers' Tales Paris, Sand in My Bra, Whose Panties Are These?, and* The Best Women's Travel Writing *(2005 and 2010).*

֍ ֍ ֍

Can I Help You?

The give and take of a twenty-year friendship.

UNFOLDING BEHIND ME, COMPLETELY IGNORED IN this bewildering moment, is an isolated Philippine valley—a certified world-heritage site complete with world-class views. If I turn around I will see brimming rice terraces, thousands of them, shining like sequins and rising step by step from the riverbed all the way to the green valley's rim.

But in front of me, stealing all my attention, lies a thigh-high pile of charred timbers and twisted tin roofing, the work of a midnight arsonist in 2006. This is what remains of a handicrafts shop that once belonged to my friend Timango ("Tony") Tocdaan, a rice farmer—and for twenty years one of the most important figures in my life.

In 1988, I strolled into Tony's life on a road paved with, I swear, the most innocent intentions. On that visit, Tony guided me on a perfect trek through these mountains, part of the hulking Cordillera range, and thirteen years later I invited him to the United States and drove him coast-to-coast—a soaring, life-changing experience for both of us.

Now, in April 2009, I stare at this rubble and don't know whether to bawl or howl. In the States, Tony had cracked open a fortune cookie and found a message we both loved, predicting, "You will become the richest man in your community." But the dream did not materialize. Tony has a houseful of kids and no steady income, and he owes his increasingly attentive moneylenders $1,500. He's standing a few yards away, studying me as I study the detritus of his shop. I imagine his thoughts: "Maybe Brad will fix it."

I have indeed sent large chunks of money that have "fixed" a few things in Tony's life. But I'm not looking to tinker any more—nor can I afford to. I've come here, I tell myself, just to visit, and perhaps to assess whether I'm partly, wholly, or not at all responsible for the scorched disaster at my feet. Or, I wonder, have I returned just to formally close down the money pipeline and run like hell?

In 1972, after completing college, I went in search of a higher education. Visits to Morocco, Iran, Afghanistan, and India led me to understand my privileged birthright. Had I been born an average guy in any one of these places, I could never have afforded to casually backpack the world. I began to develop the notion that if we in the richer countries would simply move around the planet a bit more and share small slices of our wealth, we'd heal the world.

In 1988, by then a seasoned San Francisco cabdriver and thirty-seven years old, I began my "money-where-your-mouth-is" tour: I would circle the globe and invite one member of the "other half" to visit America for one month—my treat.

One afternoon that November, I was the lone visitor at a scenic overlook in a Philippine town called Banaue (Bah-NAH-way). "Nice view," said a casual voice behind me.

"Like vegetarian wedding cake." Tony was twenty-eight and a member of the Ifugao tribe. He and his wife, Rita, had three children. For more than 2,000 years, Tony said, his ancestors had occupied this same twist of valley, living as rice farmers, woodcarvers, and, until the 1950s, enthusiastic headhunters. He pointed toward two terraces he'd inherited. "These will feed my family for maybe three months every year," he said. "And there, in the clearing, see the hut? That one is mine."

At twelve years old, Tony told me, he'd found a lucrative job carrying wood on his shoulders for the carvers. "Up and down mountains—yes, barefoot. Early morning until dark," he said. "Sleep in jungle, eat food from jungle—bird, fruit. Three years I do this, and then I understand: 'If I don't quit, this my life forever—AH-nee-mal!'"

Tony went back to school. "I was seventeen," he said. "Big. Everyone else very small." He learned history, geography, and basic English. In the early 1980s, after government efforts to promote tourism, and after the release of *The Year of Living Dangerously* with scenes filmed in Banaue, a trickle of travelers started arriving. Seeing the opportunity, Tony opened his handicrafts shop in 1987. "And," he told me, "sometimes I guide tourists up into mountains."

For the next three days of that 1988 visit, Tony led me, often by the hand, along the lips of towering rice terraces, up and down 45-degree mountainsides. We swam under thundering waterfalls and slept on the floors of his relatives' huts, in tiny villages reachable only by footpath. We became pals. When I asked about his dreams, he replied, "For me, dream only to feed my family."

It took twelve years of cab driving and freelance writing to save up for Tony's month in America. What clinched it for me was the sale, in 2000 for $8,000, of my travel memoir, *Take Me With You: A Round-the-World Journey to Invite a Stranger Home*, in which I boasted, "Travel is the best thing that could ever happen to anyone." After I appeared on national radio, promoting my book and talking about Tony's impending visit, listeners from across the country phoned in to offer everything from airplane flights and lodging to baseball box seats, river-rafting trips, and medical and dental care. It seemed that all of America was eager to show Tony its good side.

In June 2001, when I met Tony at the San Francisco airport, he told me, "On the airplane, I realize my life will never be the same again." After 150 people gathered in my backyard for a "Welcome Tony" party, Tony asked me, "What is *overwhelm*? Everyone ask me, 'Are you overwhelm?'" But to me, Tony seemed pretty comfortable. He was shocked to see homeless people sleeping on the streets ("At home, no one believe this—in America!") but he was entranced by the urping sea lions at Fisherman's Wharf, the cable cars, and hiking in the redwoods.

A cab company owner volunteered a plush taxi to use for our trip, and Tony and I cruised in style from the Golden Gate Bridge over the mountains and the prairies all the way to the White House. Our feel-good story caught the edge of the media jet stream: CBS televised our departure from San Francisco, and we often switched on the radio to catch interviews we'd just recorded with the BBC, NPR, and other outlets. One morning the Philippine ambassador read about us, tracked down my cell phone number, and summoned us to an embassy reception in Washington, D.C.

It was impossible for me not to fantasize that this high-flying month might turn my book—Tony and I called it "our" book—into a bestseller. During our epic taxi ride I asked Tony what sort of life he might imagine if I, his new "brother," suddenly had money to share? He had a ready answer. "Rita and I, many times we talk about having a guest-house," he said. "Our home site is perfect. You have seen! And Rita, she is great cook."

The instant Tony's homeward flight lifted off the runway, my cell phone quit ringing. Sales of my book turned out to be modest at best, and some eye-popping credit card bills sent me scuttling back to cab driving. But Tony's fifteen minutes continued. The Philippines' biggest newspaper splashed his wild story across its front page. A popular television news-magazine visited Banaue to trek with him and aired the segment archipelago-wide. Weeks later, over the phone, a giddy Tony told me, "Every day people still come to my house. Everybody says I am very famous man. Is like dream."

I had known in advance that bringing Tony to America would dramatically expand his sense of possibility. It would have been irresponsible of me, even cruel, I thought, to return him to his old life—with Rita and their, by then, five children—without any resources to facilitate the chasing of his dream. I sent $2,000 home with him, and over the next few months I scraped together and sent $5,000 more. In 2002, Tony's tidy four-room guesthouse, situated inside a living postcard, opened for visitors. But 9/11, and then the Bali bombings, devastated tourism. "In one week, in all Banaue, I see just three tourists," Tony reported. "The truth, my friend, we are sitting here with no food to eat. People laugh: 'You are celebrity—but no money.'

"I don't want to be famous," he continued. "All I want is to feed my family." He had a sixth child now: Bradley, my namesake! I wired Tony $100 to $200 every month, and fretted. I, too, was a family man, fifty years old with a precious five-year-old daughter, and anyone who imagines that my philanthropy wasn't causing stress at home has never been married.

And yet what are we here for, if not to help each other? Over the phone I asked Tony, "What if you had more land?" A few phone calls later he said, "I found a farm in the low-lands. Eight thousand dollars."

For several months I mulled this sobering number. The most money I've ever made in one year is $35,000. But I had pried open Tony's life, and now I owed him something, didn't I? Did I actually believe in my own share-the-wealth, heal-the-world theories, or was that all just hot air?

Then, in 2003, I received a modest inheritance. I sent Tony $10,000 and thought, "Well, that's that." Tony bought a share of the lowland farm, and soon his family's rice yield had tripled. There was never a surplus, but for several sweet months there seemed, finally, to be...enough.

In 2004, I made the eleven-hour flight to Manila and the ten-hour bus ride up through the mountains to Banaue. Tony and his family, now four sons and three daughters, led me down the 195 oversize concrete steps descending from the cluster of small businesses at Banaue's viewpoint to their spectacularly situated home. They now lived comfortably in the undervisited guesthouse that stood beside—and dwarfed—the old traditional hut, and they appeared to be almost thriving. "Thanks to you!" Tony's daughter Lynn told me. "This is your house!"

I know just two words of the Philippine language Tagalog—the two words that Tony taught me in America. At the end of my visit, he and I hugged, special brothers for life, and said them again: *"Mabuhay, kaibigan!"* Live long, my friend.

But back in California, the updates I began to receive from Banaue threatened *me* with "overwhelm": fertilizers for the lowland farm; college tuition for Tony's two eldest daughters; hospitalizations and prescriptions for Tony after an electrolyte imbalance and a snakebite. I came to dread the ring of the phone. "Two hundred...five hundred...two thousand, please, Brad." I tried to think of something that could help him become self-sufficient. During a cash crunch in 1991, Tony had been forced to sell the handicrafts shop he had owned when I first met him. In early 2006, I asked, "Can you get another shop like your old one?" I sent him $5,000, and soon he was back in business. Sales were strong, life was good, and the vigor in Tony's voice was remarkable.

It was not to last. One day a neighbor approached Tony and said, "You know that land where your shop is? That land belonged to my grandfather." An emotional brouhaha ensued, with neighbors in the small village taking sides against neighbors. Tony quickly extricated himself by selling the shop back to the person from whom he'd bought it, but the pot had been irrevocably stirred. After several contentious months, Tony phoned with some truly disturbing news: an unseen arsonist, some accelerant, and *phwoomp!* "Shop all gone," he reported.

In the fire's aftermath, I came to understand that ancient passions and jealousies do not disappear with the arrival of a few missionaries and one backpacking do-gooder. Governments and NGOs often look back on failed multibillion-dollar development projects and wonder, "What happened? Where'd we go wrong?" I had hoped that by working alone I might be more effective than they, that my involvement and my money might bring prosperity to Tony, and also to Banaue. Instead, while I may not have struck the match, I'd certainly played a key role in igniting this red-hot, village-dividing fiasco. Since his trip to America, I'd sent Tony more than $35,000, but I couldn't claim that I'd really done any good. All I knew for sure was that I was completely wrung out, financially and emotionally.

April 2009: Eight years have passed since Tony's trip to the States, and five since my last visit to Banaue. I am fifty-seven years old, cognizant of time's passage, and aware that few relationships survive on phone calls and email.

I board a plane to Manila and ride the bus up into the mountains to Banaue. I worry about our meeting, but Tony greets me at the bus station with a smile and a warm, satisfying hug.

"Kaibigan," he says. "Oh, it is good to see you." After twenty years, our link feels intact. I linger awhile at the viewpoint, studying the remains of his old shop, and then Tony carries my luggage down the steep steps to the guesthouse. Tony's adult children have gathered from their homes in neighboring provinces. Several sleep out in the hut; the guesthouse's best room is reserved for me. The doorstep is littered with a dozen pairs of sandals, flip-flops, and hiking boots, all being sniffed over by a dog and half a dozen chickens.

The poultry is not long for this world. Tony slaughters them one by one, and during my weeklong stay Rita keeps farm-fresh chicken, rice, and vegetable dishes flowing from their small kitchen. I spend much of my time sitting on the front-porch bench, eating, soaking in the view down the long green valley, catching up with everyone, and filling my notebook. Lorie, 26, runs a small bakery in Baguio City; Lynn, 24, studies for her nursing exam and tends her three-year-old; Franz, 21, is studying to become a policeman; Gladys, a quiet 13-year-old when I last saw her in 2004, is now raising an infant, Tony and Rita's second grandchild. Rowel, 15, has two more years of high school. Bradley, 8, and Scott, 6, watch for me to put down my notebook so they can scribble their names inside; when we sneak off for walks in the terraces, just the three of us, I notice they both collect litter. "I teach them this," Tony tells me later. "Last time you are here, you talk about trash. Now path is always clean."

Tony, forty-eight, still climbs the hillside steps with a youngster on his back, but an achy knee rules out long treks. We settle for day trips in the extended family's Nissan minivan and short walks near home. One rainy morning, he and I sit under a shelter in the middle of the rice terraces. Across the valley we can see his guesthouse, filled with family and choking on potential. The question of money hangs in the air like toxic mist.

"I thought people in America, they read our book, they come visit," Tony says.

"I was hoping for more, too."

"What is that word," he asks, "when plans don't work out?"

"Disappointment?"

"Yes. Disappointment."

Tony tells me he sold off two-thirds of his rice fields to pay for chemotherapy for Rita's aunt. After she died, the rest of the money went to school tuitions. "Then, all gone." Unsaid: The moneylenders are eyeing what's left of the farm.

Tony mentions new entrepreneurial ideas: a farm supply business, guesthouse improvements. "America is falling apart," I say, and look him in the eye. "I'm all out of money for you, Tony."

He says nothing for a while, and then, "I think life is not fair."

We gaze out at farmers bent double in the distant paddies. They might be the same silent stick figures I saw here five years ago—and twenty. In that time I've visited a dozen countries on several continents. None of these people has left this valley. "No," I say, "it certainly isn't."

We segue into a lengthy discussion of all the hurtful things the other has said or done. Each of us lands a few jabs, and afterward, sated, we sit for a long while in the quiet trance of the terraces, both of us pondering, I'm sure, the harsh wallop that reality delivers to just about every dream.

Finally Tony says, "Well, this is how it goes in a friendship."

On my last evening, the entire family climbs to the viewpoint and crowds into a karaoke bar. I drink a couple of beers and sing loudly and dance so hard that my right foot, my cab-driving foot, will ache for weeks.

Afterward, in a dark, dense fog, wishing we'd remembered flashlights, we begin picking our way down the 195 steps. Suddenly, deliverance: fireflies appear all around. Tiny, blinking yellow bulbs. Lemon meringue fog. Magic.

The next morning I hand Tony a check too large to justify. He glances at the amount and turns away. His shoulders quake, and he has to wipe his eyes. "Thank you, Brad." For a while, he'll be debt free. I've climbed past $45,000.

Driving to the bus station, the family clears the van's middle row for Tony and me. We sit holding hands, and when I break the silence with a song—"*I'm leaving...*"—he comes right in with me: "*on a jet plane....*"

Don't know when I'll be back again.

❧ ❧ ❧

Brad Newsham has called San Francisco home since 1982, and has driven a cab since 1985. He is the author of All the Right Places *and* Take Me With You. *There is much more about him at www. bradnewsham.com.*

JANN HUIZENGA

❧ ❧ ❧

My Roman Reality Show

It's free, and it never ends.

T HE TV SAT DARK IN MY ROME APARTMENT DURING
my ten months there. I spent all my spare time at the
window studying the players on the piazza—the Gypsy, the
Sweeper, the Cat Lady, the Reader, the Abuser, the Santas, and
the Sentries—always those ominous Sentries.

The night of my arrival in early September, a torrid wind
blew the scent of oven-baked dough through the open window, along with the wheezing melody of "My Way." I stared
at the Gypsy with a jaunty straw hat and a cigarette pinched
between his teeth. He sat outside a pizzeria pushing and pulling a red accordion like taffy over his fat paunch. A bright
moon sailed overhead.

The next morning, after a night of Roman revelry, my piazza brimmed with trash. The Sweeper turned up in orange
plastic pants. She raked a broom over the black cobbles like a
toothbrush on rotten teeth. Then she fished out her cell phone

and plunked down on a stone bench for a gabfest, as she'd do many mornings over the next ten months.

I watched a stray dog lap from the fountain—one of those big-nosed fountains (*nasone*) with no turn-off valve that Rome is famous for. The dog trotted off when a woman shuffled over in fuzzy pink house slippers to fill a plastic bottle. The sun bounced off luscious walls that made me think of Italian ices: mandarin, citrus, and melon. I inhaled the jasmine that framed my window and counted seventy-five other windows overlooking the piazza.

As September rolled along, the Cat Lady—the self-anointed concierge of the piazza—and I took each other's measure. We lived on the *primo piano* in opposite buildings, in such proximity that we could have played catch with a ball of mozzarella. She spied on me and I peeped at her, though we never made real eye contact. I suppose she'd describe me as a lonely *straniera* who hung from the window shouting gibberish into a *telefonino*. She tossed breadcrumbs to doves and kept order on the piazza by waggling a finger at littering tourists and illegal parkers. Both she and her fat pussycat had poofs of gray hair and spent their days at the window ledge nuzzling and grooming. The cat would lick her fingers clean, and she'd brush him with long, slow strokes. Hairballs somersaulted like tumbleweed across the piazza, into the melted goo of abandoned ice cream cones.

Every ten minutes or so, there was a sudden rush of Romans into the piazza from the Cavour subway exit a block away—men in sleek suits and cool shades and perfect women in tall, pointy, clacking shoes. They rode in on a powerful tide and then ebbed away, dissolving into the many tiny alleyways radiating from the piazza.

Late at night, young men would drink beer and unroll sleeping bags on the hard stone benches, stuffing backpacks under their heads as pillows. They'd crawl away each morning when the Sweeper poked them with her broom.

In mid-October I began to notice the Sentries. The first one I spied was a swarthy smoker—Turkish or Tunisian, I thought—wearing a hooded parka, an odd get-up given the warm weather. I tried to focus on my computer screen but the Sentry kept drawing me back to the window. He sat hunched on one of the stone benches, flipping through *La Stampa* and checking his watch, but mostly staring fixedly to the west. After an hour of this, I poked my telephoto out the window. I felt quite certain the *carabinieri* might someday need the evidence. What was the crime? I didn't know yet. *Click. Click. Click.* He raised his eyes. I scooted behind the curtain and into the kitchen. When I returned with a mug of hot coffee he was gone.

Another soon took his place—a wiry man with icy eyes who could have been a brother to Putin. He stood by the fountain looking in the same direction, lighting up, drawing hard on a cigarette, then throwing the butt over his shoulder. Ninety minutes passed. I snapped another photo then went to the kitchen for tea. When I returned, he too had vanished.

These same Sentries kept returning, but so did Chinese, Central Asian, and African men, most of whom parked themselves on the same stone bench and stared west. Who were they? I became obsessed. When they raised their eyes slightly, I began to worry that they were on to me.

In November, the Reader—a slender girl with platform shoes—began appearing on a stone bench. Like a heliotropic flower, she'd turn up for an hour of afternoon sun, a bit later each day as fall wore on. She'd fish her glasses from a bag, open a hefty novel that she held on her lap like a brick of gold, and sit ramrod straight, lost in a fantasy world, her silky black hair draping her cheeks like drawn curtains. The sun crawled low against the sky as she read, and when it slipped away, she did, too.

It was Roman men, not women, who would pause to primp in the side mirrors of parked *motorini*. Italian newspapers reported that Italian men were *vanitosi*, vain, *mammoni*, mama's boys, and came in last as *amante*, lovers, in some recent U.K. survey.

In early December, a crew of young workers—Romanian? Albanian?—pulled up the cobbles to lay down pipes. They worked much harder than Romans and wore sweatshirts that said Yale or Notre Dame or Michigan. The Santas arrived in December, too—not one, but a quartet of them, in single file. The lead Santa blew on a trumpet while another bawled a cheery *"Buon Natale!"* that boomeranged around the piazza like an Alpine yodel. I hung out the window and when they shouted for a donation, I tossed it into an elastic red pouch.

One day in mid-January, after days of cold rain, a ray of sunlight sliced a black cloud to flood the piazza with yellow. *Don't let the su-u-un go down on me...*

I ran to the window. The pizzeria had put speakers out on the street. Elton John's voice poured like old wine through the piazza, drawing radiant faces to every window. I inhaled meaty odors and felt wildly happy.

One morning in March, I heard the Abuser. After a terrible rant, flesh smacked flesh and then a thick high whimper pierced the piazza. I knew her as the frail woman who tended window geraniums on the *secondo piano* opposite me. Neighbors hung from windows as if from theater balconies. It went on forever. I rushed around looking for the phone book then flipped through it until I landed on a *numero azzuro*, a blue number, to report child abuse. By the time I dialed, the piazza had gone eerily quiet. The operator could do nothing, she said, no child was involved. At the police station the next day, I was handed a number to call for domestic abuse. I kept it by the phone for future reference. But within a few weeks the Abuser's windows were shuttered tight, his geraniums dead.

One morning in April, I awoke early and looked out the window. A large suitcase, open like a book, had heaved its contents onto the cobbles. A ruffly skirt printed with pink peonies, a jacket to match. A pleated skirt, a crisp white blouse. Someone had waited all her life to come to Rome, bought a new spring wardrobe, and now this. It made me sad. Back to the police station I went, but the treasure trove had been picked clean by the time an officer appeared.

The Sentries kept coming. One was a black woman in a furry white jacket and running shoes. She held a blue coat over her arm and spent a motionless hour on the Sentry bench, head craned to the west. Then she unglued herself from the bench and was gone.

In May I wandered off the piazza and into one of the dark alleys I'd never before set foot in. Girls of every race sashayed down the streets in zebra boots, blond wigs, corsets, and hot pants. But of course! That explained the Sentries.

But mysteries remained. Why was the woman in the pink beret crying on a stone bench one cold day in January? Why did a fellow survey the piazza at eye level one morning in March and then haul out his unit to urinate in the dwarf palm? Had he simply forgotten about the eyes in the seventy-five windows above him? Who had lost her suitcase? And why do Rome's *nasone* never stop running?

The hot nights came back. The Gypsy turned up again to play "My Way." I wanted to stay and see the whole show over again. But it was time to close the window and go home.

❧ ❧ ❧

Jann Huizenga has loved alien lands since the day she enrolled in a lycée *in Paris without a word of French. A three-time Fulbright Scholar, she's had stories in* The New Mexican, Transitions Abroad, A Woman's World Again, The Best Travel Writing 2008, The Best Women's Travel Writing 2009, *and elsewhere. She lives part-time in Sicily, where she can be found working on a memoir, picking fennel, or blogging at baroquesicily.com.*

DAVID TORREY PETERS

꙳ ꙳ ꙳

"Takumbeng, *C'est Quoi?*"

Beliefs are powerful, powerful.

I. ESCRAVOS RISING

UGBORODO, NIGERIA. JULY 8, 2002: IN THE WEAK, unsaturated light before daybreak, a husband's arm flopped onto his wife's side of the bed and came to rest in the indented space where her sleeping body should have been. Outside the window, female forms flitted through the underbrush on paths still muddy from the outgoing tide. Farther east, the forms gathered, here two, there four, until they converged en masse, a seething mob of women, on the banks of the Escravos River.

A short time later, an hour, maybe half that, the first of the roughneck oil workers walked groggily toward the docks to catch the *Ginuwe,* the ferry that shuttled them daily into Chevron Texaco's Escravos refinery. A surprise awaited them at the docks: hundreds of women. All shapes and sizes, ages and status, octogenarians beside teenagers, mothers alongside mothers-in-law; and the common denominator: anger.

The captain of the *Ginuwe,* unaware of the peril that awaited him on the far shore, maneuvered the thrusters until the craft slid parallel alongside the dock. Once bow and stern lines had been cleated tight, the women surged onto the dock, pouring over the sides of the ferry, overrunning the boat. The attack came swiftly; by the time the captain might have raised a response on the radio, the women were in control. "He was afraid," one of the leaders, Mama Ayo, later said, "We told him not to say anything. The guards believed it was the workers coming. Before they knew it, we were inside."

Escravos, the heart of Chevron Texaco's Nigerian oil production, takes its name from the Portuguese word for slaves. The massive complex, the size of 583 football fields, employs over seven hundred oil workers to produce 350,000 barrels of Nigerian crude daily; 10,500,000 barrels each month. Behind the concrete wall, beyond the barbed wire, one finds telephones, microwaves, fresh fruit, foam beds, and to remind the Texans of home, climate control. A runway and landing pad provide a means of direct access from Lagos—no dusty trip across the countryside, no contact with the poverty, or people, of the region.

Down the shoreline from Escravos, the village of Ugborodo slowly sinks into the sea. To construct Escravos, the engineers at Chevron Texaco concluded that they had to widen and expand the little creek that bordered the village. Foreign workers in John Deere bulldozers and Caterpillar cranes excavated the mangrove forests growing in the creek where the villagers had long buried their dead. Unfortunately, no one at Chevron Texaco had accounted for the erosion that resulted from such an expansion. The village of Ugborodo began to wash away. High tide submerged whole sections of the village ankle-deep in brackish water. When the erosion finally began to threaten the Escravos complex, Chevron Texaco came up with a solution: facing the little outhouses that dot the Ugborodo side of the river, Chevron built a concrete barrier wall that protects the complex by diverting high-tide floods into the village.

The women of Ugborodo descended in a swarm from the *Ginuwe*, infesting every cranny of the Escravos complex. They cordoned off runways, took oil workers hostage, shut down oil production, played with the microwaves, tested out the foam mattresses, and made long-distance phone calls. They kept roughly seven hundred oil workers captive outside, while the women themselves basked in the hitherto only-heard-of air-conditioning. A thirty-three-year-old woman named Roli Ododuh remarked, "The Bible describes Paradise as a beautiful place where there is everything. When we got in there, it was really like Paradise." An older woman named Anirejotse Esuku put it differently, "I saw America there."

The women of Ugborodo had not been the first group of the Niger Delta to attempt to take over a foreign-owned oil-processing facility. Before them, local villagers who had clashed with Chevron Texaco in Nigeria fared badly.

May 25, 1998: Unarmed Nigerian youths, roughly two hundred in number, occupied one of Chevron Texaco's offshore oil platforms. The youths pledged to hold the platform until Chevron agreed to provide local villages with potable water, electricity, environmental reparations, as well as employment and scholarships for young people.

In phone negotiations, Chevron officials acceded to the demands and promised to send an envoy out on a helicopter to finalize the agreements. Instead, members of the Nigerian paramilitary mobile police force, known locally as the "Kill 'n' Go," and Nigerian marines boarded the Chevron helicopters. James Neku, Chevron's acting director of security, accompanied the soldiers on the flight out to the platform.

Two activists were shot shortly after the helicopters landed. Although Chevron contends that the youths were killed after they attempted to disarm the Nigerian troops, the company held the two bodies for nearly a month, delaying autopsies. When Chevron finally returned the bodies, it appeared that the youths had been shot in the back.

Chevron Spokesperson Sola Omole in an interview on "Democracy Now with Amy Goodman":

Q: Who took them in, on Thursday morning, the Mobile Police, the Navy?

OMOLE: We did. We did. Chevron did. We took them there.

Q: By how?

OMOLE: Helicopters. Yes, we took them in.

Q: Who authorized the call for the military to come in?

OMOLE: That's Chevron's management.

Afterward, Chevron declined to provide local villages with electricity, water, or any other form of aid promised to the Nigerian youths who had taken over the platform.

January 4, 1999: Testimony of a Nigerian youth, left unnamed for his protection, as collected by Human Rights Watch:

We were here in the village. At about 2-3 P.M. we saw a Chevron helicopter flying by on the other side of the river, and then flying along the route of the pipeline. By the time it got to us, it was flying very low, and then it started firing at us. We didn't know what to do, and we ran into the bush. After thirty minutes or so the helicopter was gone. Then some of the community members came back and were calling to the others to come back from the bush. We were gathered here on the river side and were discussing what had happened when we saw Chevron boats coming toward us carrying soldiers. Three were Chevron sea trucks (two numbers were 221 and 242), the ones they normally use, and the other one was a military boat with a machine gun mounted on it. They were full of soldiers, maybe more than one hundred in all. We ran into the bush again but as we were running they started firing, it was so intense I can't describe it, *dugu-dugu-dugu-dugu-dugu*. As I was running a bullet wounded me on my leg. When we went into the bush we saw fire everywhere in the community, everything burning. Then we heard the boats leaving, so we came back carefully, crawling to see if it was safe and watching who was around. No one was there, so we called to the others in the bush to come back. We saw two people lying dead on the ground, Kekedu Lawuru, and Timi Okuru, a woman. We started crying, and called to the others to come. But some did not come back: fifteen are missing still today. Maybe the bodies are in the river. About twenty were injured, of which ten or so were from bullet wounds, the rest from branches and stones as they ran into the bush. Almost all our houses were destroyed, burnt to the ground. All our property was destroyed. We had a boat that could carry forty or fifty persons which was sunk in the river. All our canoes were destroyed. We have nothing now, no means of livelihood.

A day or two before, some of the residents of the rural villages Opia and Ikiyan had gotten into a scuffle with members of Chevron's private security forces. Chevron had previously unveiled a plan to route a pipeline directly through the center of the villages. The day following the attack, the Nigerian Army sent Chevron a handwritten invoice for $109.25, which Chevron paid, to cover expenses for "services carried out…responding to attacks from Opia village against security agents guarding Searrex."

The women of Ugborodo occupied Escravos for ten days. Jay Pryor, the American head of Chevron Texaco's Nigerian operations, arrived to negotiate with the women. According to both sides, the negotiations proceeded cordially. Pryor, originally an oil engineer from Mississippi, sounded almost enthusiastic about the takeover, "There was an organized effort to try to give us, I would say, what was characterized to me as—a try to give us some feedback, to try and get more attention to their plight."

On July 17, the two sides met to sign a memorandum of understanding. The women agreed to leave the Escravos terminal. Pryor guaranteed that Chevron would connect the village electric and water grids directly to the Escravos facilities. He pledged to build schools, a community center, and a series of two-bedroom houses. Local women who ran fish and poultry farms were awarded contracts to supply the terminal with meat. Chevron agreed to equip and staff a roving hospital-boat, able to move up the river and along the coast. Lastly, they promised to resume construction on a place called "New Town," a brand-new, uninhabited village of concrete bunkers, designed to be ready and waiting when Ugborodo finally sank into the ocean.

Q: How is it that several hundred unarmed women from Ugborodo were able to take over the largest oil processing facility in Africa, take hostage seven hundred roughneck oilmen, rebuff (in ascending order of belligerence and brutality) Chevron Texaco's own private security force, the Nigerian Police, the Nigerian paramilitary mobile police force (the "Kill 'n' Go"), and both the Nigerian army and navy, and subsequently negotiate for the most generous concessions ever granted by Chevron Texaco?

A: They were naked.

II. TAKUMBENG

Shortly after Ni John Fru Ndi won Cameroon's 1992 presidential election, incumbent president Paul Biya sent troops to Bamenda, a city in the grasslands of Cameroon, to arrest and, most likely, kill Fru Ndi. As the troops arrived, Fru Ndi fled behind the two-story wall that surrounded his compound. When the well-armed troops marched down the washed-out clay road that led to Fru Ndi's compound, they found the gates blocked by a throng of naked old women, members of a secret society of post-menopausal women called the Takumbeng. Prior to that moment, the group had not been seen publicly in Bamenda for nearly one hundred years. The naked women screeched curses at the soldiers and doused any soldier who wandered close with water from earthenware pots. Presently, some of the troops began to feel ill, others uneasy, dismayed, and frightened. The troops turned and retreated.

In 2003, after I had spent a semester studying at the University of Yaoundé, I received a small grant to stay in Cameroon to research the ties between witchcraft and politics. One of my professors at the University had been Rotcod Gobata, a writer, whose books, *The Past Tense of Shit* and *I Spit on Their Graves*, so thoroughly trash President Biya and his regime that Gobata had been required to assume a pen name. I had grown interested in the story of the Takumbeng, and once, over lunch, aware that Gobata had grown up in Bamenda, I asked him how a group of old women could have proved an unbreachable barrier for well-armed troops.

"Some of the soldiers died, so the others got scared."

"Yeah, so how did the soldiers die?"

"The women were naked."

"Why exactly did the soldiers die?"

"They were sick to the stomach."

"So some soldiers who were sick, saw some women naked and then they died—"

"—No, they died because of the naked women."

"So then the women killed them?"

"I didn't say that. They died of stomach sickness."

And so on. Finally, Gobata said, irritated, "What if I introduced you to Ni John Fru Ndi? You can pester him, instead."

Before founding the Social Democratic Front (SDF) in 1990, Ni John Fru Ndi had been a bookseller in Bamenda, an Anglophone city in the northwest grasslands of Cameroon. By 1992, the SDF had grown to become the only viable opposition to Cameroonian president Paul Biya, who had been in power over a decade. Fru Ndi ran as the SDF candidate in the 1992 presidential elections, the country's first to be monitored by independent international observers.

On election day in Bamenda, the unofficial center of government opposition, supporters of Fru Ndi's SDF party primed themselves for violence. Biya officials had leaked documents that hinted at an organized campaign of repression. One such document, circulated by MP Sammy Najeme, a Biya supporter, called for:

> Our youths, our vanguards, to beat up any stranger
> who does not vote for President Paul Biya. If you see
> any [Anglophone or Bamileke] coming out of the
> polling booth, accost him and ask him to show his
> unused ballot papers. If he has not voted for Paul Biya,
> pluck off his eyes.

On election night, both The National Democratic Institute of the United States and Transparency International declared Fru Ndi the election victor. In Yaoundé, the capitol city, President Biya's official election tally had Fru Ndi lose with 37 percent of the vote to Biya's 39 percent. The Supreme Court of Cameroon, comprised of judges Biya had himself appointed, certified the numbers.

When Biya's election results hit the airwaves, victory

celebrations in Bamenda turned ugly. Pro-SDF mobs swept through the townships, torching the businesses and homes of known or even suspected Biya allies. After a night of chaos, Biya declared a state of emergency in Bamenda and sent in troops. Heavily armed police and soldiers fought street battles, from block to block, with rioting pro-SDF demonstrators. Foreign news services published photos and reports of killings on the part of the government, killings Biya's minister of information insisted had not occurred, a claim that earned him the nickname Zero Mort (None Dead). The U.S. Department of State's 1993 report on human rights practices concluded that the police and army of Cameroon had engaged in "serious human rights abuses, including political and extrajudicial killings." Chris Mwunwe of the *Cameroon Post* wrote of "arms and legs lost in fierce confrontations with armed troops."

As the riots raged across the city, Ni John Fru Ndi hunkered down in his compound with 145 SDF supporters. In the chaos of the riots beyond his walls, the naked women of the Takumbeng beat back the mixed force of gendarmes and troops sent to arrest him. Rebuffed by the women, the gendarmes placed Fru Ndi under "house arrest," a measure that amounted to a two-month siege of his compound.

Initial Meeting with Fru Ndi 7/12/03 11:00 A.M. Under what appears to be a Chinese-style *lou*, former president-elect of Cameroon and Chairman of the SDF, Ni John Fru Ndi, enters to greet Rotcod Gobata, the underground journalist. At Gobata's side stands a young American man, with a notebook folded double in his back pocket.

FRU NDI: Who is this boy you have brought to see Fru Ndi?

GOBATA: An American student. He studies at the University in Yaounde, he hopes to ask you a few questions about the Takumbeng and their uh…assistance after the 1992 elections.

AMERICAN: Good Morning, Sir, I appreciate—

FRU NDI: [*loudly*] Is Fru Ndi the Takumbeng? Why would he come here to ask Fru Ndi about the Takumbeng?

GOBATA: No, Fru Ndi is Fru Ndi.

FRU NDI: I know who Fru Ndi is. I was asking the young man.

AMERICAN: [*pause*] Uh, what I mean is, Sir, I understand the Takumbeng aided Fru Ndi...I mean you...back in the ninety-two election and—

FRU NDI: I repeat—Is Fru Ndi the Takumbeng?

AMERICAN: Uh, no, Fru Ndi is not the Takumbeng. I'm sorry, Sir, I don't understand.

FRU NDI: There, he said it. [*Suddenly expansive, as if addressing a lecture hall*] Fru Ndi is NOT the Takumbeng. Yet he comes to ask Fru Ndi about the Takumbeng. Young man, if you want to know how a doctor cures his patients, you ask the doctor, you don't get a lesson in surgery from the patient.

AMERICAN: [*pause*] True sir, but to respond to your metaphor, I would counter that in medicine nowadays, the effectiveness of any medical procedure can be evaluated by talking to the patient about their symptoms before and after treatment to, uh, see if a given treatment or procedure had any success in alleviating those symptoms.

FRU NDI: Eh? [*to Gobata*] He enjoys playing with metaphors, does he? Clever, but it could get irritating, hmm? Never mind. Gobata, you may bring the boy to lunch with us. How does two o'clock sound?

GOBATA: Well, I sort of had previous...I was just sort of hoping you could talk to the boy, I mean him, rather, David, that is.

FRU NDI: Who?

GOBATA: [*points at the American*] Him.

FRU NDI: Does he like hedgehog? If so, by all means, he may join us.

AMERICAN: Is it like squirrel? I had squirrel once.

[*The cell phone holstered on Fru Ndi's belt rings. Before the ring has fully sounded, Fru Ndi has answered it; his removal of the cell phone from his belt reminiscent of a quick-draw artist.*]

FRU NDI: [*into cell phone*] Fru Ndi.

GOBATA: Lunch sounds wonderful, but you see, I agreed to meet my niece at two o'clock...

FRU NDI: [*into cell phone*] Fru Ndi! Of course Fru Ndi! Who else would it be? [*Covering the cell phone with his free hand*] Excellent, two o'clock it is then. And tell the boy we don't eat squirrels here. [*Strides purposefully out of the room, humming into his cell phone.*]

AMERICAN: Thank you, Sir.

GOBATA: [*to Fru Ndi's receding back*] Chairman, I really don't think I can be there because I told...Chairman?... Damn...[*pauses, then turns to the American*] Squirrels?

Eighteen years earlier, the people of Bamenda had woken up to find the stiff bodies of more than eighteen hundred people lying along the shores of nearby Lake Nyos. The dead appeared to have all died at the same moment. Their bodies lay exactly where they would have been at nine o'clock at night. Women lay crumpled near extinguished cooking fires, dead men huddled in groups over open beers gone flat. In the hills surrounding the lake, the bodies of white cattle, stiff with rigor mortis, lay in clusters. No flies on the bodies—the flies had died too.

Shortly afterwards, scores of hydrologists, geochemists, pathologists, and limnologists from across the globe flocked to the area to diagnose the cause of the disaster. Lake Nyos, 683 feet deep, sits directly atop a volcano. Carbon dioxide from magma degassing deep under Lake Nyos had percolated up into the bottom layers of water over a course of decades or maybe even centuries. The pent-up gas dissolved in the water had suddenly exploded, releasing a wave of concentrated carbon dioxide. Like its cousin carbon monoxide, carbon dioxide is odorless and colorless. At high concentrations CO_2 displaces oxygen. In air that is 5 percent carbon dioxide, candles snuff out and car engines putter to a stop. At 10 percent, people hyperventilate, grow dizzy, and eventually lapse into a coma; they gasp once or twice and fall dead. The visiting scientists generally agreed that the event had been inevitable, but that the installation of a better warning system might have saved lives. Yet, a number of people I met in Bamenda had a different take: Paul Biya had hired mercenary foreign scientists, American, or perhaps, Israeli, to explode the lake and wipe out a hotbed of political dissidents.

The eruption of Mount Cameroon in 1999 added to the evidence against Americans and Israelis. Again, villagers spotted foreigners on the mountain just before the eruption. In *The Angry Gods and the Eruption of Cameroon Mountain 1999*, a glossy pamphlet written to teach schoolchildren about the disaster, the author Jonas N. Dah writes, "One rumor about the cause of the eruption stated that foreigners went up the mountain and performed medicine in order to win the last mountain race, a practice which was against the will of the gods." Paramount Chief S.M.L. Endeley of the Bakweri tribe confirmed for me that these foreigners, Americans or Israelis, had triggered the eruption by performing occult magic on the mountainside.

The reputation Americans enjoyed in Bamenda meant that I found no one willing to disclose to me the identities of Takumbeng members. Most residents of Bamenda consider themselves good Christians; my poking around for Takumbeng rumors raised suspicions and reversed the roles I had expected—I found myself cast as a likely practitioner of the occult. Consequently, no one who had been outside Ni John Fru Ndi's compound the night the Takumbeng stood down the Cameroonian army told me what they saw. They rebuffed my inquiries with a simple restatement of local belief: any man who saw a member of the Takumbeng naked would have long since died from the accompanying curse. Therefore, if I wanted information, I had best interview the dead.

For lunch, Fru Ndi's wife, Rose, prepared and served hedgehog in huckleberry. Although there were only three of us eating, the table had been set for fifteen. Fru Ndi was not a terribly large man, but he occupied space with the same easy authority of a man half again his size. I did not get to ask many questions; the few that I did ask, Fru Ndi nimbly turned into pro-SDF polemics. His craggy face topped a green collared shirt, cut in a stylish compromise between African and Western styles. He wore his hair cropped close, more gray than evident in the official SDF photos, in which he sported a head of rich black hair or a fiercely shaven pate. He frequently referred to himself in the third person, and occasionally used his own name and his party's acronym interchangeably—"The SDF made a speech in Maroua last week."

I had expected lunch with Fru Ndi to crack the mystery of the Takumbeng, that he would describe dramatically how the woman of the Takumbeng shrieked and wailed, how the soldiers had twisted and writhed, clutching stomachs that expanded like balloons. Instead, he asked, "With all the corruption, with all the political drama, and all the suffering in this country, why would you chase a quaint, sensationalized story of African witchcraft? Do you find it fulfilling to confirm stereotypes?"

I felt very small. The vast mound of huckleberry and hedgehog steamed on my plate. He didn't wait for an answer. To prove myself, I ate more than my share of food and mentally compiled a list of the various things I decided I didn't like about Fru Ndi. When talking about the possibility of civil war in Cameroon, he made finger-guns and shooting noises, which I decided, proved he was flippant about violence. He had hung in his hallway a photo spread that documented an incident in which he had evaded an assassination attempt, a decorative choice that showed me how he suffered from messianic complex and thought he couldn't be killed. Later, he made a positive comparison between himself and Charles Taylor, which I decided, meant that had he been installed in power, he might have been a genocidal monster as well. But mostly, I sulked, because I was a twenty-one-year-old American and he had treated me as such.

Nwga Mary-Anne Ngengang had been a teenager when the Cameroonian army moved into Bamenda. Although the identities of the Takumbeng members were purportedly unknown, the nights when Mary-Anne's mother wasn't home to prepare dinner corresponded neatly with rumored appearances of the Takumbeng. It was only natural that, seven years later, Ngengang found the Takumbeng and their incantations and songs to be the perfect subject for her 1999 master's thesis. At the time I lived in Cameroon, Ngengang worked as a schoolteacher in a small village near the Nigerian border. Her thesis advisor, Babila Mutia, a professor of African Religion at the Ecole Normale of the University of Yaoundé, allowed me to photocopy one of the three extant copies of Ngengang's thesis, in which she had carefully recorded all the incantations and rites that would reputedly kill a man should he ever hear them. She even translated them into English, so that they might be understood by those who don't speak the local dialect. Her thesis could be the definitive how-to manual for performing most of the rites that have been guarded in absolute secrecy by generations of Bamenda women.

Mary-Anne Ngengang defined the Takumbeng as "a secret society of women, similar to the Anlu of Kom, that can only appear when the deities themselves have called the women together. They represent a potential force before which even eminent men must bow." Ngengang explains that members do not consider Takumbeng a secret society or a club, but rather a physical manifestation of a higher power. When Mary-Anne Ngengang's mother left the house and rendezvoused with the Takumbeng, she ceased to be Mrs. Ngengang and became an instrument of the deities.

Made up entirely of older women, the Takumbeng had been charged by the deities with preserving moral order; the women of the Takumbeng appeared most frequently in order to avenge "an insult to womanhood"—men who torture their wives. Ngengang outlines "punishments" exacted on abusive husbands that range from a small fine (for excessive beatings) to banishment and death ("in a situation where femininity is mutilated or destroyed"). Prior to 1992, the Takumbeng had last intervened in a political affair sometime between 1895 and 1901, when members of the Takumbeng aided a popular uprising against German colonialists.

Ngengang uses the metaphor of a performance to describe an appearance of the Takumbeng, although she admits that the performance could never occur before an audience because "their presence in society usually sends people running in search of safety." She then takes the reader through a "performance," a drama of justice exacted upon a man accused of mutilating his wife.

On the appointed night, the women gather in the main street leading to the culprit's compound. The women are naked, or clad in rags that expose aged breasts and genitals. They knot Bamenda grass around their heads. The younger women press blades of ijken grass between their lips to represent a "sealed oath." As whispers of a Takumbeng pass through the neighborhood, the streets clear. Windows are shuttered tight. Men abandon the plastic chairs set out in front of beer stores, aware that any man whose gaze falls upon the naked bodies of the Takumbeng, even by accident, runs the risk of death. Just a quick glance, a peek from the corner of the eye, can "render the man impotent."

Once all the Takumbeng members have gathered, they "dance naked, singing songs about their mystical abilities. People who hear their songs are left with an eerie feeling. They sing with tense, wrinkled, sullen faces which create a very solemn atmosphere." The younger women (still in their fifties) let loose with high-pitched ululations. "The voices of the Takumbeng take on a guttural nature, because by this stage, they are no longer human." From the back, as the ululations reach a fury pitch, younger women lug out earthenware pots filled with water. Older women spread their legs over the pots and bring cupfuls of water up to their genitals, washing and letting water fall back into the pots.

When every woman has had a turn, they set out for the culprit's house, "frenzied with rage as they approach." In their hands they hold long sticks of gnarled wood with which they beat out rhythms on the ground. Ngengang tells us that "anyone with eyes to see knows that the sticks are the legs of their ancestors." They surround the culprit's house. The younger women enter and drag out the unfortunate man. Stronger women bludgeon him down, keep him pinned to the ground. The mob of women engulfs the prone man. Those closest to him "list his crimes one by one." At the mention of each crime, the other women shake, shriek in dismay, or mock him for his wantonness. As the main body of the Takumbeng thrash and wail, a single woman, usually one of the eldest, recites incantations over the prone man. As she recites, other women lug out the earthenware pots brimming with the water used to wash their genitals. One by one, they hoist the pots above the unhappy man and, with a final shriek, dump the contents over his head.

The performance ends. The women go home in silence. That night the man will grow ill. By week's end, he will die.

For her thesis, Ngengang interviewed Ma Tabita Lum, a sixty-year-old member of the Takumbeng:

> Ni John Fru Ndi did not call us. We came out to protect him because he aired our grievances. He spoke the truth and still speaks the truth. We stand for the truth. When the State of Emergency was declared, we had to come out and protect our son from the Lion's fangs [a reference to Paul Biya, who calls himself *L'homme lion*]. Bamenda was crowded with military men armed to the teeth. My daughter, we had to be vigilant because the Lake Nyos disaster is still fresh in our minds.

Biya had been careful to keep the army relatively free of soldiers who hailed from the Anglophone northwest, where opposition to his regime enjoyed popular support. The soldiers sent by Biya to arrest Fru Ndi had been mostly Francophone recruits from the Muslim north and the tropical south. The Takumbeng had not been part of their local tradition, and so, when told that the Takumbeng had amassed in front of Fru Ndi's compound, a number of soldiers responded, "Takumbeng? *C'est quoi?*" Takumbeng? What's that? Or, if one extrapolates from the vocal emphasis typically given to the question: What the hell is this Takumbeng?

In Bamenda the question, Takumbeng, *C'est quoi?* has become somewhat idiomatic, a phrase that indicates that one doesn't know what one is getting oneself into. According to Ngengang, all Takumbeng performances follow a similar pattern, only the particular incantations change. Which would indicate that the scene in front of Fru Ndi's house went much like the performance she described.

Imagine you are one of these soldiers. You are sent to arrest a political figure, not so uncommon an occurrence in Cameroon. You've done it before, and the worst you've seen has been a few shots fired. Nothing like this. In front of a walled mansion, a seething crowd of old woman, dressed in scant rags or nothing at all, beat upon the ground with sticks they call legs. They shriek and wail, their voices guttural, distorted. *Mais, qu'est-ce qu'elles font, eh?* Along the fringe some of them wash themselves over clay pots. Your commander looks at you. Go tell them to move, he says. You approach, but before a word escapes your lips, a woman runs up with one of the pots, shrieks, and douses you with douche-water.

"Takumbeng, *c'est quoi?*"

Despite an implicit accusation that I missed the real political story for a sensationalized account of curses, as a favor to Gobata, Fru Ndi granted me a ten-minute interview in which he would respond to questions about the Takumbeng, although without a tape recorder. The following interview has been reconstructed from notes.

Q: The night that the Takumbeng appeared, did you know that either the Takumbeng or the soldiers were coming?

FN: This house is also the headquarters of the SDF. All my staff was here. We knew the soldiers would come, the Takumbeng do what they please.

Q: Did you or anyone of your staff see what transpired between the soldiers and the Takumbeng?

FN: Young man, if you had done any research at all, you would know that if I looked at the Takumbeng, a curse would apply to me as well.

Q: Yes, I had read that, but I also read that there were 145 people in here, roughly a third of whom were women, and as I understand it, a curse would not apply in the same way to women. Regardless, is it so unlikely that a few of those 145 people might have seen something?

FN: I had just had a presidential election stolen from me

and a warrant for my arrest had been issued over the radio. As you might presume, I was not concerned with interviewing each and every one of my staff about what they might or might not have seen throughout the course of the evening. But, as far as I know, the answer is no, no one saw anything.

Q: O.K. But how about the next day? Rumor has it that a number of soldiers were found dead in the fields around your house.

FN: Yes. I know the rumors.

Q: Did you see any dead soldiers then?

FN: I myself did not. Remember that I was under house arrest for two months. I was not in a position to go looking for dead soldiers. The house arrest was more like a siege. They cut off my water and electricity. People had to use buckets for toilets. We didn't have much food. What I most remember about the Takumbeng, and what I consider one of their bravest acts, was that they were the ones to smuggle us food and water during those first heated days. As for dead soldiers, I can't say anything one way or another.

Q: Is the time up? Wait...let me ask if you...do you feel that in some way you were not arrested that night because the Takumbeng was there to protect you? And if so, would you say they are responsible for changing Cameroon's history and placing you where you are today?

FN: The assumption in that question is that an arrest would mean the end of my political career. I have been arrested before and come away stronger and more committed than when I went in. My success depends, and has always depended, on support from a number of different sources. The bravery of those women is one such source.

III. HYSTERON PROTERON

Before September 11, 15 percent of America's oil came from sub-Saharan Africa. Post 9/11, the Bush administration sought to expand Africa's share to 25 percent. Accordingly,

Chevron made plans to pump more oil in places where—as Chevron CEO David J. O'Reilly put it—"people live on less than one dollar a day."

The women who took over Escravos had a simple demand—development. "They achieved something from this community for forty years," said Mama Ayo, one of the women's leaders. "Can't they help us achieve something?"

But Chevron delivers oil, not hopes. David O'Reilly noted, "The major responsibility [for development] is with the government. We can't take the place of the government. It's unrealistic; it's not our role." When Chevron buys oil rights in Nigeria, the contracts stipulate that the Nigerian government keeps 60 percent of the oil revenue, a concession more generous than offered by any other company. Chevron keeps 40 percent of the revenues, the Nigerians tax that 40 percent, cutting it in half, meaning that in the end, the Nigerian government nets 80 percent of the profit, Chevron 20. Then, before any actual petroleum extraction can get underway, Chevron must pass through a bureaucratic obstacle course; each application, license, waiver, certificate, and rubber stamp carries a fee. For argument's sake, one can figure that depending on the specific contract, the Nigerian government gets 82 to 85 percent of Chevron's total oil revenues. With the remaining 15 to 17 percent, Chevron must build offshore pumping platforms, construct huge terminals, pay for tankers, and train skilled workers from the local population. Meanwhile, back in the U.S., shareholders clamor for profits. Ugborodo may be sinking—but Chevron has no responsibility to make Nigeria a nice place to live. That responsibility falls on the Nigerian government—so what happened to its 80-something percent of those oil revenues?

A quick comparison: the Nigerian dictator General Sani Abacha, who died in office in 1998, managed, during his half-decade in power, to amass a personal fortune of around

$3 billion. Mobutu Sese Seko of Zaire—often held up as the paradigm of a rough, greedy dictator, a man who ruled over one of the most resource-rich countries in all sub-Saharan Africa—required thirty years to amass that same amount.

Even before the Escravos takeover, Chevron had spent $36 million to foster community development in the Niger Delta. Much of the money was stolen by contractors and dubious "development" organizations. In response, Chevron hired and funded "community liaison" officers from the local populations to police the contractors. These "community liaison" officers used Chevron money to buy themselves houses and cars. Chevron brought in American employees to oversee the "community liaison" officers, but nobody wanted to be told what to do by foreigners. In 1992, frustrated and hoping to evince some measure of goodwill, Chevron officials ordered an eighteen-bed hospital to be built and staffed in Ugborodo at Chevron's expense. The villagers burned it down in ethnic riots seven years later.

Had I not been so tender about my age and credentials, I might have actually countered Ni John Fru Ndi's suggestion, over lunch, that an investigation of the Takumbeng incident could only confirm stereotypes of backwards witchy country; that my time might be better spent looking into the attempts to alleviate the region's corruption and poverty. In fact, those are precisely the reasons the Takumbeng and the women of Ugborodo interested me.

At the University of Yaoundé, I took a tutorial on international relations and development initiatives in Cameroon, taught by Collin Ngwa, a former professor at Brown who taught at the Cameroon Institute of International Relations, where a number of Central Africa's diplomats had trained. The failure rate of development initiatives in Cameroon, Ngwa told me, hovered somewhere around 60 to 70 percent.

More projects failed than did not, and their failures generally occurred for two reasons. 1.) They tended to overlay their organizational infrastructure on top of local culture and organizations, without integrating the two, so when they pulled out, they essentially took their project with them. 2.) Being outsiders, they lacked moral authority, and so the local population did not defend their projects from corruption and theft.

With this in mind, I'd liked to have asked Fru Ndi to consider what many others already have: were a foreign NGO to team up with a traditional organization like the Takumbeng, they would begin their projects with those two major obstacles already met. The impediments to such an alliance so far have not come from Cameroonians, who recognize the power of the Takumbeng, but from Westerners, who do not. Francis Nyamjoh, a Cameroonian novelist and author of *Mindsearching,* wrote:

> Under the dominant Western export, reality is presented as anything whose existence has, or can be established in a rational, objective manner. According to this export, the world is dichotomous: there is the real and the unreal. The popular epistemological order in Cameroon does not subscribe to the same dichotomies. On the contrary, it marries the so-called natural and supernatural, rational and irrational, real and unreal; making it impossible for anything to be one without also being the other.

In other words, in order to engage Cameroon, one must engage with Cameroonians on their own terms. There exists no constant defined reality, but rather a series of collective realities. That which is collectively understood to be true, becomes, in some sense true, whether that be for Westerners and their arbitrary dichotomies, or for Cameroonians, who believe that an organized group of naked women have power, and thus, do.

Look at the proof: presidents, armies, and geo-political corporations have all backed down before such women. Could there be a more clear demonstration of power? Anyone looking to engage in a partnership with an organization that has a track record of success could (and likely will) do much worse than the Takumbeng or the women of Ugborodo. For the past few decades, governments, celebrities, and NGOs have searched their possessions for a medicine for what they believe ails countries like Cameroon or Nigeria, something to effect a change, to alleviate an entrenched suffering or combat a corrupt political system—but all along, the residents of those countries have had the cure: their voices and their bodies. They're just waiting for an opportunity to put them to use.

Of course, there might be one last consideration. What happens the day that someone challenges a group of naked women and fails to die of a curse? What happens to the man who refuses to believe? Or are we all susceptible to our own peculiar beliefs?

For that, let's refer to Jay Pryor, the American head of Chevron Texaco's Nigerian operations. On July 20, 2002, three days after the women left Escravos, Chevron Texaco appeared to renege on a number of the promises that they had made to the women of Ugborodo. That night, a bolt of lightning struck the Escravos terminal and set ablaze a reservoir holding 180,000 barrels of oil. Liquid fire spilled through the complex. Oil production halted for nearly three weeks—the exact amount of time it took Chevron officials to sign a hard copy of the verbal agreements that promised the aid to Ugborodo. Jay Pryor called the lightning "an act of God."

❧ ❧ ❧

David Torrey Peters received an MFA from the University of Iowa, where he was an Iowa Arts Fellow. His writing has been published in Epoch, Fourth Genre, The Pinch, *and* The Indiana Review. *Currently, David lives in Chicago and teaches at the Illinois Institute of Technology, but has plans to move to Kampala, Uganda in the near future.*

꙳ ꙳ ꙳

Ready or Not

Her children's origins are strangely her own.

I WASN'T SURE WHAT MY CHILDREN EXPECTED WHEN I booked our Homeland Tour to South Korea. More self aware than many teens their age, they were adolescents nonetheless. Which is to say, given to opacity. My daughter, a priestess of Asian pop—from manga and anime to gaming and "J-rock"—claimed she was on board for the music and fashion. My son, who posed as an Asian no-wannabe after years of inhaling toxic slurs (in our über-educated Maryland suburb), said he was interested in just being there. As in, being Korean in Korea.

These were all valuable reasons to go. Yet I wondered if either of them could know, let alone admit, what they hoped to find there.

My goal, on the other hand, was clear-cut: to see the towns and hospitals in which they were born. I was not bothered by having (twice) missed the Creation; but I felt remiss in not knowing where the Creation occurred. The sites listed on the adoption forms, with their variant spellings and ambiguous roles, meant (dare I admit it?) nothing to me. In that sense, I guess you could say I went searching for meaning. In lieu of meeting my children's birth mothers—the Mount Everest of primal tourism, as I have come to view such trips—I focused on finding birth*places*.

Much to my surprise, both birthplaces proved elusive; whereas meaning met up with us at every turn, most notably on a street corner in Pusan.

Half a century before our journey, my father was serving in the war in Korea when my mother gave birth to me in Florida. It made unassailable, karmic sense, therefore, that my children would be born in Korea while I was working for the government in Washington, D.C. Well, at least it made sense to *me*.

My husband, Chris, and I first held Lee Jin Ho in Baltimore-Washington International Airport. Lee was one of half a dozen babies delivered at the gate that midnight. Sprouting Munchkinesque tufts of hair at his temples, he looked like a rookie in the Lollipop League. Two years later, at Washington National Airport, we cradled our four-month-old daughter, Park Sun Joo. Julia—who lacked hair altogether but had stunning, take-it-all-in eyes—arrived with a three-year-old boy who spoke only Korean. His new parents were outgoing and upbeat, yet they spoke only English. I wondered how the three of them would cope.

As world travelers, Chris and I looked forward to learning all about the children's heritage. Lee and Julia, however, taught us otherwise: they wanted nothing to do with it. At adoption-agency events, in particular, they acted bored or acted up. One day, when we went shopping at a local Korean grocery, I suddenly understood why.

"Am I going to meet my birth mother here?" Julia blurted out, hanging back.

Nonplussed, I assured her, "No, she's not here"—only to feel the fraud. For all I knew, my daughter's mother was the clerk who rang up our noodles and nori.

And I wished she were.

If Julia was wary of the stranger who might reclaim her, Lee was resentful of the one who would not. When it came to his birth mother, he produced limitless reserves of bile. Which he delivered by proxy to me. Although he was able to meet his foster mother when she escorted a group of adoptees to the states, the reunion did nothing to assuage Lee's longing for connection. In fact, the presence of Beta Mom only underscored Alpha's absence—leaving Gamma to shoulder the emotional load.

In time, the children came to trust that Frosty the Snowman could be built in Hell before Chris and I would "send them back"; that the four of us formed our own integral family; that come what may, we were together for life. No one imagined that *life* might prove a weak link. That life might abandon us all.

Chris died when Lee was fourteen, Julia twelve.

Lee grieved pretty much the way I did: spewing emotion, as if he had taken an emetic to vomit up poison. Day after day, week after week, he tried, in vain, to return to school. After a month, I despaired: would he ever have the stomach for life again? Would I? Roiling with anger, he lamented one day, "If my birth father hadn't given me away, I never would have lost Dad."

I couldn't argue with that. If Chris hadn't swept me away in college, I never would have lost him either. Yet at least we had found someone worth the anguish. When Chris went missing, I realized how privileged I was to have been loved. *That* was the irrevocable trust—rather than the one established by his will—that would support the children and me in perpetuity. From Lee's bitter kernel of truth, however, I could see a new tendril of connection sprouting: to his birth father. Until that moment, he had never acknowledged the latter's existence.

For Julia, the bereavement was so big and close, she could not make it out. Think: watching a horror film with your face against the screen. A year passed without her shedding a tear. Then Chris's company invited us to the dedication of a fountain in his honor, at a project he had directed in Texas. As the day of our trip to San Antonio neared, Julia began to see the picture—in nightmares. After one, she awoke crying and confessed, "I've been pretending Dad was on a business trip."

Holding Julia tight, her sobs shuddering my chest, I wanted to give Chris a high-five. (As opposed to shaking my fist at him while teaching Lee to drive.) Our daughter, the one who took her sweet time with milestones—talking, teething, training, you name it—our daughter was finally grieving!

That was when I realized how perverse motherhood is. My children have had five mothers between them. Not one has failed to embrace what she believed was best for her child, no matter anyone's pain. Knowing grief delayed was grief denied, I hoped Julia would cry rivers.

Once she no longer was awaiting Dad's return, Julia asked to take a trip of her own: to Korea. To my surprise, Lee was willing. And I was when-do-we-leave ready, having talked many times about the journey with Chris, before he became ill. I phoned Julia's adoption agency and booked us on a Homeland Tour.

The morning we convened with nine other adoptive families at Dulles International Airport, the first person I spied was the mother of Julia's three-year-old fellow flier. I had not spoken to Lyndi in fifteen years, yet I felt instantly at ease.

One would have thought that we were long-lost friends. Or at least that we knew each other.

There was also another widow in the group, with a son and a daughter who was Julia's age. What were the chances of that? For the next two weeks, we warmed the empty seats next to each other during ten-hour forays on the bus, trading tales about the indecencies of death and the insolence of life, which had all the compassion of a cop shouting, "Move along!"

In Seoul, families began at the beginning: at Eastern Social Welfare Society, the agency that had placed most of our children. On a tour of the facilities, we lingered in the infant ward. Seeing the babies in bassinettes slumbering in limbo, the adoptees longed to adopt themselves. Afterward, each child had a "file review." I had not expected to learn anything new; so when the caseworker suddenly revealed the names of Julia's birth parents, I found myself searching for pen and paper.

A day later, during a question-and-answer session at Esther's Home for unwed mothers, Lee found himself searching for forgiveness.

At the group home in Pyongtaek, we were ushered into a small dining hall, where a dozen young women were already seated around a table, half with their backs to the room, one struggling against tears. After we had filled the seats at the remaining tables, which were set with juice and rice snacks, the director of the program briefly introduced each expectant mother. (Only one had already given birth). The microphone was then passed to us. One by one, we delicately probed how their lives had converged at the home away from home, while we also praised them for their courage in making their decisions, in facing us.

One adoptive mother pleaded for each birth mother to convey a photograph of herself with her infant; for a likeness would mean more to her child in the years to come than any other information. A thirteen-year-old boy, with the face and the grace of a bodhisattva, looked directly at the mothers and reassured them that he thought about his birth mother every day. When I dared to ask if the increasing number of in-country adoptions made their decisions any easier, one mother quickly replied that she preferred an international placement; for it offered the chance of later finding her child. Another birth mother tersely stated that she had not decided on re-linquishment. When she proceeded to question why people would adopt babies they abused, as reported in the news, her housemates nodded in concern. More than one adoptive parent stood and replied that, loving our children as much as we do, we could only wonder how that happened, too.

I cannot recall the point at which Lee spoke, but he caught me off guard. "I've been angry with my birth mother all these years," he confessed, and his tone and impolitic slouch said as much. The young women riveted their eyes upon him, awaiting a translation. At seventeen, Lee was but a few years younger than they were or than his birthmother was, when he was conceived. "But now, after meeting all of you," he continued, "I hope I can someday find her."

Lee's birthplace in Masan was only an hour's drive west of Pusan, where our tour was booked for two nights. Julia's, un-fortunately, was less accessible. Late in the trip, I learned that a visit to Kangnung on the northeast coast would require spend-ing a night on our own. As I second-guessed my mission, Julia made the decision easy. She had no interest in parting from the group—or, to be more accurate, a significant someone in the group. He was about her age, he loved J-pop, too, and he lived in the town next to us in Maryland. Faced with choosing between the past and the future, she chose future. So did I. We would find her birthplace on our next trip.

Once we had checked into the hotel on Pusan Bay, I set about arranging an excursion to Masan. Having spent the cost of a Hyundai Accent getting to South Korea, I didn't blink at the quote of 90,000 won for roundtrip cab fare. I just withdrew the equivalent of $100 from the lobby's ATM.

The morning our group boarded the bus to tour the Jagalchi fish market at the docks, my children and I hopped a taxi in pursuit of Fatima Hospital. Riding shotgun, as she phrased it, was the tour's translator, Susan, a native Korean who was a student at Wellesley College.

Halfway to Masan, our driver pulled into a rest stop. When we returned from using the facilities, he treated us to a bag of Korean donuts. (Picture a cabbie in the States doing that.) Back on the highway, he seemed eager to join our discussion, and Susan was happy to translate. Ever curious about prejudice, I asked if Korean parents would more easily embrace a Chinese or a Japanese son-in-law. He and Susan differed. Yet they agreed that a Caucasian was the least of all choices, given the risk of being "whitewashed."

We arrived to discover that Fatima Hospital had long since decamped. The building was now occupied by a mental-health and geriatric-care center. Moreover, Susan and the receptionist deduced that Lee was not born at Fatima but transferred there the day of his birth due to prematurity and jaundice.

Regardless of its name or function, the building had sheltered my son during his first month of life. I still wanted to see as much of the facility as possible. Apart from the lobby, we were welcome to explore a back stairway.

As we wound single-file up the spiral steps, I imagined I was Lee's birth mother on the day when he arrived. Never having given birth or had parents who rejected the child of their child, I had no ability to simulate her state of mind. And that was undoubtedly a mercy.

Aside from some ornate grillwork, the staircase revealed nothing worth seeing; yet I paused with the children mid-flight so that Susan could take the obligatory photo. When

I peered through the door on the third-floor landing and beheld floor-to-ceiling bars, I immediately turned back, thus reversing our procession on the narrow steps. Only then did I notice that the cab driver had joined Lee's birthplace tour. And he was now in the lead.

You would have thought that they were long-lost kin. Or at least that they knew each other.

That afternoon, back in Pusan, I went out alone to explore the city. To practice finding my way without Chris. Two hours later, having proved my mettle, I returned with new-found confidence—only to get lost between the subway stop and the hotel. Map in hand, I approached several pedestrians; but no one could fathom my sign language, let alone pinpoint my location. Finally, I flagged down two young men, despite the fact that, demographically speaking, they would be the last ones to consult a map themselves. They tried, though.

As they debated between themselves in Korean, another voice called out. I turned to see a slight, middle-aged man waving at us from a block away.

"I know him!" I exclaimed to my would-be guides, who looked more lost than ever.

The driver churned the air with an arm, as if reeling me to his cab, which was idling at the curb. The cab I had ridden to Masan. "Come!" he insisted, though he didn't speak English. "Service," he added, "service!"

Laughing at our improbable reunion, I obliged. Don't ask me how, but we managed to communicate as he drove me to the door of my hotel. And don't ask me why, but he suddenly meant the world to me. When he refused his fare, I realized *service* is Korean for *gratis*.

"What are the chances of that?" I later said to Susan. "In a city of more than three million people?"

"Oooh," she crooned, turning serious. "In Korea, when people find each other again like that, we call it—" She said the word for *destiny*.

I say *hide-and-seek*. The game of going missing. The game of finding people who find you.

On the flight home, Julia sat across the aisle from the boy who had traveled "home" with her fifteen years before. Beside her sat her new companion. He's been keeping her company ever since.

❧ ❧ ❧

Gaye Brown is a former director of publishing for the Smithsonian Institution's American Art Museum and National Museum of the American Indian. She subsequently served as a writer and researcher for Time-Life's history series What Life Was Like. *Her work has appeared in the* Georgetown Review, Nathaniel Hawthorne Review, *and* Adoptive Families *magazine, among other publications.*

CHARLES KULANDER

~~ ~~ ~~

Très Cheap: A Travel Writer Storms the Caribbean

He does the dirty work so envied by many.

I TRAVEL FASTER THAN BAD NEWS. I COMB MY HAIR with a plastic salad fork and use a toothbrush handle to stir my instant coffee, flavoring it with Pepsodent. A money pouch hangs inside my pants, and on my wrist is a Timex with a black vinyl strap—not to tell the time but to tell the world: I'm cheap. Go rob somebody with a Rolex.

I can't afford to get robbed. It takes up too much time, my most precious commodity. The faster I travel, the more money I make. And after ten days of reviewing resorts throughout the Caribbean, I'm back where I started, at my favorite hotel in Jamaica, the Ocean View. Pink water fills the toilet, a tattered *Popular Mechanics* from 1997 sits on the bureau (compliments of the management), and an air conditioner grumbles loud enough to drown out the jet blast from the nearby airport.

You can tell a lot about a country by its airport. Is it named after a dictator? Do the pay phones actually work? How many crashed planes line the runway? Any sniffer dogs roaming the baggage carousels?

At the Montego Bay airport, the first thing you notice are the Jamaicans themselves, a hands-on kind of people. When I landed here the week before, I sought refuge in the bathroom, which didn't stop a mob of taxi drivers from following me in, tugging at my shirt while I stood at the urinal.

"Can I please pee in private?" I pleaded. Laughing among themselves, they moved back about two inches without loosening their grips on the duffel bag slung over my shoulder.

"I don't need a taxi. I'm walking," I said as I zipped up my pants. I plowed my way through the taxi drivers, veering for the street while they pushed me in the direction of their taxis. They gave up when I told them where I was going.

"Let the cheap man walk. He go to de Ocean View."

After securing a room at the Ocean View, my first order of business was to find a means of transportation. To stay ahead of expenses, I look for the cheapest thing on wheels, which in Montego Bay was a derelict Honda 90, a step-through motorcycle with no rear-view mirror, soft brakes, and licks of foam sticking out from the seat. Instead of a helmet, I was given a plastic construction hat that strapped around my chin. For just $14 a day, I had immediately gained the social stature of a third-world pizza delivery boy.

Actually, my assignment was to review hotels. I'd walk through hotel after hotel while mumbling into a hidden microphone attached to a microcassette recorder in my pocket—*lobby carpet suffers from mange, pool murky, garden smells like malathion*—trying not to look like a crazed tourist with Tourette's disease.

Speed was essential, not just to make money, but to remain one step ahead of hotel security, whose suspicions I tended to trigger. The trick was to appear as inconspicuous as possible, which is why I dressed in Permopress. Wrinkle-free Dockers and a Van Heusen shirt gave me an anonymous middle-management look. Strangers often stopped me, demanding to know where the bathrooms were.

For four days I rode this rickety motorcycle along the north shore of Jamaica, trailed by a sputtering plume of blue smoke, a sight that never impressed the guards who stood at the entrance of each five-star resort. At these guarded compounds—each one a jungle fantasy of crashing waterfalls, rainbow-colored drinks, and party-size whirlpools—guests pay a package price that includes everything except the Alka-Seltzer. There's no need to go elsewhere. At some resorts, guests are actually warned not to leave the premises. That's the irony of the tourist industry. People pay $3,000 to be isolated from the country they came to visit.

In these compounds, inhibitions are shed right along with the sweaters, encouraged by resorts with names like Hedonism II, where young Republicans pass joints to the young Democrats in the whirlpool—and everybody is inhaling. As a travel writer, you need to brace yourself for some truly extraordinary sights at these all-inclusive resorts, such as naked people playing tennis.

Playing tennis, especially while naked, is hardly an accurate depiction of everyday life in Jamaica. Learning about the realities of this island usually comes as a crash course for anybody who leaves the compound or steps off the tourist bus. In Ochos Rios, cruise ship passengers who decide to explore on foot are met by every charity case on the north shore—the deformed, the blind, the crippled, the prostitutes, the hustlers and con men who make it a business to greet every ship of fools that drops anchor. If the tourists make it as far as the street, they are pursued by taxis, whose drivers shout out the window with a ringing laugh.

"Where you goin' man?"

"Uh, I don't know."

"Hop in, I take you dare."

White people—even those with nice tans—must come to terms with the role that color has played in the island's destitution. I had never felt particularly liable for the crimes of my ancestors until one day when visiting the Slave Museum at Port Royal. At a display case full of rusty chains and shackles, I listened to a Jamaican describe the leg irons to his son.

"De white man, he do this to us, he put us in these chains," he said angrily, as if he were still wearing them.

His young son, eyes wide with fright, stared directly at me, as if I still had the keys.

My guilt puts me at odds with resorts that romanticize the days of slavery, like the Jamaica Palace Hotel outside of Port Antonio, a white neo-classical mansion modeled after a sugar plantation.

"We wanted to recreate the colonial look," the manager told me as we strolled through the marble lobby. How do they manage that, I wondered. Put flogging poles out in back? Have the staff shuffle around in leg irons?

One morning, I sat for breakfast in a small restaurant in Gustavia.

"You want iron shoes?" asked the waiter.

Iron shoes? It was probably a traditional slave breakfast. I wondered what was in it as I glanced down at the breakfast menu. Ackee, a tree vegetable, was the featured specialty. Enjoy it while you are here, read the menu, as the U.S. Food & Drug Administration has placed a ban on ackee in all forms (canned, cooked, or frozen) from entering U.S. ports. Now that sounded like a real seal of endorsement.

"I've never heard of iron shoes," I said. "Do you put ackee in it?"

"You don't know what iron shoes is?" he replied. "Where you from, Mars?"

"California, actually," I said. "We never had slavery there."

He rolled his eyes back in disbelief, then shook his head.

"Iron shoes, man. You pick de ironge from de tree and squeeze it to make de joos."

"Oh, orange juice," I said. "Never mind. I'll stick with water."

"I'd like a window seat," I said to the attendant at the TransJamaica Air counter in Montego Bay.

"They're all window seats," she replied.

The Briton Norman Islander was built to hold eight passengers. Ours held nine. At the last moment, a huge woman wedged into the copilot's seat, her fat knees just inches from the steering column, her flabby arms embracing a basket of codfish wrapped in newspaper. I sat behind the pilot. In the seats directly behind me were two Rastafarians with glazed faces who gave new meaning to the term red-eye flight.

It's hard not to be a back-seat flyer while staring over the pilot's shoulder. As we hurtled down the runway, I wanted to ask why the autopilot had a sticker over the screen, "Not in Use." And why did the fuel gauge read only ten gallons? As we disappeared into the thick fog shrouding the Blue Mountains, I especially wanted to know why the altimeter read only 800 meters when the mountains ahead of us rose to over 2,000 meters.

The flight only lasted thirty-eight minutes, but the final approach was rough. As we broke out of the fog and swooped down over Kingston, the plane began to buck and drop violently in the thermals. The big lady in front began to panic. While the plane lurched and rolled, her hammy legs slammed around the cockpit, threatening any number of levers and dials, while her hands searched for something to hang onto, leaving the basket of fish perilously close to spilling.

"Don't touch anything!" yelled the pilot.

Now is the time to pray, I figured…but what? With cod as my copilot? The Rastafarians in back were equally alarmed, and began to shout at the pilot.

"Why dis plane bounce, man. Can't you fly de plane?"

The pilot didn't say anything, but I could see his neck clench with tension.

"Was wrong wi'da plane, man? You gonna make us crash."

The pilot still didn't say a word. His hands jerked at the stick, trying to correct for each violent lurch as the runway loomed in the window. We came down hard on two wheels, bounced up at a terrifying angle, then came down again on all three.

The pilot was the first person out of the plane. He yanked off his fingerless gloves, and threw them down on the tarmac.

"This was a good flight!" he screamed at his tormentors. "You can't judge a flight by the last two minutes."

"You can if it crashes," said one of the Rastafarians. "You almost kill us all, man."

I stepped out of the plane and saw weeds growing up through the carcass of a DC3. Dammit. Wrong airport. With my plane to Antigua taking off in less than an hour from the other side of Kingston, I jumped into the first taxi I saw.

"We might make it," said the taxi driver. "Roll up de window."

"But it's 90 degrees outside."

"We go through Trenchtown, man. And lock your door too."

For thirty minutes we cleaved through a teeming mass of poverty-stricken humanity in western Kingston's shantytown. I sat stone-faced in the front seat, visualizing green lights.

An hour later, I was 15,000-feet high, in an air-conditioned fuselage streaking towards Antigua. I always enjoyed these brief airborne interludes from the real world, which allowed me to pursue more leisurely activities; in this case, engaging in an armrest war with the tourist next to me, and pondering the message the airlines insist on posting on the back of every seat. Fasten Seat Belt While Seated. Do they really think we're so stupid that we'll fasten them while still standing? Out my window, the islands below looked like a vision of perfection, planet Earth at its most sublime, a world without poverty or crime or naked people playing tennis.

The resort industry survives on just this sort of illusion—the perfect beach, the endless summer, beautiful people—and many hotels feel it is the travel writer's duty to sustain this fantasy, even if it's not grounded in reality. At Jumby Bay, a private islet off Antigua, guests pay some of the highest resort prices in the world in order to stay at a hotel with no pool and no room service. You can't even watch any adult movies on pay TV.

"People come here to relax," said the sales manager. "That's why we allow no distractions from the outside world, no radios, no clocks, no phones."

"What'd you say?' I yelled, as a big jumbo jet roared low overhead, having just taken off from the Antigua airport. "Something about no distractions from the outside world?"

I was lucky to get a brochure before they rushed me to the boat.

Sometimes travel writers get invitations to stay at a hotel for free—getting comped, we call it. I stay away from them as much as possible, mostly because I can't afford the price of a free room. My first night in Antigua, I was comped at a five-star resort for the rich and famous. A fruit basket, a bottle of rum, and a welcome note from the manager awaited me in my room. Within minutes, the phone rang.

"Sir, shall I make a dinner reservation for you this evening?" asked the concierge in a stiff British accent.

"Yeah," I replied, "A table for one at Taco Bell."

At resorts like these, I could easily blow my week's budget on dinner alone. On top of that, there is the unspoken understanding that you are going to gush sweet compliments about the place, which is at cross-purposes with what I'm paid to do.

When I checked out of the hotel the next morning, the general manager came out to bid me farewell.

"Thank you for staying with us," he said. "And so we can be of better service on your next visit, you should know that we keep detailed guest histories on our computer."

"Oh great," I said. I knew how mine would read: *Charles Kulander, Room 212: swipes all the toiletries, leaves fast food wrappers in the bathroom, one face cloth missing, empty rum bottle found under bed.*

As the 737 streaked toward Trinidad, the cabin attendant moved down the aisle spraying us with a poisonous disinfectant as nonchalantly as if it were a can of Glade.

"Don't worry," she said, "It only affects insects."

Five minutes later, the tip of my tongue went numb, and I thought of Franz Kafka.

My sanity suffered even more once I landed in Trinidad, for it was the eve of Carnival, a wild bacchanal in which I was an unwilling participant.

After finding the cheapest place to stay—a small prison-like guesthouse in an East Indian barrio—I hopped a bus for the ten-mile trip into Port of Spain. I didn't have much work there, just six hotels to review. I'd have some time left over to watch the beginning of Carnival.

As evening fell, I followed the streams of people heading from all directions to the calypso competition at Queens Park Savannah. After Black Stalin beat out Sparrow for the crown, the spirited crowd spilled onto the street, which is when I noticed there wasn't a taxi in sight. No getting out of here. Not tonight. A knife fight suddenly broke out next to me, as people pushed me out of the way, screaming, "Watch out for the white man." So much for being inconspicuous.

I decided to lose myself for a while at one of the gambling stands where you could bet a Trinidad dollar on one of the barnyard animals painted on a roulette wheel. I put my money on the pig. And won. I put my money on the chicken. And won. I even put it on the zebra, knowing that this wasn't even a barnyard animal, and still I won. I was on the biggest roll of my life, and with thirty Trinidad dollars to the greenback, I was drowning in paper money.

This was when people started asking me for financial loans and cash dividends to be invested in the nearby rum market. This was just too much conspicuous wealth. I couldn't even stuff it all in my pockets. I'd have to walk around all night with two giant fistfuls of money. I had to get rid of it. The easiest way to redistribute the wealth would be to keep playing, knowing that sooner or later I had to lose, which I began doing—quite successfully.

Unfortunately, I took everybody down with me. Inspired by the confidence I showed in laying down giant stacks of money, everybody threw their cash on top of mine, giant piles of worn, faded bills, all of it going to the dealer time and time again till my winnings, and theirs, were completely gone. The bankrupt crowd glared at me. If looks could kill, I knew how my eulogy would read: Here Lies the Man Who Stole Carnival.

This was when I began to drink. Every fifty yards, somebody was selling beer from iceboxes, which was how I measured my progress as I wandered down the street. Three in the morning and still no taxis. Everywhere, steel bands were playing from the back of flatbed trailers while singers rapped out commands through speakers the size of NASA satellite dishes.

"Jump up an' wave. Jump an' misbehave."

This was J'ouverte, the mud festival that would last till dawn, Carnival at its wildest. As the semis moved off down the streets, I fell in behind one truck and tried to get into the spirit of it all. Before I knew it, my Permopress disguise went by the wayside, releasing my true animal spirit. After being liberally doused in buckets of gooey mud, a cardboard crest was slapped on my head. Evidently, my animal spirit was a mud hen.

The surging parade swept down the streets, setting off every car alarm in town, while the more elaborate costumes kept getting entangled in the overhead power lines. As I watched everybody writhe and gyrate with abandon, I tried to do the same, but I wasn't on such intimate terms with my loins. Some people were Riding the Pony, a dance that involved a man wrapping his arms around a woman from behind, while both simulated the motion of riding a pony at a fast gallop. Except I never saw any ponies. I hopped my way down the street riding solo.

As dawn finally streaked the sky, all of the steel bands came together at a large city square, where each tried to outplay the others—a cacophony of calypso—while the mud-covered throng, now numbering in the thousands, broke into a frenzied finale. And there I was, after countless beers, smeared in mud, my headdress askew, trying to keep up with the frenzied hypnotic dancing, flapping my wings like a true mud hen, my mind emptied of all thoughts except for one: my plane leaves in two hours.

Saint Maarten, an hour's flight north of Trinidad, is as overdeveloped as Rush Limbaugh's ego, inflated by a Customs policy whose operating guideline can be simply stated: "It's none of our business." Consequently, this investment-rich island is the little Switzerland of the Caribbean, wall-to-wall with restaurants, banks, resorts, fast-food joints, duty-free shops, casinos, and an oversupply of time-share hotels. While I was making the rounds among the many hotels, a blond-haired girl called out to me.

"Hey good-lookin'. Would you like to go to breakfast?"

"Me? I'm married," I said.

"Who cares if you're married?" she replied, raising her eyebrows suggestively. "You got a credit card?"

"Oh, I get it," I said. She wasn't after my body. She was after my scalp. She was a headhunter, one of the predators that prowl the sidewalks of every resort town. Her job was to lure gullible tourists to the time-share boiler room, using free breakfasts as the bait. These places are called time-share because by the time you realize that you've been had, you've already shared the rest of your life savings with some used-car salesman transplanted from Toledo. The trick is to eat the free breakfast, then slide out the side door for some fresh air and just keep walking.

Obtaining a free meal now and then does help the budget, especially on an island where you can spend $3 on an orange. I'd rather not eat. In fact, not eating is the best way to save money while traveling, though slowly starving to death doesn't figure into most people's vacation plans. Failing that, a bread-and-water diet will keep a person going strong for a day or two.

Still, there comes a time when you need food. Whenever I want a cheap, nutritious meal, I search out the place where all the natives go: McDonald's. The real new world order isn't geopolitical, it's a Big Mac, large fries, and a 32-ounce coke.

I arrived in Santo Domingo with extra baggage in my belly. Constipation is an occupational hazard of the traveler. I'm convinced it's an evolutionary holdover from our prehistoric ancestors who, when migrating through foreign ground, didn't want to leave any trace of their passing. It had to do with survival of the species—still does, as anybody who has ridden forty-eight hours on a Mexican bus will attest. But enough was enough. After finding a cheap hotel near the Santo Domingo airport, I walked next door to the *farmacia*.

In my rusty Spanish, I said something roughly equivalent to, "I am under incredible pressure from my lower self to relieve the stress that results from taking in more than from what comes out in the end."

"Ah, *sí, quieres* Ex-Lax," said the pharmacist, who was quite astute for being only twelve years old.

Not having much experience with laxatives, I ate one tablet and relaxed for ten minutes in my hotel room. Nothing happened. I ate another tablet, and lay down on the bed for another hour. Still nothing. So I gulped down the entire pack and went to sleep.

My wake-up call came at dawn as my intestines knotted into a pretzel. Doubled over in pain, I dropped to the floor in a fetal position, then crawled on hands and knees to the toilet, wondering if I would be the first person in history to die of an Ex-Lax overdose. Why do they make it taste like chocolate candy if you aren't supposed to eat it all at once, I fumed. What's next? Cherry-flavored antibiotics? Candy-coated Kaopectate? Tutti frutti suppositories?

The poorer the country, the larger the monument. And the Dominican Republic has one of the largest, the Columbus Lighthouse, built in the shape of a giant cross that shelters the alleged remains of the great traveler himself. On weekend nights, an immense battery of high-intensity spotlights projects a crucifix into the sky, frequently causing all the other lights in Santo Domingo to go out, including the stoplights. This wouldn't hinder the traffic, though, since nobody pays any attention to them anyway—except the police.

Still recovering from my Ex-Lax overdose and in desperate need of a bathroom, I was hopelessly ensnared in Santo Domingo's chaotic traffic. Suddenly, a traffic cop stepped out and waved me over.

"*Hay un semaforo, señor,*" he said, pointing to the stoplight.

"It's not working," I replied, already reaching for my wallet.

"When the stoplights are not working, you must come to a complete stop."

Nobody else was. A constant parade of derelict cars limped by, bumping into one another like cows on a stampede. An entire family on a tiny moped wove through the traffic—going the wrong way—the smallest child perched on the handlebars like a sacrificial hood ornament.

"Follow me to the police station."

"Can't I pay you directly?" I asked, anxious to get to a bathroom.

"A policeman who takes money on the street is corrupt," he said. He paused a moment. "Let's be friends."

We shook hands and exchanged names, and he showed me a photo of his family.

"Carlos, what is money between friends?" he asked.

"Usually a catastrophe," I said. I gave him a $5 bill and he let me go after giving me a hearty handshake.

A block later, the same policeman came up behind me on his motorcycle and flagged me to the side. My God, I thought, do I have to pay this guy by the block?

"Carlos, you look lost, and friends must help each other. Where are you going?"

"El Embajador Hotel," I said.

"*Sígame*," he said, as he turned on the red flashing light. Blowing his whistle and motioning wildly with his hands, he cleared a path through the stalled traffic while I followed behind somewhat self-consciously, trying hard not to look like a DEA agent. What a country. Where else can you buy friends like this for $5, and get a private motorcade to boot?

The Hotel El Embajador was Dictator Trujillo's glittering showplace of the 1950s. Now it looked like a container ship stranded in the backwater of time. Despite the Chippendale and chandeliers, the smell of mildew permeated the lobby.

I went to the restaurant, and noticed the same stench. The guest rooms smelled like wet athletic socks. As I was writing up notes in my car—bring noseplugs—the odor kept haunting me. I decided to investigate further. Eventually I found its source. It was the shirt I was wearing.

Laundromats are hard to find in most third-world countries, and usually cost more than my clothes are worth. Whenever my threads get too dirty, I shed them and buy new ones. El Conde Street in Santo Domingo's historic district turned out to be one of the Caribbean's great outlets for imitation designer clothes. I spent eight bucks for an Yves St. Laurent shirt with epaulets, and another six bucks for a pair of Girbaud pants with more pleats than a window curtain. A pair of ersatz Ray Bans completed my wardrobe, just in time for my next island hop to St. Barts, the fashion capital of the Caribbean. Fake designer clothes. Tres *chic*.

On Spanish-speaking islands, food and lodging are cheap and plentiful, on English-speaking ones you pay a bit more, but the French ones are by far the most expensive. What you pay for is largely an attitude and yellow sauce on your food. This trip was starting to wear on me. To keep going, I needed almost hourly infusions of caffeine. In a little sidewalk café in Marigot, I ordered a cup of coffee that cost as much as my quarterly life insurance premium, but all I received were a few drops of brown syrup in the bottom of a plastic cup the size of a sewing thimble.

"I'm confused," I said. "Do I put this on my tongue, or just rub it on my skin?" The fashionable café crowd looked at me as if I had a sign around my neck, "*Homo americanus*."

I drove the steep narrow roads of St. Barts at breakneck speed in a rented jeep with a broken windshield and a spring sticking up in the driver's seat that quickly put a tiny hole in my new Girbaud pants. I had ten hours to review twenty hotels before catching a flight back to St. Maarten. Flying in and out is the only way to visit St. Barts without spending the night, as the ferry only runs in one direction once a day. In this way, the island weeds out ordinary people from among the rich and famous.

At the most expensive hotel on the island, the Taiwana, they don't even publish their rates. When I insisted on knowing what it cost to stay there, the exasperated owner said, "One thousand dollars a night to start. Would you like a room?"

This drew a giggle from his bronzed guests lounging around the pool.

"One thousand bucks for one night," I said. "About what it takes to keep a Haitian family alive for five years."

He rolled his eyes, and dismissed me with a wave of his hand while letting loose with a mouth fart, a uniquely European habit in which a pocket of air bursts up from the lower lip, a contemptuous gesture often accompanied by a theatric closing of the eyes, a facial drama meant to convey a subtle existential message: you're dog shit.

When I turned to leave, the oiled people around the pool erupted in laughter. I stormed out of there, my pants flapping in the breeze. They didn't know it, but the Red Brigade had just found a new recruit.

At the hotel next door, the receptionist asked me in that charmingly blunt way of the French, "Monsieur, you have had an accident with your pants?"

"Just a little rip," I said, but as I reached back to check the seat of my pants, there was just bare flesh. My Girbauds had ripped from the belt loop all the way down to the back of my knee and I hadn't even noticed. So that's what people have been laughing at. On an island where the women brazenly expose their breasts, my thigh seemed to be getting all the attention.

Travel fatigue had definitely set in, my body numb of senses yet moving one step ahead of an overactive mind. I should have recognized the first symptoms that morning at the St. Maarten airport. Whenever I had flashed a big smile, people recoiled in horror. Little children ran to their parents. Perplexed, I went into a bathroom and looked at myself in the mirror. My teeth and gums were colored inky red from sucking on a pen already weakened by so much high-altitude flying. Leaking pens are another occupational hazard of the travel writer. My wife is always threatening to buy me a pocket protector. What I really needed was a pocket protector for my mouth.

The last hotel on St. Barts I reviewed while making a new fashion statement: bare-chested, with an Yves St. Laurent shirt looped around my Girbauds, revealing just a flash of lower thigh—the deconstructed look. This is when I formulated my latest travel rule: Never look back, somebody's laughing at you.

I arrived in Kingston on a midnight flight—the last leg of my trip—and went straight to the Indies Hotel.

"One room, yes," said the night-shift receptionist. "But you have to pay cash, and leave before 6 A.M." A carpenter was coming to put a new door on.

"Come on," I said. "On a Sunday morning?" He shrugged his shoulders, and checked me in on my MasterCard.

Scamming is the most popular pastime in Kingston, explained a man who invited himself to eat breakfast with me the next morning. He warned me about strangers who appeared to be friends. After half an hour of pleasant conversation, he wanted to know if I wanted to make some quick money. "You look like a smart man," he said.

Now I knew he was scamming. After inspecting 180 hotels in ten days, I didn't look very smart. I looked like a travel-crazed idiot, an addict warped on speed, a travel junkie who dreamed of hotel bathrooms in his sleep.

But I was almost done. Only five more hotels to review and it would be time to go home. I stepped out into the street, and brushed past the group of touts who have set up a cottage industry in front of the Indies Hotel, dedicated to the fleecing of tourists. I turned the corner down a long boulevard, and paused. Not a soul in sight.

Lapse of judgment is the final stage of travel fatigue. I've learned the hard way never to walk down empty city streets (Filling out police reports is the less glamorous side of travel writing). Oh, big deal, I told myself. It's Sunday. Nothing bad happens on a Sunday.

I strode off purposely down the empty boulevard. About halfway—just when I thought I was home free—a huge man pedaled up behind me and jumped off his bike. He held it over his head, then threw it to the ground with enough force to gain my immediate attention.

"Gimme your money," he said. "Take your wallet out, dat one dare." He pointed not to my wallet but to the secret money pouch I wore inside my pants. This guy had job experience.

"Are you robbing me?" I asked.

"No, I'm not robb'n you," he yelled. "Just give me your money and I won't mess you up."

"Don't bother," I said. "I'm already messed up."

One of his bulging biceps was wrapped in a bloody bandage held together with duct tape. What the hell. I reached in my pocket, and gave him some loose change.

"Dis aint shit, man," he said, throwing it to the ground.

He had a point. I had forgotten how worthless coins were in Jamaica. I had just given him the equivalent of two-and-a-half cents.

Does God have a sense of humor? Right in front of us stood the Ministry of Tourism, its doors padlocked, the glass windows plastered with travel posters. "Jamaica. Come Experience the Warmth of Our People." This guy wasn't just warm, he was boiling over and frothing at the mouth.

I fished out thirty Jamaican dollars from my pocket, the price of a Red Stripe. "Here, buy yourself a beer and cool out," I said.

Then I turned and walked off at a fast pace. He stared at the money, then measured my resolve, which he apparently miscalculated. Given that bloody wound on his arm, I was good for at least another $5.

A cab suddenly turned the corner, and I flagged it down.

"Where is everybody?" I asked the driver.

"All the folk be in church," he said. "Only hustlers and fools be out on the street,"

"And which are you?" I asked.

He laughed without answering. Then asked if he could make a detour to stop at the Bob Marley monument. "I have to meditate on my man here," he said. He sat down in a cross-legged position, closed his eyes, and hummed a reggae tune for ten minutes while I waited impatiently in the front seat. Then he charged me for a sightseeing tour of Kingston. Like he said, only hustlers and fools.

From the veranda of the Ocean View, I can see an Air Jamaica 737 landing, tail heavy with tourists. I'll be taking that plane home in another two hours. It's been a long 240 hours away from my family. I sometimes imagine that I am not actually traveling so much as running in place, just trying to keep up with a world that is spinning under my feet.

There are, however, aspects of travel I do enjoy, such as the assimilation of varied cultural traits I pick up along the way. On the flight over from Kingston, I talked with a couple who were just returning from a week at Sandals, a couples-only resort, about our respective trips. "But what you do isn't really traveling," said Mr. Banana Republic, smugly smiling to his wife. "You never really stay long enough to know a place, do you?"

I rolled my eyes back, waved my hand dismissively, and let a pocket of air burst up from my lower lip.

≈ ≈ ≈

Charles Kulander is a former editor of the Mexico City News *and* Baja California *magazine, and he is now a Utah-based freelance travel writer, and a contributing editor for* National Geographic Traveler. *His work has been published widely in newspapers, magazines, and books, including the Travelers' Tales anthology,* A Dog's World. *He is the author of* West Mexico: From Sea to Sierra.

❧ ❧ ❧

L'Inondation

Helping them dig out of it in Nîmes.

THE YEAR WE WENT TO LIVE AND WORK IN A SMALL village in Provence the weather was glorious, except for October. It rained and rained every day, all day, in October—or at least that's how my memory has it. The village square directly in front of the house where we were living, which consisted of finely crushed stone, mostly vanished under water. We had only arrived in mid-September, and here we were forced to stay inside, day after day, watching the relentless rain and fixing not a few leaks in our house. Early on, the rain was especially relentless, and we began to wonder where it all came from. The day following one particularly ferocious downpour, we got a copy of the local paper, the *Midi-Libre*, and saw pictures of devastation in nearby Nîmes. There had been a flash flood the day before. A villager who had come to help repair the leaks had spoken of *l'inondation*, but my French was nonexistent at that point, and my girlfriend's, though better, was still not attuned to the bouncy, thick accent of the South of France. So she missed it, and we did what we usually did in the circumstances when we couldn't understand what the villagers were saying: we smiled and nodded.

We didn't need to know French to understand the photographs. It looked like the world had been turned upside down in Nîmes. The streets were under water, cars had been tossed about, and you couldn't even see some of the doors to apartment buildings the water level was so high. It was when we read the word *Inondation!* in the paper that our minds went back to the word we hadn't understood. Then we realized what the villager had meant.

Nîmes was about twenty minutes from our little village. It was the nearest decent-sized, interesting city; we had already driven there a few times just to see what it was like. Nîmes, in fact, would be our salvation in many ways. Eventually we would discover a squash club there, not far from the arena, run by an Englishman, and that convivial place would be the source of many friendships and good times. Nîmes is an old Roman city, and it has a spectacularly well-preserved arena. It always sent chills down my back to drive or walk down the main street, rue de la République, make a turn, and suddenly see this perfectly-formed two-thousand-year-old Roman edifice, massive and indomitable. I was impressed by it, awed by it, but I found it impossible to love. It represented for me all the relentless force and resolute authority of the Roman Empire. I could see why Simone Weil hated the Roman Empire and wrote about it as if the Romans had just left.

Nîmes is also home to the Maison Carrée, a Roman temple built about eighty years before the Arena. This temple was an inspiration to Thomas Jefferson who saw it on his journey to the South of France in 1787. On March 20 of that year, he wrote to his friend, Madame de Tessé, "Here I am, Madam, gazing whole hours at the Maison quarrée, [sic] like a lover at his mistress." He took the Maison Carrée as his model for the design of the Capitol of Virginia, in Richmond. I was not as inspired by the temple—but never mind. Jefferson was, and look what he did with that inspiration. The Capitol is a pretty building indeed.

It was far too early in our stay to have these opinions. We barely knew Nîmes at this point. We looked at the photographs in the paper of houses destroyed, cars overturned and stuck in mud, trees awash, all due to a flash flood. The extent of it had had overwhelmed the city's inadequate drainage system. Nine people died. We looked at the photos of a city that we didn't really know, but which nevertheless we knew would be part of our lives in France, with a sense of dread. Then I turned to my girlfriend and, without thinking, said, "Let's go help."

She nodded. We changed into old clothes, put on our working shoes, got some gloves, and ten minutes later, we were on our way.

Out little Peugeot 104, which we had recently bought used, intrepidly made its way through the brooks the weather had created and that populated the roads. We got onto National Route 106 and made the twenty-minute trip to Nîmes. We had no idea what we were going to do once we got there, or what condition the city was in. We didn't know anyone. No one had asked us to come. When we drove into the city we saw that, for the most part, the water had dissipated. We found parts of Nîmes absolutely untouched and parts of it devastated. Such is the indifference of nature. It wasn't so much that buildings had been destroyed but that the water had entered houses and stores up to the second or even third floors and brought hundreds of gallons of mud and detritus and God knows what else and left it there.

We parked the car, got out, and simply began walking. The city was certainly not normal, but it wasn't without life, either. We walked down streets, and as we saw people in their houses trying to sort out things, we simply called out to them, in French—I had asked my girlfriend how to say this: *"Est-ce que nous pouvons vous aider?"* Can we help you? Most people said no. They said it politely, but it seemed to me that for them this was a private devastation. The inundation had entered their domicile or their store, and they wanted to be the only ones to attend to the mess. At first, especially when we saw them trying to make their way through the tremendous muck inside their homes, stumbling over furniture they couldn't see, we were surprised. But after a while, it made sense. Would we want some strangers coming into our home and poking about in *our* bedroom, in *our* children's room?

But not everyone refused our help. We came to a house that had a sizeable front yard where a man was hauling an almost unrecognizable record player to the side of the road. He was streaked with mud, and sweating. We uttered our line in French, and, without hesitation, he said, *"Oui."* This is where we spent our first day in Nîmes after the flood. He led us into the house. Though there was no electricity, there was enough light coming through the windows to see. The mud on the floor was thick and resistant, and the place smelled of fetid dampness. The man's wife joined us from the kitchen, a mud-streaked plate in her hands. The man said something to her in French, and she smiled. Then she outstretched her arm and must have said something like, "You see what has happened to our home."

What I did that entire day was to haul mud out in buckets. They had a basement, and that was particularly done in. I spent most of my time going down there with a bucket, filling it with sluggish, heavy mud and hauling it up the stairs and outdoors and emptying it into the street. It was not only hard work to haul a full bucket of mud, but it was slightly treacherous as well. The stairs were slippery, and I lost my footing more than a few times. My girlfriend stayed upstairs and helped the man's wife sort out things in the kitchen. And indeed there *was* something intimate about this experience of working and cleaning in someone's home all day, of having unrestricted freedom to poke and pull and move whatever we wanted to in a place where two people had built their lives in all the private and particular ways people build lives. The man and his wife were so vulnerable—nothing had been left of their home to shield them from the daily assaults of the world. Now there were no touchstones of familiarity that tables and photographs and rugs and even wood floors provide. It made me realize anew how much a home provides beyond mere shelter. Here it was all gone.

We took breaks from time to time, and cobbled together some facts about the couple's history. We asked them to please speak slowly in deference to our French. They had lived in that house for thirty years. They had two sons who were grown who had moved away. The man was retired—he had been a policeman—and he had a bad back. Hence, the hauling of mud he asked me to do. They had some food that neighbors had brought them, and they gave us a lunch of cheese and bread and fruit and bottled water. Nothing I have ever eaten has tasted better. We—or rather my girlfriend— told them we had come from New York and were living in a small village not far away. "Why?" they asked. Living in a village in the South of France? How is there a "why" needed for that? But to them, village life was uninteresting. Only farmers lived there. And obviously we weren't farmers. We left it at that.

After lunch, we went back to work. When we finally told them we had to leave, around five o'clock, we were spent. I felt about ninety-five years old. Both of us were filthy, and stunk. I could see my girlfriend's eyelashes had been painted brown, and her cheeks were rouged with mud. And our hands? I could feel the welts from the bucket's pulling metal handle. I walked with a stoop. We shook hands with the man and his wife, and we said goodbye. I'm not even sure we had exchanged last names. They thanked us, but it wasn't

effusive or melodramatic. It was simple. They still had much
to do—weeks of work at least. That's what they were thinking about. I'm sure they were still stunned. We walked back
to our car, looking and feeling like miners. Although we were
exhausted, the two of us agreed to come back to Nîmes. We
did, twice more, each time helping someone different all day
long. We never told anyone in our village what we had done.
And we never saw those people we helped again. We did not
seek them out in any kind of macabre reunion months later.

Provence is a land of matchless gifts. That year we spent
living there, it gave them to us bountifully. It gave us sun, pel-
lucid air, perfumed mornings, land to grow things, simplicity,
tradition, and the privilege of work. I am still grateful. Our
gift in return was meager. But it was the best of us. It was
heartfelt, unrestricted, and, until today, twenty years later,
anonymous.

❧ ❧ ❧

Richard Goodman is the author of French Dirt: The Story
of a Garden in the South of France *as well as a contributor
to* Travelers' Tales France; Food: A Taste of the Road; *and*
The Road Within. *He wrote the Introduction to* Travelers'
Tales Provence. *He has written on a variety of subjects for
many national publications, including* The New York Times,
Creative Nonfiction, Commonweal, Vanity Fair, The Writer's
Chronicle, *and* The Michigan Quarterly Review. *His new
book,* A New York Memoir, *will be available soon.*

❧ ❧ ❧

Living Among Incompatibles

The mind of Japan is the best the author
has encountered in a lifetime of travel.

I WALKED INTO THE CENTER OF OLD KYOTO NOT LONG
ago and found myself in a scene from a Hiroshige painting. Huge floats containing ancestral treasures stood on the
narrow lanes at the heart of the ancient capital, while rows of
lanterns bobbed above the wooden houses. Old men played
piercing melodies on bamboo flutes, and little boys, wearing
blue headbands to match their *yukata*, or cotton kimono,
thumped away on drums. Along the Kamo River, which
runs through the "Moon Capital" like a lifeline, couples were
seated on wooden platforms under the stars, red lanterns
(with white plovers on them) lighting up their faces as in
a novel by Yasunari Kawabata. Even at the busiest inter-
sections, women in indigo kimono were standing, picture
perfect, under parasols.

Yet when the floats began to move through the busy streets, in the great summer festival of Gion Matsuri, I started to notice other things below the classic surfaces. Many of the men in white-and-blue *yukata*, chanting a traditional song in unison, had the dragon tattoos of gangsters across their bare chests. Many of the young women running after them were teetering on eight-inch platform heels, their hair bright yellow and their skins artificially tanned in the fashion of the moment. Even some of the tiniest little boys were calling their mothers on tiny cell phones. The ancient rites were observed solemnly, with dignity and elegance; but they were woven into and around and through the most garish of modern Western artifacts. As if (as often happens) a geisha were carrying a boom box into a traditional inn.

When first I came to Japan, more than twenty years ago, these contradictions—and the serenity with which the culture lived among them—startled me every day. If the test of a first-rate mind, as Scott Fitzgerald once wrote, is the ability to hold two opposed ideas at the same time, and still keep going, then Japan, I thought, had the best mind I'd encountered in a lifetime of traveling. And in the years that have followed, the extremes have in some ways intensified, as much of Japan streaks into a mongrel, high-tech, science fictive future, while the rest remains more firmly rooted in the old than any culture that I know, including China's. There are TVs on the dashboards of taxis in Kyoto, but most Japanese people were slower to get onto the Internet than the people of Cambodia were.

As I've stayed longer in Japan, though, living here on and off for almost a decade, I've come to think that contradiction is in many ways in the eye of the beholder, and that part of the magic of this place is that it invites, and sometimes forces the foreigner to leave his assumptions at home. We tend to think that cultures, and people, must be one thing or the other (modern or traditional, themselves or imitations, elegant or crude); the Japanese are happy to see them as both things simultaneously. They adhere, that is, to a belief in both/and more than in either/or. And this allows them to collect an almost indefinite number of selves and surfaces without remaining any less themselves within: at a typical wedding over here, the bride still changes costume three or four times in a day, shifting from classic Shinto maiden to white-dress Eastern Cinderella to typical Japanese young woman (with many traditions alive in her).

This is, of course, a skill prized in all ritualized old societies—it's little different from the England where I was born—but nowhere is it managed so efficiently as in Japan. In countries like America, for example, the emphasis is on "being yourself"; in Japan, it's often on the opposite. Being "not yourself," but just a kind of impersonal actor playing the part the moment requires (to this day my Japanese wife doesn't know the name of her immediate boss at work, because the boss is always and only known as "Tencho," or "Department Head"). And this is all made easier, perhaps, by the fact that the Japanese tend, I believe, to think in images rather than in ideas, and where ideas need to be consistent, images can sit side by side, belonging to different worlds, like parallel lines in a haiku. It's not uncommon, near where I live, to see a Zen abbot stepping out of a late-model Mercedes on his way to his favorite bar in the red-light district. In Europe, such behavior might be seen as hypocritical; in pragmatic Japan, a Buddhist priest will perform every last rite demanded of him at funerals and ceremonies immaculately—like the Platonic image of a Buddhist priest; but when he is finished, he will go home to his wife and children, and pop open a beer in front of the baseball game on TV. He's played his role, he's allowed to slough off his robes.

The first thing to remember when coming to Japan, I therefore tell my friends who visit, is that everything is reversed here. The Japanese read their books from right to left and from back to front (as it seems to us), and they take their baths at night, before they go to sleep; even their baggage carousels move in the opposite direction. And so, naturally enough, what is exotic for them, and what is normal, is the opposite of the way it might be for us. Sometimes, here in Nara where I live, I go out at dusk and walk along the great park that surrounds Todaiji Temple, home to the largest bronze Buddha in the world. As night falls, the only beings visible are deer, grazing under trees or pricking their ears at me, like ghosts come down from the hills. The place is largely deserted because most of the local Japanese are heading in the opposite direction, to the "Dreamland" amusement park ten minutes away.

The other thing to recall is that the Japanese keep their different selves perfectly organized (as everything else is here) by drawing strict lines between different worlds. There is one set of rules and expectations for men, another for women (and, indeed, one set for "normal" women, and a very different set for those who belong to the "*mizu-shobai*," or water-world of the night district); in the same way, there are firm divisions between the office world and the play world. That is why the same Japanese businessman who is so flawlessly polite to you in a meeting will vomit in the street; and the one who fashions a delicate *ikebana* flower arrangement will be incomparably ruthless when it comes to war.

Yet within these strict rules, too, things are very different from in the West. The Japanese woman, for example, still enjoys almost no power in the workplace; yet at home she controls all the household finances and makes most of the big decisions (even the highest-ranking "salaryman" often hands over his entire paycheck to his wife). There are cartoon figures on screens in many public telephones, yet the figures bow when you put down the receiver. Japanese men are encouraged to be as macho and even gruff as possible; yet 40 percent of them, I recently read, pluck their eyebrows.

The thrust of all this, then, is that appearances, of every kind, are even more deceiving in Japan than elsewhere, and the biggest "contradiction" of all is the one that separates surface from depth. If you go into a McDonald's in Kyoto, and see the kids dressed all in surfer shorts and Chicago Bulls t-shirts, watching a baseball game on TV, you may begin to tell yourself that Japan is "Americanized." But the baseball players smile when they strike out (as seldom happens in America). The McDonald's salesgirls offer you Moon-Viewing Burgers and "Corn Potage Soup," and pear sorbets (and cup your hand when they return your change). And the girls in the Chicago Bulls t-shirts still eat with a delicacy and demureness you'd never find in Chicago.

This is how Japan can take in scores of Mexican restaurants, Iranian immigrants, Indonesian fashions, and African rhythms and still remain as Japanese as it's always been (and farther from the world at large than any culture that I know). It is why many Japanese you meet in the street will be too shy even to answer a question, though nearly all of them have learned English for six years in school (while the villagers of Bali, Nepal, and Thailand chatter away in French, Italian, German, and English). And it's why the Japanese in some ways seem to have the best taste in the world (when they're working in their own distinctive and elegant tradition) and the very worst taste (when they adopt the trappings of the outside world). Japan is the fastest culture in the world to gobble up the latest fashions, and the slowest when it comes to change deep down.

The newcomer arriving in Japan will probably find more that she didn't expect than in any other country in the world (even as much of the country looks exactly the way it's supposed to in every photograph). He will find, for example, a quiet people who (maybe for that reason) love nothing more than noise. Not far from one of the two thousand temples in Kyoto, where you find a stillness and calm unparalleled in the world, are the brightly-lit, clanging arcades of pachinko parlors—the local equivalent of pinball—which could put Las Vegas to shame. The more low-key the ancient spaces are, the more revved-up are such places as Shinjuku in central Tokyo, or Shinsaibashi in Osaka. And though it is rare to see young couples kissing—or even holding hands—here, Japan famously has unabashed swingers' clubs that would make a Parisian blush.

So, too, the visitor will find people more uniform in their public behavior than anywhere around, and yet more eccentric underneath, and unexpected behind closed doors (a female neighbor of mine here flew all the way across the world to see Jon Bon Jovi's house, before turning around and flying back, and one Zen priest I know is famous for his collection of videos of every episode of the American cop show CHiPs ever filmed). She will see exquisitely dressed young women in the latest from Dior, with Snoopy key-chains around their Gucci bags.

I no longer think of any of this as contradiction so much as a special gift for knowing how to honor each self in its own place. In some ways, in fact, this practical gift is what has allowed the Japanese to stay true to their traditions while devouring the new, to remain lovers of beauty while surrounded by some of the ugliest things on Earth, and to remain inalienably themselves while importing everything from everywhere. When you walk amidst the festival flutes and lanterns on a Kyoto summer day—even when I walk among them, after all these years—they have the capacity to move and transport you as if nothing had changed since the ninth century (when the Gion Matsuri began). The men around me are using at least three different words for "I," and the women at their side are using different words—or, as often as not, none at all. It's all a way of telling us that the self, whether it belongs to Mrs. Suzuku or Japan, is a pliable, fluid, mutable thing in Japan, less like a monument than a river. Try to put a Western frame on it, and everything slips through your hands.

≈ ≈ ≈

Pico Iyer is the author of several books about his travels, including Video Night in Kathmandu, The Lady and the Monk, The Global Soul, *and* Sun After Dark. *His most recent book,* The Open Road, *describes thirty-three years of talks and adventures with the 14th Dalai Lama.*

JEFF GREENWALD

❧ ❧ ❧

The Facts of Kathmandu

A symbolic search lights the way back
to an adopted home.

"THE WILDEST DREAMS OF KEW," WROTE KIPLING,
"are the facts of Kathmandu." I've never been to Kew
Gardens (except the one in Queens), but Kathmandu is woven
inextricably into my dreams.

I first visited Nepal in July 1979. My journal entry that first
day, written in the garden of the Kathmandu Guest House,
was just two words long: "Welcome home." I stayed for five
months before tearing myself away and returned in 1983 on a
year-long journalism fellowship. Ever since, I've divided my
time between Oakland, California, and Nepal.

Twenty years ago, I combed the shops of Kathmandu and
nearby Patan looking for a specific sculpture, a meditating
Buddha in the "touching the earth" pose. The image would
serve as a point of concentration, and a hedge against the

demons of distraction. My search evolved into a book called *Shopping for Buddhas*, written in 1988 and published in 1990. The slim volume describes my quest for a "perfect" Buddha statue—an ironic theme that serves as foil for exploring Nepal's art, culture, and halting steps toward democracy.

In the twenty years since the book's publication, the Himalayan nation has changed dramatically, from the royal massacre of 2001 to a civil war that claimed about twelve thousand lives; from enormous growth of urban Kathmandu to the emergence of China as an eager and bossy ally. The Kathmandu Valley is no longer the place of innocence it seemed to be in the 1980s, when visitors explored hidden lanes as sacred cows eyed them warily from carved wooden doorways. When the monarchy was abolished in 2008, and a true republic created, even the country's exotic tag line—the World's Only Hindu Kingdom—became obsolete.

But despite its trials, Kathmandu can be as beguiling as ever. During my latest visit, paper kites filled the air, fragile squares bouncing in the breeze. In the labyrinthine alleys near the Indrachowk market, necklace weavers await customers amid shimmering curtains of glass beads. And along the funky streets of Thamel, or near Patan's beautifully restored Durbar Square, rustic shops still display a pantheon of fabulous deities: masterworks in copper, brass, wood, and silver.

This visit, I'm not sure what I'm shopping for. It will have to be an object symbolic of my relationship with Nepal itself: something to help me endure the changes, and focus on the magic that remains.

As much as I love Kathmandu, the city today is the product of fifty years of bad choices, one after another. Concrete box architecture, gridlocked traffic and acres of billboards all attest to a lamentable lack of urban planning or regulation.

Much open space has been lost. Even the field of flowers beneath my once-peaceful flat has been leveled, and leased to a scrap metal salvage crew.

I pack up my laptop and escape to Kathmandu's newest oasis: the Garden of Dreams. Once the private estate of Field Marshal Kaiser Shumsher Rana, the garden fell into neglect during the 1920s. After years of restoration by expert landscapers and architects, the walled compound opened to the public in 2006. With its fountains, grass terraces, and shade trees, the garden is now a refuge for creatures of every stripe—from songbirds and squirrels to love-struck couples and agitated journalists.

Here, I'm able to indulge my favorite Kathmandu pastime: listening. The spectrum of sounds is amazing: a toy whistle, barking dogs, an occasional firecracker, a taxi horn, shouting voices, crows, bicycle bells, singing children.

That aural tapestry is one of the things I love most about Nepal. Perhaps, then, I ought to buy myself a statue of Milarepa: the twelfth-century Tibetan poet/saint who is portrayed with his right palm cupped to his ear, listening to the music of the spheres.

A few blocks from the Garden of Dreams, the curio shops along Durbar Marg are filled with enticing statuary. I stroll down the boulevard, ducking into showrooms.

In the always reliable Curio Corner I find a meditating Buddha with an expression so uplifting that the shopkeeper has to peel me off the ceiling. I'm also taken by a small figure of Guru Rinpoche, the great Indian sage who brought Buddhism to Tibet in the eighth century. Snow lions and clouds swirl on the sorcerer's robes. His face conveys a view of pure transcendence, clearly immune to the vagaries of change. I'm tempted, but the price (about $2,000) is prohibitive.

Later that afternoon, I ride my rented motorcycle across the Bagmati River and up the long hill to Kathmandu's sister city, Patan. Until recently, Patan was the home of Sidhi Raj, one of the most venerated sculptors in Nepal's long tradition of masters. Though Raj died in 2008, his students are still producing work of head-turning beauty.

Scores of shops line the cobbled streets near Patan's magnificent *durbar* (palace) square, selling exquisite statuary. As enticing as the figures are, none seems to embody my affection for this fragile, beleaguered valley.

Giving up the search, I duck through a low passage and into the compound of Mahabauddha: The Temple of a Thousand Buddhas. The architecture is unusual: an ornate South Indian *gopala*, rather than the traditional Nepalese pagoda. But what intrigues me most is a hand-lettered sign, nailed on a wall across the courtyard:

YOU MAY TAKE PHOTOGRAPHS FROM

THIS BUILDING GET THE BEST VIEW OF

HIMALAYAS THERE IS NO CHARGE

Climbing a flight of pitch-dark steps, I emerge onto a small crow's nest overlooking the Patan rooftops. Many are planted with thriving flower gardens, islands of color in a brick and cement city.

On an adjoining rooftop, a father and son are preparing a kite. The father holds the square of paper in one hand, and a spool of string in the other. With a gleeful expression, he tosses the kite up into the breeze. The little boy watches, agog, as it dances into an updraft. When the kite is stable, the boy is handed the spool. Imitating his father's gestures, he soon assumes control of this emissary to the clouds.

Watching the interaction, I'm struck by a realization: That little kite's string is the backbone of the Himalayan spirit. The Nepalese (and neighboring Tibetans) have a miraculous ability to create links, visible and invisible, between heaven and earth. With their incense and prayer flags, their

sacred architecture and tantric rituals, the residents of the
Kathmandu Valley have spent centuries forging bonds between the worldly and ethereal realms.

Driving in Kathmandu is a surgical skill, accomplished
along narrow roads shared with vagrant dogs, taxis, badmin-
ton players, housewives in saris, rolling fruit, rickshaws, ice
cream carts, balloon sellers, and hundreds of other motorcy-
clists. There's no room for error—which is why one friend
refers to the exercise as "meditation at gunpoint."

Riding home from Patan at sunset, I glance at the northern horizon—and nearly run into a florist's cart. The entire
Himalayan range, from Ganesh to Gauri Shankar, towers
above the foothills. I pull over. It is impossible to concentrate
on anything but the staggering beauty of those sun-washed
peaks, the smallest of which dwarfs the highest mountain in
North America.

This, I realize, is why I keep coming back. I forget the bad
bits, the stuff that's subject to change. Yes, there's a salvage
yard under my living room window. True, it now takes an
hour instead of ten minutes to ride home from the Monkey
Temple. O.K., I have dysentery. These things shall pass. But
the frosty peak of Langtang, looming over the valley like a
white tent—that's always going to be here. What seems eternal is Nepal's ability to thrill me, offering moments of sheer
bliss between one trial and the next.

How hard can it be to find one perfect statue—an image
of a god or goddess, saint or sage—that will bring back these
memories?

The five-day celebration of Tihar, the Festival of Lights,
honors Laxmi, the goddess of wealth, who bestows her blessing on freshly cleaned homes and shops where a flame burns
in her honor.

A few decades ago, the only lights seen on Tihar were but-ter lamps: small ceramic bowls arrayed near windows and on rooftop ledges, each with a woven cotton wick. This year, as I wander with the crowds filling Asan and Indrachowk, most of the lights are electrical. Garish Christmas-style decorations blink and flash, creating ostentatious displays. They're eye-catching, but soulless.

Suddenly, there's a deafening explosion. An overloaded transformer shorts out, showering the street with sparks. The square is plunged into darkness. Or near darkness; hundreds of traditional clay lamps, previously obscured by their electric cousins, flicker into view. They glow from windowsills, roof-top planters, and the wooden workbenches in cobblers' and electricians' shops. A reverent hush descends on the crowd. Children reach for their parents' hands. Everyone seems transfixed—transported back to an almost mythical time, not so long ago, when Kathmandu Valley was still a place of enchantment and mystery.

Without warning, power is restored. The electric lights blink back on. But at that moment, I hear something extraor-dinary. A collective groan rises from the streets—as if a magic carpet has been snatched away from beneath us.

At that instant I know what I must bring back from Nepal. It will not be another Buddha, Ganesh, or Tara; it won't be Milarepa, or Manjushri, or even a paper kite. Only one object—tiny and fragile, but timeless—can symbolize my at-tachment to Nepal and affirm the eternal spirit for which I always return.

Near the packed intersection of Indrachowk and Asan I find a small ceramics shop. I step inside and purchase a dozen little clay lamps—and a package of woven wicks.

❧ ❧ ❧

Jeff Greenwald is the author of five books, including Shopping for Buddhas *and* The Size of the World. *He also serves as executive director of Ethical Traveler, a global alliance of travelers dedicated to protecting human rights and the environment (www.ethicaltraveler.org). Jeff's newest book is* Snake Lake, *set in Kathmandu during Nepal's 1990 democracy uprising. Please visit www.jeffgreenwald.com for details.*

GARY BUSLIK

☙ ☙ ☙

In or Out

All politics are local, but especially on an island.

I WAS IN BARBADOS WRITING AN ARTICLE ABOUT horseracing for a British travel magazine, when its editor offered me a job writing an article about Caribbean cockfighting. It would pay pretty well, but since the magazine had no intention of reimbursing me to traipse back and forth from Chicago, I'd have to research the cockfight piece while I was already in the islands. Since Barbados, the most British and, therefore, the most civilized of the former colonies, didn't participate in such barbarity as chicken fighting, could I, you know, just pop over to Grenada for a look-see? Lots of barbarity there.

This might have seemed like a great gig, except that it was in September 1983, when Grenada was in the midst of a vicious political power struggle that had all the earmarks of impending bloodshed. The deputy prime minister, a Marxist revolutionary and best friends with Fidel Castro, was threatening to publicly eviscerate the real prime minister, a reformed socialist who was tired of their Cuban advisers fornicating with local livestock. Literal and figurative red flags were all over the place, which is why I wasn't totally excited about the assignment. On the other hand, my cunningly parsimonious editor suggested that if I didn't write the bird article, my horse article would wind up in a glue factory in Liverpool, along with my check. "Are you in or out?" he wanted to know.

Which is how I soon found myself checking into the Sunrise Guest House overlooking the bay on the outskirts of St. George's, Grenada's picturesque capital. Unfortunately, the seaside city did not lately feel so picturesque. Since the Cubans had come—to train Grenada's military and build a new airport, which, to American eyes at least, seemed more of a size to accommodate long-range bombers and troop transport planes than tourist puddle-jumpers—the town was deathly quiet. Cruise ships, normally two and three a day docking at St. George's lively and colorful quay, had, for the past six months, given the island wide berth. Spider webs laced sagging spice stands. Fruits and vegetables rotted in stalls. Souvenir shops were locked and abandoned, their owners hunkering down at home or in church, girding for the worst.

Near the bottom of the geographical question mark formed by the Antilles archipelago, the 133-square-mile island of Grenada rises from the Caribbean Sea like the back of a dragon, its vertiginous cliffs, emerald rain forests, and ancient volcanic folds fiery in the tropical sun. Between 1967 and 1979, under the aegis of his Grenada United Labour Party (GULP), a tyrannical prime minister named Eric Gairy lorded over the island, mauling anyone who challenged his authority. His security force, the "Mongoose Gang," terrorized his opponents, especially those who dared speak up in newsprint or at the ballot box. While ordinary Grenadians languished, Gairy siphoned off the public treasury, holding lavish parties, draping sinuous women on his elbows and, when he wasn't strutting around in garish ceremonial garb, donning white suits made of the finest English fabrics. The mercurial leader, acting more like an escaped mental patient than a head of state, insisted on being called "Honorable Doctor Sir Eric Gairy"—although what kind of doctor or from whom he had acquired the title was never clear. He openly practiced voodoo, sacrificing chickens to stay in power. He harangued the United Nations to do something about extra-terrestrials. One local psychiatrist who fearlessly testified that Sir Eric had completely lost his marbles had to flee the country in fear of his life.

The United States ignored Gairy's antics because, for one thing, he was a fervent anticommunist. But in Gairy's own country, a revolutionary spring was beginning to swell. Not even the honorable doctor himself could kill the hopes and dreams of long-suffering Grenadians. Not that he didn't try. In 1974 an outspoken Gairy critic named Rupert Bishop, while leading a peaceful antigovernment demonstration, was butchered by the prime minister's thugs. Rupert's son Maurice, a London-trained lawyer, silently vowed revenge.

He would get it.

Sunrise's owner, Mrs. Wilsmith, an elderly, genteel black woman as fragile as a banaquit, insisted on carrying my bag to my room. Her skin was the color of wet hemp, and the dying sunlight tinged her gray hair red. I followed her over a narrow path of coral stones, overgrown with tropical bramble. When I tripped over a half-empty jug of Weed B Gone, her smile tightened to a wire. "We had to let Alford go," she apologized. "Couldn't pay him anymore. Things have been difficult, you see."

"Alford?"

"Our gardener. Crazy Bones. But I've known him since he was a boy, before they called him that dreadful name."

"He's the guy my editor wants me to see about cock-fighting."

She hefted my bag onto the bed. I offered her a dollar, but she coughed with gentle indignity. "I'll ring him up for you." She stopped at the door and turned. "You might want to offer *him* a little something, if you find him particularly helpful. Are you a communist?"

I made a face.

"Things haven't been well lately, I'm afraid. I'll call Alford. He isn't really crazy."

Handsome, unassuming, sincere, Maurice Bishop became a spokesman for the poor and oppressed. Perhaps because of his comfortable upbringing, unlike Gairy, young Bishop had nothing to prove. Soft-spoken, intelligent, and charming in a way that the stentorian Sir Eric could only envy, "Brother Bish" drew working Grenadians to his side like pilot fish.

After his father's murder, Maurice's left-wing party, the New Jewel Movement (NJM), bedeviled Gairy like a fighting cock—circling, pecking, jabbing, and retreating. Despite police brutality, imprisonment, death threats, and the usual electoral irregularities, in 1976 Maurice managed to win his St. George's parliamentary seat. It was probably because of Brother Bish's enormous popularity, and the backlash it would have surely caused, that the honorable doctor didn't kill him outright.

But when, in the spring of 1979, rumors crackled that a fed-up Gairy had put the word out to his heavies to get rid of the commie Bishop once and for all, the NJM made its move. During the early hours of March 13, while Sir Eric was in New York talking little green men, Bishop and his armed NJM cohorts, calling themselves the People's Revolutionary Army, overpowered what remained of the few policemen and soldiers still loyal to the flaky dictator—resulting, with breathtaking speed, in the first elected Caribbean government to be deposed militarily. As Bishop, having secured the army barracks and the radio station, redubbing it "Radio Free Grenada," announced that the army had eagerly surrendered to the new "People's Revolutionary Government," Grenadians took to the streets to celebrate Gairy's overthrow—dancing, figuratively, on the madman's grave.

Later that day, in his first formal address, the new prime minister promised his countrymen:

> "People of Grenada, this revolution is for work, for food, for decent housing and health services, and for a bright future for our children and great-grandchildren. The benefits of the revolution will be given to everyone regardless of political opinion or which political party they support."

After years of suffering under Gairy's buffoonery, thuggishness, and sluicing off the national trough, Grenadians had reason to celebrate. Socialism did not sound bad at all.

But Bishop's promises soured quickly. No sooner had he guaranteed free and fair voting, than he suspended elections altogether—"until the principles of the revolution are firmly in place." No sooner had the NJM pledged the blossoming of a new society in which the democratic rights of the people would be fully restored, than it began rounding up and imprisoning its enemies, real and perceived. "In any situation of a revolution," the new prime minister explained over Radio Free Grenada, "there must be a necessary period of dislocation. The choice is between a firing squad, pretended 'accidents,' or detention."

The trustworthy and charismatic Brother Bish was beginning to sound suspiciously like Brother Fidel.

Many leaders around the Caribbean found Bishop's refusal to seek an electoral mandate and his immediate restricting of civil liberties contemptible. Still, after the NJM had rid them of the Gairy kleptocracy, working-class Grenadians were willing to give their new prime minister plenty of leeway. Bishop was so mild-mannered and earnest and likable that the islanders cheered him when he soon demanded an end to the Monroe Doctrine. They cheered him when, establishing relations with Cuba, he proclaimed, "No one, no matter how mighty and powerful they are, will be permitted to dictate to Grenada who we can have friendly relations with. We are not in anybody's backyard." They cheered him when he ringingly declared that Grenadians no longer needed to kiss America's backside.

This was, after all, the last flush of Soviet geopolitical ascendancy: the crushing U.S. defeat in Southeast Asia and the glory of a unified Vietnam; revolutionary fervor in Angola; Sandinista victories in Nicaragua; East German and Cuban Olympic teams that could not be beaten. Gold medals and more gold medals. The Soviet hockey team. Teófilo Stevenson's murderous left hook.

As the newest coin in the Soviet pocket, Grenada did for a few years shine. Not only rubles but pesos came pouring in. As he had in Angola, Castro sent over a long line of "advisers": doctors and nurses and platoons of red ants to arm and train the Grenadian military, to build roads, hospitals, and schools—and, oh, yes, an airport.

Until the Cubans came, Grenada's only airfield had been a cinder-block shack at the edge of a stubby, unlighted runway, on the opposite end of the island from the capital, St. George's—an arduous trip over the country's mountainous spine. In 1979 Castro's construction crews began laying a long, thick strip of macadam and erecting an enormous steel terminal at Point Salines, on Grenada's southwest coast, twenty minutes from St. George's over breezy flatlands. This project, more than any other—more than Grenada's new arsenal of AK-47s and antiaircraft guns, spiffy new army uniforms, revamped radio station, more even than their new roads and clinics—best symbolized Grenada's transformation from a backwater, shuffling, former colony to a modern, muscular island-nation. Where previously only puddle-jumpers could find refuge, soon thunderous jumbo jets would be bringing bushelsful of dongs and rubles and zlotys. Bringing *respect*.

National pride was running high. The future was as cheery as rum punch. Soon boys would no longer have to dive for nickels in St. George's Harbor or beg for candy on the quay. Thanks to Brother Bish, soon the whole world would know that the name of this minuscule country was pronounced with a long *A*.

Instead of attending voodoo ceremonies or lavish cocktail parties, Bishop attended cricket and soccer matches, always sitting with average Grenadians, eating hubcap chicken and drinking local beer. Unlike Gairy, he never showed the slightest inclination to monogram the national treasury with his initials. His house at Mt. Wheldale, modest by usual head-of-state standards and smaller than many other homes in the area, sat cozily next to its neighbor, the home of Maurice's best friend and deputy prime minister, Bernard Coard.

Maurice and Bernard had grown up together; their families had been neighbors, too. Now that the lads ran the country, it was perfectly right that they should carry on the tradition. Toward the back of their lots, a utility gate allowed them easy and private access to each other, whether for official business or just friendly visits.

Like Brother Bish, Coard dreamed of a homeland that would blossom through socialism. Stout, thick-spectacled, and not very handsome, Coard idolized his lifelong friend. The two leaders were seen everywhere together, smiling, laughing, enjoying each other's company and high spirits. They donned identical white guayabera shirts, made similar gestures, sported the same close whiskers, wore the same style wristwatches and hairdos. They worked in sync, wooing and welcoming the Cubans, promising their fellow Grenadians abundance from the socialist fertilizer, and, like their amigo Fidel, haranguing against the United States.

Coard's wife, Phyllis, and Bishop's girlfriend, education minister Jacqueline Creft, didn't like each other much but managed to keep their peace. For the nearly four years the families lived next to each other, their backyard gate got a good, neighborly workout.

Then something strange happened. Something very strange.

Carlysle's backyard was noisy and animated, filled with tobacco smoke, the sound of clinking bottles, and people shouting over a tape player. Carlysle's wife, Eulalie, her head wrapped Martiniquan style, stood next to a wobbly Formica table, overseeing a Maxwell House can overflowing with U.S. and E.C. dollar bills, two half-gallon bottles of Mount Gay and Pusser's rum, three listing stacks of plastic cups, a liter bottle of Canfield's seltzer, a dusty box of M&Ms, and a box of White Owl cigars. On the ground behind the table hunkered a case of Carib beer, a case of Coke, and a galvanized tub of mostly melted ice.

Crazy Bones recognized a couple of girls from St. George's. Holding a cigarette and plastic cup in one hand and nothing in the other, Tulia, a prostitute from Grand Anse, cha-cha-ed over and, smoke burling out of her nostrils, kissed our cheeks. Cutter Laidlow, a taxi driver whose wife ran a spice shop on the quay, and Bullfoot, a stevedore with a nutmeg-size forehead tumor, came over to pat Bones's back and issue encouragement. They checked me out glancingly—more with curiosity than suspicion. As Bones's friend, I was all right. But Père Marcel, a priest from Concord, eyed me like an iguana.

Carlysle came out to greet Bones. "You the first fight. Get going." Carlysle's eyes darted around the yard. Something was going on. Marcel said he didn't know what.

The airport construction foreman, Hernandez, straddled a folding chair on the other side of the pit, pretending not to notice us. Bones went to the Cuban and offered him a look at Ivan, his fighting bird.

Hernandez blew smoke at Ivan's cage. "I'm surprised you showed up with that goose," he chuffed, flicking ashes at Ivan and spitting on the ground. The foreman wore new jeans tucked into ostrich cowboy boots, a green-and-yellow floral shirt with papers sticking out of his pocket, and a straw hat with a sprig of cock feathers. He had a ferret face, and although he was skinny on top, his belly stuck out, the rhinestones on his belt buckle catching the light. He offered us Cohibas, but we declined. He unwrapped one for himself, lit a U.S. twenty-dollar bill, and, with exaggerated suckings, lit the cigar.

Father Marcel didn't like Hernandez. It wasn't bad enough that his Cuban cocks had beaten all the other local birds; the foreman was arrogant and insulting. When there were no worthy contenders left, he insisted on fighting the biggest rooster in Grenada—Ivan the Terrible—boasting that even a six-and-a-half-pound Grenadian cock was not worthy of being considered a main event against his three-pound, one-eyed Spanish bankiva, El Diablo. Hernandez knew that although Ivan was the underdog, the locals were stupidly going to bet on him.

Next to the Cuban, at the cock display area, twenty cages were stacked into a pyramid. Half-cut plastic milk-jug water bowls, resembling human skulls, poked through the cages. Spectators, filliping the wire mesh, goaded the combatants. Furiously the roosters scratched the floors of their cages, thrust out their chests, flung their heads back, flapped their wings, and bellowed. If, on prodding, a rooster lunged at a finger or threw himself against the mesh to get at a neighboring bird, it roused a hefty bet.

It was almost nine. Bets and counter-bets flew across the

yard. Father Marcel offered thirty dollars on Ivan. A Cuban answered with a wad of American bills on El Diablo. The cocks pecked hard at their cages.

On one fitting table, Diablo's handler, a runt named Pescador, finished attaching the bankiva's spurs and headed to the pit—a more-or-less round ring Carlysle had constructed out of stakes and chicken wire. The floor was honey-colored sand from Petit Caillou Cove, which, Marcel claimed, absorbed blood better than sand from other beaches. A string of light bulbs drooping between palm trees cast hangman shadows over the pit.

When Pescador stepped over the chicken wire, the spectators became subdued. El Diablo panned the crowd with his one dark, glinting eye. He had a small head, sinewy white legs, a rust-red torso that looked like a mortar shell, and a brilliant yellow ruff. His tail had been trimmed, making him look even smaller. Pescador set him down to get him warmed up and impress the Grenadians. Diablo swaggered around the perimeter, his steel spurs trailing like comets, his ruff distending lionlike. There was something mystical about him, something foreboding. He was a bankiva cock—pure Spanish—and, said Marcel, cruelty was in his blood.

As Bones brought Ivan to his fitting table, the priest, standing close to me and reeking of garlic, provided a running explanation. Bones wrapped two cotton balls and slipped alloy shoes over the sawed stumps of Ivan's natural spurs. Next he fitted two-and-a-half-inch curved sabers into the shoe slots. Over these he fixed squares of chamois and leather gaiters. With eighteen-inch lengths of gaff string, he bound Ivan's armory to his feet, checking and rechecking the angles of the gaffs with every loop. Bones, the priest explained, had thinned out Ivan's back and vent feathers so he wouldn't overheat. His long yellow legs shone from Bones's warm rum-and-herbal massages. His comb was short and erect. Ivan was an older bird, and he had not fought in over a year. "But he stands tall and dignified, *n'est-ce pas?*"

When Bones carried Ivan to the pit, the crowd momentarily hushed, then broke out into wild cheering and a frenzy of bets.

Pescador scooped up El Diablo and left the ring while Bones exercised Ivan.

Poised, neck extended, back taut, the local rooster strode back and forth in the ring, his magnificent tail resembling a Mayan headdress. But he was a huge, ambling bird, and there was something slightly comical about his gait. Some of the Grenadians winced. Ivan the Terrible, though, obviously remembered what it was to be a fighting cock. His eyes shone, taking in all around him, searching for an antagonist. He spotted El Diablo in Pescador's arms, struggling to get at him. Ivan stood motionless—noble, thoughtful, sedate. The crowd did not like the fact that their bird did not act perturbed.

Carlysle stepped into the pit and made his announcement. He motioned for the handlers to approach. He stuck his nose into each bird's feathers, smelling for poison. Some were almost impossible to detect, but Carlysle, Marcel swore, had an unfailing nose. The host gestured for the men to bill their birds.

Holding their roosters like bowling balls, they approached the near score lines—poker chips nailed into the ground two feet apart. They rocked the cocks back and forth so the birds could get a good look at each other. El Diablo's neck stretched and writhed like a snake's. His eye flashed and his beak snapped malevolently. But Ivan the Terrible was unaroused. Bones jostled him to get him to show some fighting spirit, but the Grenadian bird remained placid. Perhaps something about Diablo's missing eye threw him off.

Suddenly El Diablo sprang out, grabbed Ivan's comb, and shook the bigger rooster's head like a scrap of garbage.

Ivan squawked in pain, but Diablo held on viciously until
Pescador jerked him away. Ivan was no longer apathetic. He
became frantic with rage, snapping futilely at Diablo, and
Bones had trouble holding him. The crowd went wild. The
odds narrowed.

"Pit your cocks," Carlysle instructed.

The men walked to the far score lines—eight feet apart—
put their roosters on the sand, and quickly stepped back.

Despite their murderous hatred for each other, the birds
did not attack at once. They spent the first few seconds looking over each other's style, searching for an opening, trying to
intimidate the opponent. These were not barnyard brutes but
highly skilled warriors. They circled the pit clockwise, their
neck feathers raised, closing toward the center of the pit like
a maelstrom. El Diablo threw out his chest and swaggered.
Ivan took advantage of this momentary narcissism and bolted
toward the smaller bird.

The crowd stretched to see the first blow.

In November 1982 President Reagan went on U.S. television to discuss communist penetration in the Caribbean,
singling out Grenada, showing maps of the new airport at
Port Salines, then more than half-finished. The president
claimed that the Cubans were building the airport to "export
revolution." Much bigger than needed for peaceful purposes
on such a small island, its oversize terminals could only be
intended to handle large numbers of foreign soldiers. A nine-
thousand-foot runway could only be meant to accommodate
military planes, intent on transporting Cuban and Russian
arms throughout the West Indies, South America, and even
Africa. Huge underground storage tanks would be capable
of refueling long-range bombers, surveillance planes, and
squadron after squadron of fighter jets. Every Cuban now in
Grenada, President Reagan claimed, whether he be a doctor,
artisan, dentist, construction worker, architect, or diplomat,

was, in fact, a highly trained soldier. Bishop and his cohorts were Soviet thugs.

Predictably, Deputy Prime Minister Coard put on a public display of outrage and defiance at this American provocation. Clearly, he ranted, the U.S. would never countenance the birth of another Cuba or Nicaragua in the Caribbean. Therefore Reagan's pronouncements could only be regarded as a prelude to invasion. But, Coard vowed, the cowboy president would learn that Grenada was one steer that would not be roped.

Mysteriously, though, Prime Minister Bishop did not get aroused at Reagan's charges. On the contrary, over the next few months his behavior toward the U.S. grew more and more conciliatory. He declared that free-market capitalism was not necessarily incompatible with socialism, that profits and prophets could coexist. Openly he began to wonder what it would take to lure foreign investment back to the island. As Deputy Prime Minister Coard looked on in horror, Bishop went so far as to formally request that the U.S. reconsider Grenada's exclusion from Reagan's regional economic-stimulus package, his Caribbean Basin Initiative. The prime minister even invited an American delegation down to discuss the situation and make recommendations.

Coard, growing ever more frustrated with his boss's overtures to Western democracies, retaliated by taking an even sharper turn left. His revolutionary rhetoric became more strident, and he began calling secret meetings with militant factions of the NJM, branding as traitors those who tried to establish friendly relations with the United States. He was not yet naming names.

He formed a blood alliance with "General" Hudson Austin, a former prison guard who, as leader of the covert military wing of the NJM, had helped overthrow Sir Eric Gairy. Now, as Commander of the People's Revolutionary Army, Hudson—a squat, square man whose uniform pants were too short and who saluted with stiff arm to chest, as if hacking himself with a machete—was only too glad to be Coard's muscle should things start getting ugly.

Which they were about to do.

With a contentiousness that quickly worsened through the first half of 1983, for every step that Bishop took to the right, his former friend Coard took a longer stride to the left. Each time Bishop trotted closer to Washington, his deputy cantered faster toward Moscow. Their chasm grew rapidly unbridgeable. To any casual observer, the former friends'—and still-current neighbors'—sudden rivalry seemed not just political but personal. They had stopped hanging out together. They began sniping at each other by name—first in private, then publicly. Phyllis Coard and Jacqueline Creft stopped talking to each other. Then so did their men.

In June 1983 Bishop suddenly announced the establishment of a commission to study the drafting of a new constitution that would lead to a return of parliamentary democracy.

With Hudson Austin in his pocket, Coard began openly to express his belief that he, not Bishop, was destined to rule Grenada. In August the NJM Central Committee blamed Bishop for the "collapse of national morale" and for the country's "development plans being off target." It named Coard as best able to direct ideological development of the nation. Not wanting to give Bishop time to see positive results from improved Grenada-U.S. relations, Coard demanded that the NJM leadership vote to force the prime minister into a power-sharing arrangement with the hardliners. On September 16 the Central Committee complied.

In retaliation, Bishop called for the immediate formation of a constitutional government and the holding of free elections.

Coard and his militant Marxists could never allow that to happen.

At the end of September, Bishop traveled to Hungary and Czechoslovakia, where he negotiated an aid package for Grenada. On his way home, he stopped in Cuba to meet with Castro. Some say this was at Fidel's request, to take his comrade to task for playing footsies with the United States. Others claim that Castro, as befuddled by the Bishop-Coard rift as everyone else, wanted to find out what the heck was going on. Still others swear that El Maximo was keeping Brother Bish distracted in order to give Coard and Austin time to set their trap.

Something foul was in the air. Ominous broadcasts were crackling out of Radio Free Grenada.

> "Brothers and Sisters of the Revolution: Our progress as it develops is becoming more complex. Recently, the NJM Central Committee leadership and the entire membership of the NJM took certain firm decisions on internal party changes which were aimed at strengthening the work of the party and revolution. Comrade Maurice Bishop refused to accept and implement these decisions.... As much as we of the People's Revolutionary Army love and respect Comrade Bishop, we will definitely not tolerate this development in our country. Principle is principle."

But despite the hardliners' howls, the American delegation Bishop had invited down, preparatory to readmitting the island into Reagan's Caribbean Basin Initiative, was scheduled to visit Grenada on October 13. What's more, Bishop was on the verge of declaring a date for holding elections.

Convinced that he had the army's support, Coard made his move.

On October 12 the NJM Central Committee declared that Bishop and girlfriend-cum-education minister Jacqueline Creft would be confined to their home and disconnected their phone to further isolate the prime minister from his supporters. In the meantime, Coard was making radio statements about "the need to maintain ideological purity."

By the next day, rumors were washing over the island. While Radio Free Grenada, now in the hands of Coard, was announcing a Bishop plot to murder the deputy and his wife, the people in the streets were murmuring instead about Coard and Phyllis's plan to kill Brother Bish. Austin's soldiers disarmed the police, who mostly supported Bishop.

The American delegation stayed home.

On October 14 the minister of national mobilization, a Coard crony, formally announced that a "People's Military Council" was now in power and Bernard Coard was Grenada's new prime minister.

But Grenadians didn't buy in. Unrest rumbled through St. George's. Hundreds of people refused to work, instead taking to the streets shouting, "We want Bishop!" Government ministers loyal to Bishop resigned in protest. "If Maurice is not freed by Monday," labor leader Kenrick Radix frothed, "there must be no work, no school, and no play in Grenada." He alluded to Coard's delusions of grandeur and personal disloyalty to his former friend. He was promptly arrested.

The next day, Coard fired back, commandeering the radio station microphone to make this statement:

> "Brothers and Sisters of Revolutionary Free Grenada: The Revolutionary Armed Forces have noted that some opportunists are seeking to fool the people by spreading lies that this is a personal struggle between two individuals. The armed forces are presently investigating the personal involvement of Comrade Bishop in the starting of these vicious rumors, which, were it not for the swift action of the armed forces, could have led to bloodshed on the streets of Grenada last Wednesday.
>
> "It must be clearly understood by all concerned that the People's Revolutionary Army and armed forces as a whole will tolerate absolutely no manifestations

whatsoever of counter-revolutions, no matter what
state or form it shows itself."

This did nothing to deter the masses. Worse for Coard,
demonstrations now attracted international attention. So
on October 16 the NJM kicked out of the country all journalists attempting to report on Grenada's power struggle.
Information about Grenada's chaos would now be difficult to
get to the outside world. But one thing was certain: more than
five hundred students, U.S. citizens, were attending classes at
the St. George's University Medical School, believing themselves to be safe but beginning to get nervous.

Three days later, all hell broke loose.

Diablo leapt four feet off the ground. But Ivan had gotten
just enough of a running start to meet him in midair before
the smaller bird could gain an edge. They slapped together
with the sound of a wet umbrella opening in the wind. They
locked in a wing-flailing, leg-kicking, beak-slashing convul-
sion of fury, blowing away the cigarette and cigar smoke that
had descended on the pit.

They landed together on the sand, rolled over and over
and on top of each other so that it was impossible to tell
where one left off and the other began. They bounced off
the chicken-wire wall and finally knocked themselves apart,
jumped to their feet and faced each other, pecking and stabbing and hacking, darting backward and forward trying to
find the flaws in each other's defense.

Without warning Diablo was off the ground and soaring. Ivan went up with him, vaulting with his back parallel
to the ground, his spurs positioned for a thrust at Diablo's
underside. But as he fell, the smaller cock's gaff caught Ivan
in the face. Ivan buckled, and a squawk of piercing pain tore
from his throat. Feathers burst over the pit, and both birds
dropped. Blood spurted from Ivan's forehead.

Three, four, five times they clashed in midair, their gaffs flashing, Diablo leaping high and Ivan following. As the birds put their spurs into full play, the crowd's excitement rose to a murderous, fist-flailing frenzy.

But Ivan was too big and clumsy to fight above the ground for long. Soon, when Diablo leapt, the bigger cock was a beat behind. Diablo was light and elastic, and when he got above Ivan, his legs were a blur.

Ivan adjusted. When Diablo vaulted, the local bird flipped back on his tail and hooked upward like a cat. In one exchange, his left gaff grazed Diablo, and his right pierced the bankiva's shoulder. But it was the smaller bird who scored the real damage, driving both spurs into Ivan's breast. Ivan twisted free, throwing Diablo. Before the bankiva could get into the air again, Ivan drove a hard blow with his beak to the smaller bird's face. This stunned Diablo, and they fought for a few seconds on the ground. When Ivan got up, the sand beneath him was shiny with blood.

Again, Diablo jumped high above his rival. Ivan saw the shafts of death heading toward him. He darted back and half-turned to meet them, but he was too slow, and Diablo drove both gaffs into his back. This time Ivan could not shake the smaller cock—the blades were stuck. Ivan rammed Diablo into the chicken wire to try to get him off, but it was useless. The bankiva kicked madly, working his spurs deep.

"Handle your birds!" Carlysle shouted, seeing that the combatants were hopelessly locked.

The handlers were not allowed to touch the opponent's bird. Ivan was on the bottom, so it was up to Pescador to lift Diablo and separate them. When he did, he twisted the spurs to tear a little more into Ivan's vitals. We all saw it, and Tulia, the Grand Anse prostitute, strode to the pit with raised fist.

"Cut it out!" Bones warned Pescador.

"Cut what out, *pendejo*?"

Bones looked at Carlysle to say something. But the damage was already done. Carlysle glanced at his watch. The rest period had begun.

Bones brought Ivan to his handling table, where Marcel and I stood. First he assessed the damage. Diablo had hit Ivan's face but had missed his eye. Blood was bubbling at the base of his bill, dripping down his beak and forming pendant globules. Diablo had ripped half the feathers from Ivan's ruff and had pierced his back. His soft gurgling meant his lungs had been hit. Blood was filling the air sacs and making each breath sound like percolating coffee. He was trembling with pain.

Bones washed the congealing blood from the rooster's face, dabbing the puncture and caressing the wound with a towel. Ivan perked up. He straightened his neck, and the gleam came back in his eyes. Bones stroked his neck, and the bird purred. He stopped quivering, and his breathing became regular. Bones dabbed Ivan's skin wounds with a chalk stick to help stop the bleeding. He took a mouthful of water from his Hinckley and Schmitt bottle and doused the rooster.

Across the pit, Pescador was blowing a bubblegum bubble. El Diablo looked unhurt and eager. They were both watching Ivan.

"Pit your birds!" Carlysle called.

This time the men did not have to bill the cocks. The birds' eyes locked in a killing gaze. The handlers put them down at the far score lines and stepped back.

On the overcast morning of October 19, 1983, a band of recently resigned government officials led a phalanx of Grenadians to Bishop's home, intent on liberating their true prime minister. In the face of this mob, the surprised guards put up little resistance. Hoisting Bishop onto their shoulders, and with the newly freed Jacqueline Creft at their side, the crowd marched their leader toward town, where they hoped he would address a waiting throng.

But instead of going to the marketplace to make a speech, Bishop and his loyal ministers whisked themselves to Fort Rupert, the old citadel overlooking the harbor, headquarters of the armed forces. Bishop knew that if his restoration were to succeed, he would first have to win over Austin's military. Besides, what more stunning symbol of victory, what more stinging slap to Coard's pudgy face, than for Bishop to re-take his command from the thick-walled ramparts named in honor of Maurice's murdered father?

Bishop's detour, though, gave Coard and his cohorts time to regroup. Inside the fort, Brother Bish could be accompa-nied by only a small group of supporters, instead of the masses in the marketplace. Worse still, in the central command room of the fort, he was cornered.

Exactly what happened inside that room will always remain a matter of speculation. Some swore that while his supporters waited outside, Bishop was on the verge of peace-ably convincing Austin's soldiers to hand over their weapons. Coard would later claim that Bishop's people took the guns by force. Whichever it was, it gave the general time to lead a platoon of heavily armed men to the fort, where they barged through the clot of Brother Bish's supporters to the com-mand room, rifles cocked, ordering Maurice and his follow-ers to come out with their hands up. When, unarmed, they did so, the soldiers brought Bishop and (some say pregnant) Jacqueline back into the room and beat them badly, cutting off the prime minister's ring finger. Then they dragged Maurice and Jacqueline back into the courtyard, lined them and six other leaders against a wall, and tore them apart with automatic rifle fire. At the fort's entrance, the soldiers opened fire on Bishop's supporters. To get away from the hail of machine-gun bullets, many jumped from the ramparts, only to dash their brains out on the rocks below.

In Market Square, meanwhile, Austin's armored personnel carriers and AK-47s were wildly firing into the pro-Bishop crowd, killing dozens—just to make sure everyone got the point.

If you weren't in, you were out.

Ivan took two quick steps forward, but this time it was Diablo who rushed first, flying across the ring as if shot from a cannon. There was no sparring. He leapt high, flapping his wings and slashing forward with his legs. Ivan tried to meet him but only got a few inches off the sand and landed badly.

The smaller bird uncorked a fusillade of lightning kicks at Ivan's underside. Ivan pinned Diablo and tried to hammer home his own. But something was wrong with his right leg. The gaff hung at an odd angle and bounced off harmlessly. Diablo counterpunched, and his gaff sunk deep into Ivan's chest. The blade came out red to its hilt.

The crowd hushed. We knew Ivan the Terrible was in trouble. His thigh was broken and flapping. His left eye was swollen shut, and his ruff was plucked bald. His lungs sounded like a balloon letting out air.

"Get the cooking oil ready!" Hernandez taunted.

Diablo's thrusts and parries were still crisp. Like the rest of us, he sensed that his opponent was mortally hurt. He sprang into the air, his eye gleaming, his gaffs shimmering as they extended for a fatal blow.

But Ivan stood his ground, watching the spurs come down at him. He reached up and slashed with his good leg and caught Diablo in the ribs just under the wing. When the crowd saw that Ivan still wanted to make a fight, their fists rose once more. I, though, wished Ivan would soon be out of his misery.

With Ivan's gaff hung up in Diablo's armpit and his right leg dangling uselessly, the bankiva slugged away with impunity, his spurs plunging time after time into the bigger bird's flesh.

Despite Ivan's great will and determination, he was doomed. He fought lying on his side, trying to beat Diablo with his wings, but only sapping what little strength he had left.

With one last tremendous effort, he broke free. Enraged, Diablo leapt up straightaway. Ivan staggered and strained to meet him, but his good leg buckled, and he keeled over in his own blood.

Diablo's spurs sank deep into his enemy's back and scissored through the meat. Ivan was too weak to do anything but squat down and take it. The eye that was not already swollen to a slit closed dreamily.

Again, Diablo's spurs were hung up in Ivan's flesh. Ivan rolled over like a sinking ship and inadvertently pinned the smaller cock to the ground. The lockup was ugly, and the crowd groaned. I looked away.

Carlysle gazed plaintively at Bones. Any other handler would have stopped the carnage. But Mrs. Wilsmith's former gardener refused to concede.

The Bishop murders and coup caused an outpouring of condemnation the likes of which had never been heard in a West Indian political context. Caribbean leaders expressed abhorrence at the barbarity of the acts and called for various degrees of isolation of the illegal Grenada regime: halting regional airline service to the island, blocking its access to money from the Eastern Caribbean Central Bank, even expelling Grenada from all Caribbean federations.

But in the face of these threats and continuing unrest on Grenada—dozens more demonstrators were killed; the general had Bishop's, Jacqueline's, and the other murdered ministers' bodies dumped into a mass grave and burned—the new leadership dug in its heels. On October 20 General Austin made a statement over Radio Free Grenada, accusing Bishop of having provoked the massacre, of firing on the soldiers first, and of "openly linking up with counter-revolutionaries." Stunningly, he went on to declare:

> "Let it be clearly understood that the Revolutionary Armed Forces will govern with absolute strictness. Anyone who seeks to demonstrate or to disturb the peace will be shot. An all-day and all-night curfew will be established for the next four days from now until next Monday at six o'clock. No one is to leave their house. Anyone violating this curfew will be shot on sight."

Grenada was now not only a prison island, but every Grenadian was a prisoner in his own home. Fear gripped the islanders. Many were stranded where they had been when the twenty-four-hour curfew began. Family members had no way of finding out who was alive or dead. Not only were Americans locked down with everyone else, they seemed to be attracting special attention. In St. George's, one terrified American woman had rifles pointed at her when she stuck her hand out to feed a dog. The medical students were now isolated, out of touch with home, and afraid: "They had us all under house arrest. There was no way people could wait to see how things worked out."

Least of all Ronald Reagan.

Carlysle shouted for the men to separate the birds. This time the parting was silent and deathlike.

Bones brought the once-proud Ivan back to the handling table. The bird was a mass of blood and matted feathers. There was no point assessing the damage. Ivan was cut to shreds. The gardener nuzzled his face into what remained of his rooster's back feathers to give him warmth and comfort.

He lifted him up, spread his tail feathers, and blew into Ivan's anus. Ivan raised his head and straightened his neck. His tongue began to palpitate.

"Get ready!" Carlysle shouted.

Bones cradled Ivan in his arms and rocked him like an infant. "You a brave bird," he whispered.

Father Marcel pointed across the pit. We saw something. Bones saw it too. Instead of holding Diablo at the edge of the pit as he had after the first handle, Pescador was at his table working feverishly on the bankiva. With one hand he was fanning the cock with a flattened six-pack container. With the other he had Diablo's wing stretched and was peering at the area where Ivan's heel had hung up. Something was wrong. Pescador spread Diablo's ruff feathers and scanned the bird's neck, looking for a puncture. He turned to Hernandez and shrugged.

"Get ready!" Carlysle shouted again to Pescador.

Pescador asked for another minute, but Carlysle waved him to the score line. "Either in or out! Pit!"

The handlers released their birds. Ivan took a single gallant step and collapsed on his chest. He would make a last stand from where he fell. Diablo ran toward him with a killing glint in his eye but, mid-ring, staggered and toppled like a drunk. No one was more startled than Diablo himself. He got up, flapped his wings to shake off the sand and restore his dignity, and charged Ivan again. But his gait was off; he got a little airborne and flew right past the larger cock. The crowd gasped. Ivan turned his head to see Diablo slide into the chicken wire. The local bird perked up. He turned and faced the bankiva.

Diablo leapt at Ivan. His spurs flashed and Ivan braced, but this time Diablo's gaffs only slid off Ivan's back. He landed awkwardly, beak first. Something was very wrong. His neck jerked, and his head turned. Excitedly, Father Marcel whispered that a nerve had been struck.

Ivan dragged himself on his belly across the score line, braced himself with a wing, and sideswiped at Diablo's head, sticking him near his eye. Diablo pecked twice and missed. He tried to get off the ground but fell over on his side. Ivan didn't even have to move; he reached over and grabbed Diablo's comb and held him while getting his good leg into play. Diablo pulled free and spun crazily into Ivan's gaff. Ivan drilled the rapier deep. Diablo jerked away and into the chicken wire. Ivan dogged him, hopping, and pinned the bankiva against the wall. He climbed atop the smaller bird, sunk his gaff into the bankiva's throat, and hacked away at his eye socket. Diablo cried piteously as his nostrils squirted blood. In a minute the Spanish bird stopped fighting and lay motionless.

Hernandez hurled his cigar butt at his rooster. "Get up, you fucking pigeon!"

But it was over. Still atop the mound of the bankiva's bloody flesh, Ivan held up his head and squealed victory. The spectators—most of them—crowed their approval. I kept quiet.

"Over!" Carlysle shouted, extending his arms.

Bones had to untangle Diablo's guts from Ivan's foot. He lifted the local rooster high in the air and pivoted so everyone could get a look. Again Ivan tried to crow, but more blood came out of his mouth than exaltation. By the time Bones got him to the handling table, Ivan too was dead.

A few days before the St. George's massacre, a terrorist bomb killed 241 Marines in Beirut, and President Reagan was itching for a fight. With the revolution in Grenada taking a hard left turn, and with concern for the safety of its citizens there, the U.S. administration quickly forged a coalition of Eastern Caribbean countries, at whose "invitation" the U.S. would invade Grenada, its stated purpose being the liberating of the American medical students. Using nearby Barbados as a staging point, the coalition launched a "freedom flotilla," code named Operation Urgent Fury, led by the massive aircraft carrier USS *Independence*—by itself carrying more firepower than most of the world's nations. On October 25 an invasion force of seven thousand, including the armies of the United States, Jamaica, and the tiny islands of Dominica, Antigua, St. Lucia, St. Vincent, Barbados, and St. Kitts-Nevis, hit Grenada's beaches.

The invasion—or, as Grenadians themselves apprecia-tively called it, "the rescue"—was a calculated risk. Would the Soviets send troops and even more sophisticated weap-onry to fight for their new puppet? Unlike during the 1961 Cuban Missile Crisis, would Russia, bolder now, make a stand on their dab of Caribbean soil?

This time, too, though, Moscow left its marionette flap-ping in the trade wind. Coard, Austin, and their Fidelistas were on their own. Still, coalition forces met stubborn re-sistance. Aided by stockpiles of arms and munitions Castro had been exporting to Grenada for the past four-and-a-half years—rifles and machine guns and grenade launchers and crates of armor-piercing bullets, which the locals derisively called "Cuban rice"—the People's Revolutionary Army, bul-warked by Castro's fierce and skilled fighters, under orders from El Comandante to fight to the death, dug in.

But the antiaircraft guns ultimately could not stop the waves of American jets surgically bombing any commie stronghold they could identify. While the American bombs left surrounding buildings unscathed, the radio station was reduced to a pile of rubble. Coard and Austin would be mak-ing proclamations there no more. The police station in down-town St. George's was strafed to a smoldering ruin. Russian artillery cannons and armored personnel carriers—the same ones that had fired on Grenadians in Market Square—lay burning and useless.

Ironically, the citizens the Revolutionary Military Council now called on to come to the defense of the motherland had been driven out of sight by the house arrest under which they had been placed. General Austin's militaristic madness had come back to bite his backside. Desperately and diabolically, he ordered his army to transplant the PRA flag from Fort Rupert to the St. George's Mental Hospital, arming its patients and instructing them to fire at American planes. The result—the one Austin had hoped for—was predictable: the Americans, believing the building to be a hostile military installation, obliterated it, along with eighteen patients.

Meanwhile, in an Entebbe-style raid, U.S. Marines were evacuating the students at the medical school.

When, three days later, on October 28, coalition troops occupied St. George's, leaving a trail of dead Cuban and Cuban-trained fighters, Grenadians led their liberators to where Coard, Austin, and other members of the RMC were hiding. The Americans handed the despots over to legitimate Grenadian authorities.

Overall, the coalition's attack was so swift, severe, and precise, that even amid the bullet-riddled roofs, bombed-out buildings, pock-marked walls, shattered windows, and smoldering debris, not a single American civilian, and, with the exception of the mental hospital patients, no Grenadian noncombatants were killed. Nineteen American and thirty-one Grenadian fighters lay dead, with several hundred wounded. Twenty-nine Cubans died, many more were wounded, and many more still were captured.

The first military planes to land on the Cuban-built Point Salines runway were American.

The following January, I returned to Grenada to research an article about the aftermath of Operation Urgent Fury. It was high season in the Caribbean, and Grenada was back in the game. In St. George's Harbor, boat taxis skittered like bugs. Cruise ships were in port, their mooring ropes taut and singing, gangplanks rolling rhythmically on the pier.

Creaky wooden skiffs, loaded with fresh fish and bananas, chugged toward the quay. Sleek yachts collected like sand-flies. Dinghies etched the bay. In town, stores were thriving, stalls were pyramided with fruit, burlap bags were plump with nutmegs, cloves, and sachets of coconut-oil soaps and incense. Grenadians welcomed American tourists with hand-fuls of spices, tureen smiles, and creole as sweet as papaya. They called President Reagan "our cowboy."

My taxi driver gave me a tour of the bombed-out govern-ment buildings. We stopped at St. George's Mental Hospital, and he told me about the tragic trick that had cost the inno-cent patients their lives.

"You knew Crazy Bones?" I asked.

He seemed surprised. "Alford?" He looked down and frowned. Then he perked up. "He have one hell of a bird."

"Ivan the Terrible."

He beamed. "How you know Ivan?"

I didn't answer.

He turned to the asylum. "Bones wasn't crazy."

"They put him in there anyway."

"Hernandez figure it out. He try to get his money back, but—"

"Poison," I said.

He looked at me as if for the first time.

"Weed B Gone."

"How you know?" he asked.

But I was already halfway out the door. I walked the rest of the way to Sunrise Guest House, where Mrs. Wilsmith greeted me with a planter's punch and a hibiscus blossom. "From our garden," she said. "No more bramble. Our flowers been liberated."

What really happened between longtime best friends Maurice Bishop and Bernard Coard to have led their cause and themselves to such rack and ruin? Historians have their theories. The one most often heard is that because at heart the two men leaned toward different ends of the socialist spectrum—Bishop a left-of-center pragmatist and Coard an ambitious doctrinaire—even in the glow of their lifetime friendship and political successes, they could repress their ideological differences only so long.

Some say Brother Bish finally faced the fact that with the loss of tourism and international trade—inevitable in the face of Grenada's new ties with Cuba and the Soviet Union—his country's economy was bound to shrivel and die. Loving his people above himself, he sought a middle ground between the ideals of communism and realities of capitalism—a compromise likened to immersing one foot in freezing water, the other in boiling water and expecting that, on average, he'd feel comfortable.

Many think that the rift began when Bishop got sick and tired of the Cubans defiling his island. Castro's advisers-on-loan had a persistent tendency to eat in St. George's restaurants and help themselves to items on store shelves without paying. Some were said to fornicate with local sheep and goats, shooting at any Grenadian catching them in the act. Bishop began pushing for the Cubans to go home. But Coard, seeing Grenada as the jewel in El Maximo's crown, balked.

Others speculate that their friendship was doomed because as boys Bernard and Maurice attended fiercely competing secondary schools, and deep-seated rivalry was bound to surface. What's more, Coard's father had once worked for Rupert Bishop. Did Bernard harbor unconscious resentment? Or had Coard, longing to play the dashing leading man instead of the sycophantic sidekick, simply grown weary of standing in Bishop's shadow while the beloved prime minister basked in political sunshine?

But "tabay" or "ole talk"—local scuttlebutt—has a different story to tell. In *The Grenada Massacre*, a regional magazine published just after the military intervention, there is a photograph of the backyard service gate between Bishop's and Coard's houses, with the caption:

THE GATE OF CONTENTION. BERNARD COARD HAD MOVED INTO A HOUSE RIGHT NEXT DOOR TO MAURICE BISHOP'S. GRENADIANS SAY A DISAGREEMENT FOLLOWED BETWEEN THE TWO AS TO WHICH WAY THE GATE SHOULD SWING — IN OR OUT.

❧ ❧ ❧

Gary Buslik writes essays, short stories, and novels. He teaches literature, creative writing, and travel writing at the University of Illinois at Chicago. You can visit his latest book, A Rotten Person Travels the Caribbean, *at www.arottenperson.com. You can write to him at arottenperson@earthlink.net.*

~&~ ~&~ ~&~

The Train at Night

An entire world is riding those rails.

ACCORDING TO HASIDIC TRADITION, THIRTY-SIX "saints" (*lamed vavnik*) are hidden in the world at all times, holding it together through their secret good deeds. Disguised as socially marginal figures—peasants, porters, and homeless, nameless wanderers—they appear among strangers and, through their seemingly trivial actions, or even through nuisance they cause, bring about shifts in people's perception that create community and lighten human sorrow.

I wish I could sleep every night on a train. Not alone in a berth, but in the coach with everyone else, our seats tilted back, the long car dim. I love listening to the sound of the rails at night, that *da doom, da doom, da da doom* and sometimes *chuh chuh CHUNG,* and the way you sometimes get that little shuffling, wheezing noise, or maybe a sharp little bark like a small dog. Or a little piping noise, like somebody hiding between the coaches with a flute. I enjoy most of the

227

sounds the passengers make, too, when it gets dark and they turn on the little rectangular white-and-cobalt night lights in the ceiling—the blue end pointing in the direction of the train so nobody gets lost coming upstairs from brushing their teeth. People rustling and whispering as they get ready to sleep, dropping their pillows in the aisle, lifting up their foot-rests, reclining the backs of their seats. "Put on your socks!" "Do you want some more?" People stealthily zipping and rezipping their fanny packs, someone eating something out of a box, trying to be quiet. It's cozy and it makes the world seem not so lonely. It would be good to sleep every night on a train.

Some nights aren't as quiet. The *Capitol Limited* had pulled out of D.C.'s Union Station in the early evening. At eleven we were just beyond Martinsburg, Pennsylvania, the lights dimmed, the coach snug. I was sleepless as usual, trying to look out the window but mostly seeing us passengers re-flected back, young sweethearts curled up tight under a thin pink blanket, friends stretched across a whole row with their feet in each other's faces, old couples asleep holding hands. And then me, alone, the only one awake, with my glass of merlot, looking out onto the dark river, maybe an occasional houseboat light or a lighted buoy bobbing alone on the dark water. The seat next to mine was empty: my son was sleep-ing in a vacant row he had found far down the aisle on the other side.

It was summer. My twelve-year-old son and I were riding the train home from Washington, D.C. via Chicago after set-tling my mother's estate. I was shaken by my mother's death, and on this trip, I'd hardly seen my son at all; from early morning to very late the kids joined up, all backgrounds, all ages, and roamed the train (under the kindly eyes of the coach attendants) teaching each other card games, sharing their Skittles, and laughing at Wile E. Coyote and Road Runner cartoons.

You'd think I was the only mother whose boy ever grew up. Because that evening I kept remembering this same trip with him when he was six, how we'd leaned together against the window and pointed out the scrap metal barges, the horses galloping away from the train, the colorful tags spray-painted on warehouses. How we'd shared little pepperoni pizzas from the café. And when it got dark, after we'd brushed our teeth and put on our sweatshirts, how he'd put his head against my shoulder and needed a story. You'd think I was the only woman whose marriage ever faltered.... I was feeling lonely, the kind of existential loneliness where you feel the wind blowing through your insides, and you're so desolate you've got to hug yourself and double over.

Suddenly I heard a loud snore two seats up. Then a gurgling sigh like a bad drain. Silence for a moment. Then a passionate bellow-snore, wet, vibratory, with a choking gasp of panic at the end. Now everyone was awake. Rasping, chain sawing, "I'm-going-to-die-now" snores. The train was slowing and I read "Three Rivers" on the station wall. The snores abruptly stopped.

A lanky man in a flannel shirt helped himself to water in a tiny paper cup at the stair-head water fountain. While he sipped it, he turned with friendly eyes to inspect the snorer. "I thought I saw a sign that said Three Rivers, but I'm not sure. You going to Chicago?"

"No," responded the snorer, now awake, and he and the man exchanged a few more words. The train pulled on. I put away my wine glass, tucked my pillow into the corner between the seat and the window, and tried to sleep.

Suddenly I—we—were wrenched wide awake by an alarmed snortle from two seats up. Then another volley of raucous, wet snores. I looked at my watch—1 A.M. We were passing the West View Authority Water Treatment Plant; a chimney pumped out orange flames.

"Give his seatback a good shove!" I whispered to the

woman in front of me. Several seats around us suddenly emptied as people rethought their seating arrangements. I wandered, sleepless and dizzy, downstairs to the bathroom. There I amused my haggard self by practicing mobster faces in the mirror. Should we loom over him and hiss, "Stop snoring, or we'll have to kill you"?

I came back up the stairs, paused near his seat to glare at him. Fast asleep, his mouth open, he looked pasty and unshaven, like somebody homeless or just out of jail. Vulnerable. His right arm was lying flat and white down his big belly. And now I noticed that it wasn't an arm at all, just a white fin that tapered at the end.

I stopped at my son's seat. "That man is making me crazy," I whispered.

"It's really kind of sad," he whispered back. "His arm is *mutated*." Then he rewrapped his head with his ingenious noise-abatement device—two little train pillows tied together with a length of string—and shut his eyes.

I continued up the dim aisle to my own seat. The woman ahead of me had moved her son to a quieter row, but she stayed behind the snorer. "Me he don't bother at all. My husband snored for twenty years," she announced cheerfully to the coach. Again I felt the pang of deep loneliness.

Now the snoring had stopped. Up and down the aisle, seats were tilting back again. Meanwhile, the Monongahela River gleamed by. A gibbous moon rose on a long, silver, rippling stilt, and three lights on the flank of a dark houseboat threw on the water three rippling shafts of illuminated gold. I began to drift off....

A raucous snort broke the silence. Then a tense quiet in which one passenger said, under his breath but distinctly, "Dickhead." Then abruptly the snorer was at it again with renewed vigor. The ones who hadn't noticed his hand were no doubt wishing him dead, and we, the elect who had, were exchanging gently pitying smiles with strangers. Elect or not, none of us slept.

Early the next morning, passengers from our coach began to wander into the lounge to get coffee and exchange amused or exasperated notes about the night's ordeal. We smiled and nodded or shook our heads at the wonder of having made it through the night at all, and then struck up conversations. We had been kept awake half of the night, and yet everybody seemed cheerful and refreshed. At an unusually early hour, the lounge car was alive with conversation.

When the snorer himself walked into the lounge with his white flipper hand tucked against his belt, everybody was really nice to him. We were nice because of his hand and because all of us shared a secret to keep from him: that at 2 A.M. he innocently had every one of us wide awake, cussing in our seats. And we were grateful to him because his snores had brought us together. His snoring had transformed a coachful of strangers into a community—and had made me forget my lonesome sorrow.

Everybody was nice to his buddy, too—a jowly, seedy, middle-aged, outgoing man who looked like he'd done time—because he *was* his buddy, bringing him a soda from the downstairs café, striking up friendly conversations with other passengers and then drawing his disabled friend skillfully in. So with corn fields and crossroads passing outside the big windows, and the golden morning light streaming into the lounge, and Porky Pig cartoons playing cheerily on the tube, with cups of sweet hot coffee, we all felt tender toward the man with the flipper hand. There he was, salt-and-pepper stubble on his round blanched face and a stale white undershirt, like a vagabond, really, an ex-con, most likely—and all sorts of people from our car, simple or sophisticated, were chatting warmly with him and his buddy. Diffident at first, he gradually expanded in the warmth, smiling and nodding, and soon he was circulating shyly in the lounge as a sort of guest of honor.

His buddy turned to him affectionately. "You were sawing logs pretty good there last night, pal. So loud I got up and went down to the café car." I held my breath; I felt all our coach holding our breaths. Our secret was out: his phenomenal snoring was exposed. Would he and his buddy suddenly shrivel up—poof!—and disappear, leaving us all strangers again? But their magic was good; if anything, the camaraderie in the lounge car increased—soon people were sharing their life stories and ham-and-cheese sandwiches.

"Ah, got a book, eh?" the buddy said when I walked past them. They were both drinking beer now and chuckling at the cartoons. I suddenly felt that they had no destination; they were just riding the rails.

"Yes," I said, showing them the cover. "*Nonfiction Prose*. It's a collection of essays."

"Oh, yeah, I read this book once—I recognize it," said the buddy, taking it gently in his hands and turning it over. "It was white, like this. Yeah, I'm pretty sure it was the same book. Had a white cover." From then on, whenever they'd pass my seat, they'd stop. The snorer would smile and the buddy would ask me kindly, "Still reading that book, eh?" They asked me so many times, I began to dread their passing. I put my book away. Then I felt bad because they were so friendly and trying to be kind, so I got it out again. Perhaps they thought I was lonely since I was reading a book. Well, Chicago in a few hours was the end of the line. My son and I would board the *Southwest Chief*, and they'd be getting on another train or a Greyhound bus. And I *was* lonely: now that the day was wearing on, my loneliness was creeping back, so much that I was already dreading the night, wondering whether I'd be able to sleep at all.

At Chicago, as the crowd gathered at the gate for the *Southwest Chief*, I was a little disconcerted to suddenly find them just a few yards away. But it was a long train, dozens of cars, and no doubt they would be assigned seats in a faraway coach. They both looked pale under the fluorescent lights, different from the other travelers, as if gravity were somehow heavier for them. The snorer reminded me suddenly of a merman lost on human shores with liquid warm brown eyes and a desolate white flipper. Now I felt certain they had done time. When they saw me, they both nodded, smiling approvingly at my book.

We left Chicago. In a few hours I was sitting in the lounge car, looking out the picture windows. To our right, the sun was setting scarlet. Our train ran along the Mississippi River, flushed rose and silver from the almost full moon on our left. The river was a mile wide with low forested banks on the opposite shore. Huge black tree trunks floated on the silvery water; rusty, flat barges slid slowly and imperceptibly down the middle of the river, pushed by a white boat. Big lotus swaths lay wherever the shore curved in, their pale blossoms shut up for the night. Little black islands. White herons. One or two lights blinked on the distant wooded shore. Shreds of mist lifted off narrow inlets. The sky dimmer, the moon now radiant yellow. Slow, the quiet wide dusk river. So lonesome, wandering without a home. So peacefully flowing, so softly by.

"Five minutes to Fort Madison," the attendant announced. There was a stir in the car. According to the route guide, we were about to cross the Mississippi on the world's largest double-track, double-decker swing span bridge. I loved the phrase; I wrote it down—a talisman against grief. We crossed, and darkness fell.

The coach was dim and half empty when I went back to my seat. Everybody was asleep, my son down the aisle in an empty row he'd found for himself. For a long time I sat with my glass of merlot and my white book, watching for the dark river outside the window. Finally I closed my eyes, but as I had expected, sleep refused to come. I turned the little reading light back on and, hoping to catch glimpses of houseboats with their golden lights, pressed my face against the window. But of course the river was far away now. Loneliness swept over me again, seized me, and I hunched down in my seat, wide awake and desolate.

Suddenly our coach door slid open and two men came bumping down the aisle toward me. The buddy and the snorer. Dear God. I closed my eyes and pretended to be asleep, afraid they would stop at my side. "Still reading that book, eh?"

"Here's our stuff," said the snorer in a thick voice. "And our seat." They must have been drinking all evening in the café car. They stumbled into the row directly behind me, next to the stairwell.

The buddy said, "Hell, we're not going to sleep at all with that fucking stairwell light." They may have thought that they were whispering, but they weren't.

The snorer laughed and asked whether the bathroom was still locked downstairs. When the buddy said yes, the snorer yelped. "You mean I have to go all the way to the next car every time I wazoo? I'm not going to make it. I might just have to wazoo right here." Oh, God, I thought.

"Man," the buddy laughed, "I feel sick. I just might puke."

The snorer was struggling with his footrest. "I can't get it to stay up!" he laughed.

And the buddy said, "You can't keep it up? What do you want me to do? *Hold* it for you?" He giggled. "Can't keep it up, huh? Maybe *she*"—and I knew they meant me because I was pretending to be sound asleep—"maybe *she* can get it up for you." Alarming giggles from both of them.

And then the buddy belched and said, joking but not laughing now, "I hope some gang-bangers don't come up those stairs and sit on my lap." As they settled bumpily into their seats, it suddenly seemed to me that they were like men secretly carrying a terrible cargo, one they could discuss only between themselves, late at night, when everybody else was asleep and only, perhaps, when they were drunk.

Then I realized I was the only one in the whole car awake, and these men, so gentle and kindly during the day, were now staggering drunk and making lewd remarks. Men who'd probably done time. What if they made a pass at me? What if the buddy threw up on me (I pulled my sheet right up under my chin) or if the snorer snored all night, right behind my head? At the same time, I felt oddly braced and cheered by my position, like the heroine in a fairy tale facing the Three Dangers. What should I do, then, with ex-convicts at the back of my neck? Get out my Mace?

But I felt too cozy to move, and besides, if I moved, they'd ask me about my book.

Then I thought, what dangers? Why, these men are like the wandering Mississippi. For us secretly-awake or peacefully-sleeping passengers they are carrying the weight of innumerable dark and broken things, things we cannot guess: black uprooted trees, the world's debris, barge-loads of loss and loneliness and grief. Homeless, nameless, they carry our burden, keeping the darkness at bay, so that for us the darkness scarcely presses outside or inside the windows of our quiet coach.

And then I knew, both that this was unfair beyond all human understanding—and that we—all of us in the coach—were blessed by these two drunk and seedy men. Blessed that of all the coaches in a long train, it was our coach they'd found. And my heart was suddenly comforted, light and free and protected. I let the sheet slip down, carelessly from my chin. "*Da da doom, da da doom, da da da doom*," went the train in the beautiful night.

Then the buddy whispered to the one with the white flipper, bitterly and passionately, like someone in a Shakespeare play: "Those fucking gang-bangers. They'll tear the heart right out of your chest."

And we all fell asleep.

❧ ❧ ❧

Gina Briefs-Elgin is a professor of English, teaching composition and creative nonfiction at New Mexico Highlands University in Las Vegas, New Mexico. Her delights are her artist husband, her artist/DJ son, her women friends, teaching, traveling, riding Amtrak, exploring the mystics, cooking, fishing, and reading Dickens. Her dream is to spend a month each year in India. Gina thanks her friend Sukey Hughes, writer and editor extraordinaire, for her compassionate and insightful suggestions for revision. This story won the Grand Prize Bronze Award in the Fourth Annual Solas Awards (www.BestTravelWriting.com).

MICHAEL McGEE

~ ~ ~

The Two~Dollar Difference

Frugality on the road is its own reward.

I'VE FOUND CERTAIN THINGS TO BE TRUE IN LIFE.
For instance, when traveling, coincidences tend to pile
up—making life far more magical and unpredictable than it
ever is back home. So often, one curious happenstance leads to
another and another until, before you realize it, you've reached
a spot that in hindsight seems like a minor miracle.

Long before I planned my trip to Jordan, I'd relished a visit
to Wadi Rum, which one fellow traveler had called the most
beautiful place on the planet. It's a vast expanse of desert and
dunes, alternating in sands of orange and red where enormous ridges of rock burst from the desert in every direction.
"Wadi" means "valley" in Arabic, and Rum was a favorite
haunt of Lawrence of Arabia, who occasionally waxed rhap-
sodic in his memoirs about its otherworldly beauty. During
World War I, the armies of the Desert Revolt were based
there as they campaigned to push the Turks back into Turkey.

The Bedouin nomads, who helped lead the charge, still live there in their desert tents today, and part of my reason for visiting Rum was to find out what desert life was like for the Bedouin, an existence fast disappearing.

After spending my first night in a pup tent on the dunes and watching an enormous spotlight-bright moon rise from the sands amidst a silence so perfect and awesome even the flies ceased their buzzing, I returned the next day to the village of Rum. Rum sits at the desert's rim, populated by some four hundred Bedouin and dozens of camels, the animals' ranks arranged like receptionists at its front entrance. I planned to return to Aqaba that afternoon, the nearest bona fide city, and had to choose between fighting my way onto the only available bus, or taking a private cab for a few dollars more. Logically speaking, I should've taken the cab—it was air-conditioned, plush compared to the bus, and the driver had so reduced his fare to win me over it would've scarcely paid for the gas used. Instead, I chose the bus. Don't ask me why. I'm cheap, I guess. Whenever I can cut costs, I do, because it all adds up in the end—in unexpected ways. Which turned out to be particularly true on this occasion.

When I boarded, three young Jordanian men made room for me, and on the way asked the usual quota of questions: where was I from, what was my job, how long was I staying. Turned out they were teachers, and they told me if I returned to Rum later that week I should visit them at their school. They even paid for my bus fare when we reached Aqaba.

The following Wednesday, I found their tiny school, and upon entering, immediately ran afoul of the school's superintendent, a fellow in full military dress named Abdullah. Tripping over my words, I told him about the teachers and how they'd invited me, but for the life of me I couldn't remember their names. Bad form. Abdullah and the other personnel, all in military uniforms, seemed a few sentences away from officially ushering me out when, by chance, one of the teachers from the bus appeared. A friendly handshake transpired, and with my story confirmed, Superintendent Abdullah warmed significantly, asking if I'd sit in on their classes. I'd barely agreed when they whisked me upstairs to marvel at the little Bedouin children, most around eight years old and many in army fatigues themselves, sitting for their English lesson.

When the class ended, I returned to Abdullah's office for tea. The officers and teachers, twelve in all, drew a circle of chairs around me and launched a barrage of questions about how I thought they could improve their classes. Talk about intimidating. I'd never taught a day in my life and here were a dozen men, dressed like army brass, hanging on my every word. Racking my brain, I recalled the successful marketing tactics of my own early teachers (with their reading contests and creative projects), but Abdullah and the others thought the ideas too frivolous, too much "fun" for the kids.

Our brainstorming ended, Superintendent Abdullah surprised me again by asking if I'd return the next day to teach classes to the children. I agreed, a bit shell-shocked. As I mentioned, I'd never taught before, and in a way it scared me. I'd been best man at two weddings and despite elaborate preparations, I froze during my toast to the groom on both occasions. Speaking in front of crowds, or antsy eight-year-olds dressed for combat, sounded akin to appearing before a firing squad. In the end though, as so often happens, it turned out to be one of the most rewarding things I've ever done.

From what I'd seen, the classes at the school were too formal. The teachers sometimes barked at the kids as they led them through their ABCs, so I loosened it up, got the kids involved, hoping to make the material more memorable. I brought in charts, posters, drafted children to the front of the class to illustrate body parts—arms, legs, hands. They had a blast.

When my first class finished, I noticed a shy second-grader

in fatigues standing beside me. He was a tiny fellow, his black hair cropped short, and when I left for the next class, he followed, toddling behind and coming to stand beside me at the blackboard. A teacher who was guiding me asked the boy something in Arabic, then chuckled and explained, "He just wants to be with you." I smiled at the little guy. He was there later, too, when I crossed the school grounds and the boys suddenly ceased their playing and lined up, wanting to shake my hand and say *"merhaba"* or "hello." Needless to say, to be employed regularly this way, and get paid for it, suddenly seemed the best job in the world.

Amidst all this, another boy named Salem (pronounced Sah-lehm), Abdullah's assistant, told me that if I was interested, I could come live at his father's tent in the desert for as long as I liked. This is typical desert hospitality, something which the Bedouin, besides being lauded as magnificent warriors of ages past, are renowned for. Still, such a thing is rare. Apparently I'd mentioned wanting to write about Bedouin life in the desert when I first explained myself to Abdullah, but I'd completely forgotten it. Nevertheless, I jumped at the invitation. And as the day closed, Superintendent Abdullah bid me a warm farewell, telling me I was welcome back whenever I liked and that henceforth I should consider myself one of the school's teaching staff.

The following afternoon I left by pickup for the tent of Salem's father: total bumpy commute time, forty minutes. The tent was shaped like a candy bar, made of black goat hair (woven by Salem's mother), and twenty meters long. It was an open-air tent, with no flaps over the entrances; its floor, the desert sand. There were no toilets, you simply picked a sand dune or rounded a convenient corner of rock. Between the tent and the mountain ridge it nestled were the livestock and belongings of Salem's father: a hundred sheep and goats, a dozen camels, two dogs, and an enormous water tank which was occasionally replenished by trips to Rum village.

Salem, who resembled every dime-store villain you've ever imagined, with pencil mustache, stick-thin frame, and overly white smile, took great pride in his Bedu upbringings. His was a big family: three brothers and eight sisters, many of whom studied at Rum's schools.

After showing me about, Salem departed with instructions to his youngest sister, Rbyah (rub-ya), a spunky, cocoa-haired nine-year-old, to take me into the desert near sunset to find her sister, Amira, and the lovely, funny Jefoolah (wife #2 to Salem). The two women were out tending the sheep.

For an hour we wandered the desert searching for them, Rbyah occasionally pointing out abandoned wells or empty shells of snake eggs. Occasionally, she'd scale a rock cliff, walking the skimpy ledges (in her sandals, no less), me close behind, as we sought a better view in hopes of spotting the herd. Still nothing.

Later, with Rbyah constantly joking and laughing as we climbed the dunes, we began a small song exchange. She'd belt out an upbeat Bedouin song and then I'd sing "Oh, Susannah." She'd produce a lilting Bedouin ballad, and I'd warble "Home on the Range." This continued until, as the sun neared the horizon turning the cliff rocks into candy apples, Rbyah made a bold prediction: we'd find the goats over the next dune. Now, I had every faith in Rbyah and her ridge-climbing sandals, but I had a hard time believing she'd pegged this one. Sure enough, though, as we reached the dune's crest, there, between a defile of rocks, were Jefoolah, Amira, and the family's herd. While the sheep and goats grazed, the women had settled down and built a fire, making tea as Amira sketched Jefoolah in her notepad.

Drawing is a favorite pastime of the girls. Since there's no TV or other electronic entertainment, the girls often spend their fireside hours sketching one another, drawing people from memory, or anything else that comes to mind—after all, things can get pretty monotonous once the sun calls it a day. They're actually pretty talented, considering they have no training and no models besides bored siblings and unco-operative sheep. They're quite proud of their work, too, and I returned with a bounty of drawings, the girls excited at being able to actually give them to someone. Their sketches were also incredibly romantic—like any teenage girl's in America—filled with fantasies of finding true love, which sometimes centered around the image of a young country-man in white, his face warm and loving. And even though the girls barely spoke any English, the words "I love you" often adorned the drawings, the phrase amply backed by bright pink hearts of various sizes.

Having found Jefoolah and Amira, all four of us, along with the dogs, sheep, and a couple of burros to carry supplies, departed for the tent as the sun sank into the sand. Rbyah kept trying to clamber onto the lead burro and eventually ended up backwards on the thing as it bolted off down the dune, the nine-year-old hollering as she tried to hold on and flip herself around. The sheep and goats meanwhile moved out like an advancing army, surrounding us in numbers that felt far larger than the hundred they were. Occasionally, some would leap and buck like colts, excited to finally head home for a full meal. It was a strange sight, and we laughed aloud every time another bounced into the air. Little to no herd-ing was required of us. Once the mob started to move, the rest—except for a few stragglers whom we'd chase down, chiding them with "Tet-tet!"—fell into line.

Rbyah had since righted herself on the burro, and as the sun's glowing rays turned the dunes and cliffs into reds and purples worthy of a Maxfield Parrish painting, and the sheep and goats kicked up their heels as they flowed past in fluffy rivers of cream and gray, Rbyah began singing another jubilant Bedouin song, clapping her hands and shouting above the flock's jangling bells. The rest of us looked on and laughed—the view glorious. Indeed, I had to blink a couple times to prove I was really there—awash in such beauty. It was one of those moments of bliss—times so rare in our lives, but times nonetheless that remind us of just why we climbed out of bed that morning—and which serve as a reminder of why we should do so in the future.

I stayed on with Salem's family another three days, occasionally helping where I could, visiting other nearby Bedouin families, and teaching the girls English in between their chores...and all of this arising from a tiny decision days earlier to save myself two dollars by taking the bus instead of a cab.

Never let anyone tell you it doesn't pay to save.

≈≈ ≈≈ ≈≈

Michael McGee is a writer and book editor who has swum with dolphins off the New Zealand coast, worked with elephants in the jungles of Thailand, lived through the SARS epidemic in Beijing, and danced with geishas in Kyoto. His work has appeared in the San Francisco Chronicle, San Jose Mercury News, *and other publications. He is also a winner of the* Amelia Magazine *award for best short fiction. His travel story podcasts appear on The Great Big Bungalow website (www. greatbigbungalow.com) and on iTunes, and full-cast radio play productions of his short stories and novellas, some of which have appeared on radio stations in the U.S. and Canada, can be found on iTunes and at his website, The Theater of the Midnight Sun (www.theaterofthemidnightsun.com).*

❧ ❧ ❧

Ashes of San Miguel

There's bones on the beach. There's ashes in the jar.
Ghosts in the air laughing at fools in the bar.
But somewhere inside, this river don't run
to the sea no more.
Give me a sign, amigo, can you tell me,
Did you go down laughing when you finally fell?
—"Ashes of San Miguel" by Roger Clyne

LET US BEGIN WITH DEATH. THAT IS THE PLACE THAT, for me, everything seems to begin in Mexico, or at least the place where everything eventually winds up. In San Miguel de Allende, behind every elaborately carved wooden door, the specter of death lurks in one of its guises, which are many. Sometimes death menaces. Sometimes it mourns. Mostly, in Mexico, it laughs.

To understand why this matters, it is necessary to rewind, let's say two years, to the onset of my midlife crisis, which is not, it turns out, the variety that induces one to acquire German sports cars and sculpted twenty-five-year-old Adonis husbands, but is instead, the true-blue, perhaps distinctly American, variety that induces a crippling fear of death. There I was, sequestered in my sanitized home, diligently fondling my breasts for ominous lumps, making friends with my freckles and moles, watching them for oozing or weeping or creeping, jolting awake in the middle of the night certain the pain in my right arm was a sign of a heart attack even though I could distinctly remember slamming it against a rock during a volleyball game, eating my veggies, riding my bike, slathering on sunscreen like a mad woman, when the universe, that mother with an elegant appreciation for beauty but a sense of humor that can only be described as sadistic, decided to plop me in the middle of Death-Ville for a month-long writer's workshop.

I first dubbed San Miguel Death-Ville when I dropped my suitcases in my hotel room, which was strangely elongated and sparsely decorated, but made up for these defects by boasting a gorgeously tiled bathtub. Also, it featured a heater that resembled an archaic toaster, with an article posted beside it titled, "Carbon Monoxide: Secret Killer That Takes Sleepers before They Awake."

In addition to this melodramatically-worded literature (though I'd be damned if I dared try to turn on the heater, even if arctic winter hit), I saw a painting. I say "saw a painting" as if I had the option of missing it. I didn't. It was an oil original the size of a sofa, hung over my narrow bed, painted by some authentic Mexican named Smith in 1994, according to the signature. It boasted five figures, four disturbingly happy clowns and a cackling skeleton (at least I think she cackled—she seemed to do so mostly at night) wearing a crown of flagrant orange flowers. If you want to get your blood going, try waking up in a bitterly cold room, shivering in a narrow bed, to the sound of church bells clanging and strange birds squawking and the sight of four clowns and a hippie grim reaper leering down at you in the moonlight. It's a page right out of Stephen King.

Death has a long and honored tradition in San Miguel. Well, death has a long and honored tradition in all places, whether we like it or not, but in San Miguel, they like it. They celebrate it. Little laughing skeletons are everywhere, dressed up like whores and window washers and Elvis, reading and dancing and laughing. Mostly laughing. Why are Mexico's dead so happy? It could be because they are never forgotten.

Over margaritas, a Mexican painter told me that death, for the Mexican, is not an ushering out of the land of the living. Rather, it is a change in form, the way a river, say, might turn into steam on a hot summer day. The Mexican dead are still citizens of their communities. On Dia de los Muertos, the living wander up into the hills where the dead are buried. There, they offer them gifts, sing with them, laugh with them, dance with them.

In the next town over, Guanajuato, they celebrate Dia de Los Muertos as well. But there, every day is death day, for every day, their museums display gape-mouthed mummies and their churches flaunt the yellowed bones of saints. In Diego Rivera's house, the guides will tell you that Diego ate human flesh for inspiration, that he went to cemeteries at night and filched meat from corpses. He did this because he wanted to get in touch with his Aztec history, which is featured a few hours away in Teotihuacán, in the form of crumbling pyramids.

There, you can climb the narrow stairs to sit in the place where priests cut out the hearts of human sacrifices, offering the still-beating organs to the gods in hopes of warding off apocalypse. Macabre, yes, undeniably so, but history tells us that many of these sacrifices were volunteers. According to Aztec religion, the honored dead—warriors who died in battle, women who died in childbirth, and those who died as sacrifices—became gods and goddesses. These honored dead visited the living again and again, in the forms of butterflies, hummingbirds, bright things with wings. The dead still visit the living in Mexico. In fact, it seems they never left. Mexicans maintain an intimate relationship with death.

Since I am old enough to have acquired a midlife crisis, I am also old enough to have made a certain personal acquaintance with death. I wouldn't say that I know it exactly. It mystifies me, haunts me, the way that men did when my skin was smoother, my limbs leaner, my body making an ascent into full bloom instead of gradual descent to dust. I saw death first when I was twelve. I think, perhaps that acquaintance with death was the most positive I have had, for I was not afraid, only fascinated, as I stood over my grandmother's embalmed body, poking her skin, entranced by the waxiness of her skin, the way her face had morphed in death into that of a stranger.

Later, at the age of twenty-one, I stood over another body, my beloved father's this time, minutes after his heart attack, horrified at the bolts of purple that had crept along his skin, at the stillness of his cold chest pressed against my cheek, at the cuts on his fingers that would never heal. We had planned a trip to the zoo that day.

Five years later, I encountered death again as I stood beside the tiny grave of my favorite kindergarten student, two days after a horse's wayward hoof stopped his heart. I was enraged as I watched his mother scream, "My baby, my baby," while they lowered his pint-sized casket into the ground. I wanted to kill death.

I have met death, and though our first acquaintance was cordial, I have come to view him as a thief, a plunderer of lives. Never have I stood at the bedside of an ailing loved one, watching him suffer, begging for the mercy of death. For me, death has shown no mercy. He has always crept in on jaguar's feet and stolen suddenly what, in my mind, was not his to take. And I have hated him for his work.

If I could, I would pull that leering skeleton from the painting over my bed and slap him.

"Who do you think you are?" I would ask.

And I suppose he would laugh, maybe adjusting his flowery crown with knobby, skeletal fingers. "I am death," he would say, offering no more explanation than that. He would only laugh again, the way he does in the little figurines that stare out from the carts of street vendors in San Miguel. In a fit of peevishness, I yanked the painting off my wall and thrust it behind my dresser.

But death is persistent. He appeared to me over and over in many forms, in the face of the Aztec god Quetzalcoatl, whose macabre visage was carved on the walls of the pyramids in Teotihuacán. In the skulls of sacrificed humans displayed in Teotihuacán's museum. In the final tortured works of Frida Kahlo displayed at the Heart of Frida Museum in San Miguel.

The site of this museum is lovely, holding at its core a peaceful courtyard in which one can sit and peruse one of the many-featured Frida texts. Around this courtyard, various rooms flaunt a collection of Frida's letters and a handful of her drawings, scrawled on the backs of losing lottery tickets. As a self-proclaimed Frida enthusiast, I had placed a visit to this exhibit at the top of my "San Miguel To-Do List."

My first exposure to Frida was in my mid-twenties, when I was more than open to being impressed by wanton displays of fetuses and feminine sacrifice. As a college sophomore, my teacher, an avid feminist, showed slides of Frida's paintings, and I wept quietly at my desk as vision after gory vision flashed in front of my eyes, each painting doused in blood and buckled with pain. Later that semester, I gave Frida a mental standing ovation and wrote a fiery paper dedicated to the power of her work.

So years later, when I, now a tenured Frida acolyte, wandered the halls of the Heart of Frida exhibit, I was surprised by my reaction to her childish love/hate letters and scrawled Crayola protests. I was surprised, most of all, however, by the fact that I would label anything created by St. Frida as childish. And yet, the only thing with which I walked away from The Heart of Frida exhibit was a resounding sense of pity. No. Pity is too kind. Disgust. I am ashamed to say, I was disgusted with Frida Kahlo, that celebrated painter of indelible images, for her abominable lack of vision, her crippling lack of imagination, her ignoble inability to see anything in life but pain.

And as I walked down the narrow cobblestone streets that led back to my hotel room, with its resident manifestation of oil paint death, I wondered if death had not, in fact, already shown me some small mercy. Breathing the gardenia-perfumed air, listening to the laughter of children dressed in red, watching the slow progress of a mongrel dog contentedly sniffing its way past Kool-Aid-colored buildings, I wondered if my current obsession with death had, in fact, endowed me with an unprecedented ability to appreciate life.

Of all of Frida's paintings, the one that is most applicable to my current state of mind is the oil painting entitled *Thinking about Death*. I have been thinking about death incessantly, whether I like it or not. And yet. And yet. Something about the way Frida thought about death, the way that she exulted in the macabre and doused her metaphorical body in pools of blood while her physical body was still working, more or less, made me want to slap her.

"Frida," I want to say to the painting, "you are still alive. Why all the death talk?"

She only stares, frozen in agonized thought, with a little

skeletal manifestation of death sneering from the center of her skull.

"Frida, your eyes still see. There are butterflies and bananas and blazingly blue beetles to be admired, and all you do is ruminate on the sewage in the street. Your ears still hear, and yet, you drown out the sounds of the wind flutes, craning for echoing screams. Your skin still feels, and you ignore the cool rain trickling over your shoulders, the wind licking your throat, the sun slipping its fingers up under the hem of your gorgeously colored skirt. I know what you think. Life is pain. Life is ultimately pointless, ending, as it inevitably does, in death. And I know what you mean. I get you, Frida. I am almost as old as you were when you wrote those tortured letters. I am old enough to have made an acquaintance with death. I am old enough to know that life is not all butterflies and wind flutes and cool rain. And yet. And yet. Along with the sewage and the screaming, those things are here too."

My most recent acquaintance with death came only two years ago. It was perhaps the most brutal encounter I have had thus far. I could argue, probably accurately, that it induced my aforementioned midlife crisis. My last encounter with death began with a phone call.

"Hello," I said, and the voice on the other end, "Tawni, Dea is dead." Just like that.

Dea was dead, and I threw the phone. Dea, the beautiful one I remember best hip-hop dancing during a lightning storm, wearing a gauzy yellow dress and flowers in her hair. My Dea, the one with the Grumpy dwarf tattooed on her calf, the Dea who sang like Macy Gray and did a dead-on pterodactyl impression. Laughing Dea, the girl who stood beside me in blue at my wedding, the girl who gave me the honor of standing beside her while she gave birth to her son. That Dea. She was dead.

I had seen her the day before, and she had laughed, like always. I had seen her the day before, and hours later, she had hanged herself from a porch, at night, watching, I imagine, as she died, the dancing of van Gogh stars. Thirty years of life reduced to a can of ashes, and at the funeral, I saw my own bewildered rage mirrored in the eyes of her nine-year-old son, who had found her hanging. Dea was dead. Dead from impetuousness and impulsiveness and unadulterated self-pity. Dead from exactly the kind of self-indulgence Frida Kahlo displayed in those letters at the Heart of Frida exhibit. Dead from a lack, perhaps, of ever having bothered to live.

The day after Dea's death, I awoke to see a jade-colored hummingbird flitting outside my window, and I wept, because it occurred to me how lucky I was to be there to see it. A hummingbird, the Aztec symbol of everlasting life, hovered outside my window, and I knew that because Dea had never bothered to live, I would live for both of us, sucking up, along the way, enough color and song and sun and love for two.

It turns out that Dea's death has given me, along with a fear of death, an irrepressible love for life. Every breath is a miracle. Every morning I wake to hear the whir of hummingbird wings, I am keenly aware that this day could be my last. And I am thankful all day, for the blazing of the morning sun, for the banging of the lunchtime boom boxes, for the meandering of the evening traffic jams. Yes, even for the traffic jams, I am grateful.

And yet. And yet. During my last week in San Miguel, I woke up in the middle of a black night ripped by gashes of moonlight. I woke up, and my liver hurt. I woke up, and even though death no longer stared down at me from that painting over my bed, I felt him in the room. I felt him, and I worried about the way I had been drinking while in San Miguel, about night after wild night of margarita after margarita after tequila shot after margarita. I wondered if one could acquire cirrhosis in a month.

Staring into the darkness, spinning and dizzy, I held on to my pillow like a drowning woman clutching a floating bit of

wood. I held on and wondered if one could fall off the edge of
the world. And I knew one could. I knew Dea had.

What scares me most about death is this. Some nights, I
am standing on the edge of that dizzy ledge where Dea stood
that one night when all of this—the pain and the pretty—became too much. I am standing, looking down, into an abyss
that goes on and on into forever, and I am remembering the
Sunday school stories about hell, and even now, even after all
of these years, I am still that little girl kneeling by her bed,
praying to a god that never hears, begging him not to throw
his little girl into hell.

I wonder about my Dea. I wonder where she is now, if
that night, when she was standing on the edge, and her foot
slipped, if she just kept falling and falling, with no one to
catch her. I wonder what will happen to me if my foot slips.
I wonder if the god that judges after we die was even more
cruel, to Dea, to Frida, than I have been, if he judged them
more mercilessly, if he cared less about their pain.

I wonder if Frida is in hell. I pray that she is not, because
for all of my pretty words, on those nights, after I wake up
and research cirrhosis on the internet, after I wake up and
stand, hands against the tile, crying in the shower of my little
San Miguel cubicle, letting the hot water shatter my skin,
after I stand there like that, the pain of my life, the pain of
my impending death, washing over me like the water—in
that moment, I am Frida. And I pray there is a god who is
kinder than I.

The Aztecs, for all of their bloody sacrifices, believed, a
tour guide told me, in a kind afterlife. There was no concept
of punishment after death. Only heaven. Heaven for everyone, regardless of the lengths to which they were driven when
the pain became too much. That kind of death is a death I
want to believe.

The week before she died, Frida painted a different kind
of picture, a lush montage of watermelons too beautiful to

eat, and she called her final masterpiece *Viva la Vida*. And I wonder if Frida, in those last moments, looking back over her pain, knew something I didn't know. Did death, standing there, staring over her shoulder as she painted those last strokes, whisper something in her ear, something sweet and warm that erased those years of agony and made her life, in retrospect, beautiful?

I wonder if Dea, while dangling and looking out over those van Gogh stars, saw things that I had never seen, beauty unimaginable. I wonder if in that moment, life became bigger for her, if it was like all the stories say, if a tunnel of light stretched out in front of her, out and into forever, and she danced away, through that tunnel, into something too big and beautiful for words. That is the way I want to see it.

Those laughing skeletons, a museum curator said to me, do not represent death. They represent the life of one who has lived. On Dia de los Muertos, people build altars for their dead, altars laden with gifts that symbolize the lives of the dead ones.

For Dea, I would build an altar, an altar decorated with Grumpy Dwarfs and pterodactyls, an altar with a silver *milagro* of a nine-year-old child's hand, an altar to hold that yellow dress she wore that night she danced, laughing, flowers in her hair, under a night sliced by jagged lightning. I would build that altar, and I would sit by and wait for her to fly over, the way the Mexicans say she would, fly over and sweep down, maybe to touch me, maybe to sweep my face with a gentle kiss, a breeze or a raindrop. I would ask her questions.

I would say, "Dea, beautiful laughing Dea, broken bleeding Dea, how did you go down? Did you go down laughing? Are you laughing now? Was that laughing skeleton hanging over my bed a picture of your face?"

≈ ≈ ≈

Tawni Vee Waters is a writer, actor, and gypsy. When she is not on the road, she makes her home in Albuquerque, New Mexico, with her two children and a menagerie of wayward animals. She has an MFA in Fiction from the University of New Orleans. Her work has been published in Bridal Guide Magazine, Ft. Lauderdale Sun-Sentinel, Albuquerque Journal, *and* Albion Review, *among others. She recently won The Editor's Award for Fiction from* Ellipses Magazine, *and her last novel won first place in the Southwest Writer's Contest. Her most recent novel,* Empire of Dirt, *is poised to become an international bestseller, poised being a loose term meaning "rejected by every agent in America and two in Canada." In her spare time, she talks to angels, plays Magdalene to a minor rock god, and humanely evicts the spiders living in her floorboards. This story won the Grand Prize Gold Award in the Fourth Annual Solas Awards (www.BestTravelWriting.com).*

⚛ ⚛ ⚛

Freewheelin' Liberia

Feeling at home in the land of the Americos
is a snap, Uncle.

"**D**ID AMERICA COLONIZE LIBERIA?" MY BUSH-
taxi driver asked me as we hurtled deep into Liberia
at dangerous speeds.

I'd heard this question many times, both in the United
States and in Liberia. The two countries' shared history is
only vaguely understood. I told the driver that Liberia was
the only sub-Saharan African country that had never been
colonized. In the 1820s, though, Congress awarded a grant to
the American Colonization Society, which promoted sending
freed slaves back to Africa, to purchase the area that is now
the capital, Monrovia (named after President James Monroe).
Thousands of American ex-slaves, known as "Americos," re-
settled in Liberia (for "liberty"). In 1847, the country became
the first independent republic in Africa, but it's still often
dubbed America-in-Africa.

I delivered this history lesson between gasps. There were four passengers squeezed into the Nissan Sunny, and I sat in the worrisome shotgun seat, whose occupants are most frequently killed in traffic accidents. Worse still, the driver kept turning the key in the ignition every two minutes, causing the engine to roar wildly.

When I asked him why he was doing that, he smiled broadly and explained: "To shoot in fuel." I reached again for the seat belt that was no longer there and suddenly felt that I should have stayed in my air-conditioned hotel in Monrovia. As if vacationing in Liberia weren't adventurous enough, I had decided to traverse the entire country by the only means available: bush taxi, motorbike, and foot.

The driver shot in fuel, scowled hard and asked: "Why'd America never colonize us?"

"Bossman," I said, switching into the Liberian English I'd picked up while living here as an aid worker a decade earlier, "you vexed because America did not colonize you?"

"Ivory Coast got plenty factories and trains, from France-o," he said. "What we get?"

"Gentlemen!" a voice suddenly boomed from the back seat. "I am Samuel Jefferson."

I turned to see a distinguished man of about sixty, with glasses and a graying Afro. He said, a little boastfully, that his ancestors had arrived from North Carolina in 1842.

With this, a hush of respect blanketed the bush taxi. In Liberia, slave blood is blue blood; here, saying that your ancestors picked cotton is akin to letting it casually slip in the United States that your forebears had founded Princeton.

Jefferson boomed out: "I want to ask you a single question!"

He allowed a dramatic pause. The driver used his key to shoot in fuel. The speedometer hit eighty, and I vise-gripped my seat. Screeching hornbills soared through the rain forest canopy above, and I imagined us hitting a ramp and flying,

Evel Knievel-style, up with those prehistoric-looking birds, airborne to Guinea. Finally Jefferson said: "What did our forefathers—the Afro-Americans—do for this country?"

The driver shrugged. "Nothing," he said.

"Exactly! And that's our endowment. They didn't take out the gold, the diamonds, and the timber. Instead, they left it right where it is, for us."

Samuel Jefferson cleared his throat. "Gentlemen," he said, gesturing out the window as one of the world's poorest nations raced by, "Liberia is rich."

One week earlier, I'd landed at Robertsfield International Airport, built by the United States in 1942 as a military base. But this was very much a postwar Liberia, former president Charles Taylor's dreaded Anti-Terrorist Unit troopers long gone.

"Welcome to Liberia!" the immigration officer exclaimed.

"How da'body?" I replied.

"Body fine!" he answered, reaching out to shake my hand. I was ready. I knew the ubiquitous Liberian snap-shake: after a regular handclasp, each person uses the other's middle finger to snap his own. The result is a satisfying double-pop. But I'd been out of Liberia too long. My snap-shake wouldn't snap. The officer shrugged. "Keep tryin'," he said.

In Africa, the world is constructed on a larger scale. On the hour-long drive from the airport to Monrovia's center, I gazed at the ultramarine vault of sky that stretched over rolling grasslands and forests. Far out over the Atlantic Ocean, an electrical storm flashed, but the landscape around us was dotted with reassuring baby blue: the helmets of U.N. peacekeepers, reminding me that I was safe and on vacation.

Well, I wasn't just on vacation. I was here to help prepare an ecological trade agreement between Liberia and the European Union. But my contract stipulated a week of vacation, and I would spend it in Liberia.

"Are you nuts?" colleagues had said, unable to put the words "vacation" and "Liberia" in the same sentence. "Hop a flight to fabulous Dakar."

Alas, they were thinking of the old Liberia. The new Liberia is now open for adventure travel. Taylor, the infamous gun-running strongman who ruled the country from 1997 to 2003, is far, far away—on trial for war crimes in The Hague—and Africa's first female head of state, the Americo Ellen Johnson-Sirleaf, leads a democratic nation that has been at peace for five years. Economic growth has soared, and the U.S. Peace Corps is coming back after a two-decade hiatus.

I checked into an oceanview room at the Mamba Point Hotel and plopped down on my comfy bed. It's not a bad time, I figured, to explore what is squarely African here—like Liberia's tribal cultures and its virgin rain forests, full of forest elephants and pygmy hippos—as well as what's American, from a plate of ribs at Sam's Barbeque in Monrovia to the country's red, white and blue flag, with its stripes and single star.

I drove to the sleepy town of Clay-Ashland, on the banks of the St. Paul River ten miles outside Monrovia. It's named after Kentucky slave owner Henry Clay who—quite conveniently—favored a gradual approach to abolishing slavery, and his Lexington estate, Ashland. In the early nineteenth century, the Kentucky affiliate of the American Colonization Society raised the cash to resettle slaves who had been freed on the condition that they leave the United States. In 1846, Clay-Ashland was founded as part of a colony called Kentucky-in-Africa.

I spoke to an older woman sitting on her wraparound porch. She pointed out plaques in town that celebrate such famous former residents as William Coleman, Liberia's thirteenth president, whose family immigrated to Clay-Ashland from Kentucky. The woman's accent was laced through with the lilting cadence of the antebellum South. She was clearly Americo, a term that is now applied to the descendants of the original freed slaves who settled here.

Though they've never comprised more than 1 percent of the country's population, the lighter-skinned black Americos have dominated Liberia. Zealous Christian missionaries in the early days, they built plantation houses in the style of their masters, with gabled roofs and dormer windows—sometimes even with grand fireplaces, unusable, of course, in the humid tropics—and affected top hats, white gloves, and parasols.

The Americo True Whig Party, founded in 1869 in Clay-Ashland, ran the country for more than a century, and Liberia's black-on-black apartheid rivaled the white-black apartheid of South Africa. It got so bad that in 1930 the League of Nations condemned the Americos for using native Liberians for forced labor, a scandal so fraught with irony that it forced the resignation of the country's then-president, Charles King.

The next day, my fun-loving Liberian friend Doegbazee announced that he was taking me out on the town in Monrovia. After fried chicken at Sam's Barbeque, we headed downtown for some Liberian Star beer at a packed outdoor dance joint. We sipped to a hip-hop beat, soaking up the humid, globalized funk of it all. Many of those dancing would don Speedos and bikinis the next day on one of the city's half-dozen beaches; some would perhaps ride the waves up the coast at Robertsport, the world-class surfing spot featured in the recent documentary film *Slidin' Liberia.*

Then Paul Simon came on. And man, do Liberians love Paul Simon. A pair of girls grabbed Doegbazee and me, and we boogied it all the way to Graceland. The moon above us blushed in antique pink, telling me it was Christmas season, harmattan season. As the harmattan winds carry the Saharan sands over West Africa, they mute the edge of things. The next day I'd leave the comfortable coast and head into the relatively little-known interior.

Cuttington University, 120 miles north of Monrovia, has a touch of small American black college to it. Campus fashions are similar to those in the United States. The college is made up of quaint, single-story white buildings interspersed between rice paddies and electrified by a USAID-donated generator.

"Brother!" exclaimed the slightly plump, thirty-eight-year-old Barzai Moore as he wrapped me in a hug. "Your mother is my mother, too," he said, "so we're brothers."

It shocked me to see Barzai in a tie. He'd been a janitor at my aid organization. My mother had visited Liberia in 2000 and, impressed to see Barzai diligently teaching himself computers after all the toilets were scrubbed, had offered to pay for his education. She used her Social Security checks to put him through Cuttington. Barzai graduated at the top of his class and now works as a well-paid accountant at the university.

But there was a downside to Barzai's prosperity. "Everybody uncle-ing me," he lamented as we strolled the campus, referring to the practice of addressing someone as "uncle" as an indirect way of asking for money. A sense of dependency, which may have roots in plantation culture, still exists in Liberia.

Later that day, a young man approached me and declared: "Compliments of the season!" We shook hands, but still no snap.

"Compliments...of the season," I replied, managing to force that nineteenth-century Southern artifact out of my twenty-first-century mouth.

"Where's my Christmas?" he asked, in another form of widespread begging.

I grinned and said, "I don't see it-o."

He laughed, slapping me on the back and added: "My New Year?"

"Uncle," I said, feigning exasperation, "you didn't come soon." Translation: Someone else beat you to it. My Liberian, or Simple, English was kicking in now. Instead of "both of them" I heard myself saying "all two of them." Once I even referred to the nation's finance minister as "the bossman of Liberia's money business," as they do on Monrovia's Simple English newscasts.

I spent the next night at the Methodist mission guest-house in the trading town of Ganta. George Way Harley, an American missionary and physician, established the mission and hospital after arriving in 1926. I toured the chapel and then relaxed in a wide, silent clearing near the school. But the tranquility was soon broken as a team of cell phone sales-men from Monrovia tore up in a 4X4. Their company, as one of them told me, was throwing "mobile phone parties" in the villages to "connect them to the civilized world." Their missionary zeal for the Flat World rivaled that of Harley for Christendom.

But their tune changed that evening when the mission generator sputtered out and the place went pitch dark. "We paid for electricity!" one of the salesmen yelled at the mission staff.

By candlelight, I talked with the mission cook, who told me about Harley's interest in indigenous culture, his Liberian mask collection (now housed at Duke University) and his fascination with the "bush school" initiation ceremonies that are still common today.

Little did I suspect that I'd stumble into an initiation myself.

Two days later, while walking a stretch of high jungle north of Ganta, I stopped to observe a phosphorescent tree orchid. The flower had me in such meditative thrall that I

hardly registered the pounding of drums in the forest beyond—until a shrill cry rang out.

For explanation, I looked to my guide, and he gave it to
me in the form of two terrifying words: "Country devil!"
Then he bolted back toward the village through which we'd
just passed. I didn't stick around to ponder anthropological
theory. I took off after him.

We finally reached the village. Just twenty minutes earlier
it had been full of people; now it was empty, everyone gone
into the surrounding bush. We didn't stop running until we'd
cleared that ghost town. I collapsed at my guide's feet, and he
exclaimed between heaving breaths that "the devil's coming
to town" and that we were lucky to have been able to cross
back before he entered.

Staring down at my sweaty body on the forest floor, he
asked: "Y'all right?"

Shooing away mosquitoes, I could only mutter: "Tryin'
small."

I reached the extreme edge of Liberia—the hilly mining
town of Yekepa—on New Year's Eve.

The town immediately seduced me. Yellow birds darted
around about one hundred nests hanging on the mango tree
across the square; beyond a row of market stalls rose forested hills. I checked into Noble House, a basic hotel on the
square.

Prince, the bossman of Noble House, joined me for a luke-
warm Guinness on the hotel porch. "There's chimpanzees
on the French side," he said, referring to Guinea, the former
French colony a few miles away. He explained that these wild
chimpanzees walk on "funky baboon paths" paralleling the
roads, climb palms for their tender cabbage, spontaneously
join soccer games and even sneak into the Guinean town of
Bossou to snatch market-stall bananas.

Prince's girlfriend served us bushmeat-in-sauce with *fufu*, a dish of pounded cassava. When she left, he explained that his wife had died suddenly a year back and left him to raise three children. "We're watching each other," he said of the girlfriend, "to see if we fit."

I spent most of the day listening to reggae with Prince and his waitress, Patience. That evening, two Catholic priests, one Liberian and the other Nigerian, rolled into Noble House to say New Year's Mass in the town church. Accompanying them was the first white person I'd seen in days, an American lay missionary running an antiabortion campaign in Liberia.

"The fetus screams when it's vacuumed out of a womb," she said. "It's in the videos we're showing the villagers."

The Liberian priest sipped his beer and then said, ambiguously, "God is in the small things." He smiled, staring into the foam in his beer glass. "Not the big things."

The next day I rode a rented motorbike along the dirt road to France, as some Liberians in that area refer to Guinea. There were no other travelers at the border. The immigration officer on the Liberian side asked whether I had a visa for Guinea, which is required for Americans. "It's another country, you know," he said.

I told him I didn't have one. Then we both forgot about it as we talked about the Bossou chimpanzees I was going to see, and the news from Monrovia. Behind him, the Liberian flag flew on a tree pole; it brought to mind James Monroe's enigmatic prediction that Liberia would become "a little America, destined to shine gem-like in the heart of darkest Africa."

I finally rose to leave and shook hands with the official. The thump of our mutual snap was so forceful that it echoed off the border post walls. "You know our Liberian shake!" he said.

I motored up a dusty road to the Guinean crossing and handed my passport to an official. He wore knockoff Dior sunglasses and a beret. A couple of other stylish officials lazed on a king-size mattress on the ground. Without asking for a visa, they waved me through. Strangely, as I crossed into Guinea, it felt a bit like leaving home.

≈≈ ≈≈ ≈≈

William Powers is the author of the Liberia memoir Blue Clay People: Seasons on Africa's Fragile Edge. *His website is www. williampowersbooks.com.*

❦ ❦ ❦

For the Spirits of Guinaang

A search for headhunters does not go
entirely unrewarded.

WHEN TWO VEHICLES MEET GOING THE OPPOSITE
direction along certain stretches of the Halsema
Highway in the northern Philippines, one has to back up to
a spot where the other can pass. Somehow, our bus driver
managed to do just that and allow other buses and trucks
to pass a dozen times on our trip without backing off a cliff,
though once he was within inches of the edge. There are few
guardrails along this mountain trail, and at places the drop off
is a thousand feet. But oh, what a drop into such beauty, down
past rice terraces and river gorges and smoky clouds hanging
below jagged mountain peaks.

I was traveling this treacherous road all because of a story.
My traveling companion, Lawrence Reid, told me this story
several years earlier at a dinner party in his condo in Hawaii
Kai on Oahu. The story concerned a gong in his possession;

part of the gong handle was made from the top of the skull of an American G.I. from World War II. The G.I. was one of two who escaped a Japanese prison camp and made their way up north to the village of Guinaang. The people of this village welcomed the G.I.s, and eventually the two moved on to another nearby village, Mainit, which means "hot," so named because of its volcanic hot springs. There, one of the soldiers took a wife, and all was well until one night the soldier named Taylor became drunk and threw out all the rice stores that one family owned. The village elders decided that Taylor had to be killed, and as it was their practice to take heads, they quickly dispatched Taylor to the afterlife by spearing and beheading him. Seeing that the other G.I. was miserable without his companion, they decided to behead him as well so that he could join his friend.

At least one of the soldiers, or part of him, became a music-maker after his death, and I listened to him make sounds so unlike the sounds he made in life as Laurie, as Reid is known, beat him on the gong at the dinner party. Such music often accompanied sacrifices to the spirits in Guinaang, but in Hawaii Kai its music was more ambiguous, its listeners never having heard such a tune before, made of an instrument of misunderstanding. To have been given such a gift seemed both horrific and something of an honor. But Laurie, of all outsiders, undoubtedly deserved such an honor, and could put such horror in the proper perspective. Laurie, a renowned linguist and specialist in Austronesian languages, had been coming to Guinaang since 1959, when as a young lay missionary for the Summer Institute of Linguistics, his job was to learn the local language and translate the New Testament into Bontoc. He lived with the Guinaang people about eight years, earning a doctorate in linguistics in 1966. In 1970, he quit SIL and had taught ever since at the University of Hawaii, from which he recently retired. Now he lives in Japan with his wife Ritsuko, also a linguist.

Why the story fascinated me, I suppose, has to do with the ironies, of this particular clash of cultures. By American standards, the people of Mainit had certainly overreacted by beheading the soldiers, but by the standards of the people of Mainit, the Americans had overreacted as well. Laurie related that after the war, American soldiers, hearing of the deaths of the G.I.s, traveled to the village and summarily executed eleven of the village elders.

I'd wanted to make this trip the previous year, but an inconsiderate mosquito had bitten me and I'd come down with dengue fever on Valentine's Day as I was having dinner in a restaurant in Manila with my wife. For the next eight days, I'd languished in a Manila hospital, receiving five bags of platelets, my only company my wife's brother Joe and the BBC on the TV. The theme music of the BBC still makes me feel ill. My wife, of course, visited me when she could, but we had a newborn child she had to stay at home with, and so I sprawled in bed as though I were modeling for the *Pieta* and received a few doleful visitors, including Laurie.

Over the next year, I corresponded with Laurie and we arranged to meet in Manila the following May. If all worked out, he'd take me to Guinaang after all, though we had a short window this time. I was arriving in the Philippines on May 6th and Laurie had to leave for Japan on May 15th—if we left on the 9th, we'd barely have time to trek to Guinaang, stay a couple of days, and then make the two-day journey back to Manila. National elections were on the 10th, not an ideal time to travel, but I had little choice.

On the bus, Laurie told me stories about Pakoran, the man who would be our host in Guinaang. Pakoran had been Laurie's friend almost from the first day Laurie set foot in Guinaang in 1959. In the sixties and early seventies, the two roamed widely through the Mountain Province, Laurie negotiating a peace pact between two villages, delivering countless babies and mending wounds, building a couple of airstrips on ridge tops to bring in supplies for the villages. The two had been inseparable.

"Pakoran is a great storyteller," Laurie assured me. "Once you get him going, he won't stop."

When we reached the town of Bontoc, we arranged for a van to bring us the rest of the way to Guinaang. But first, we purchased eggs, vegetables, Spam, and a kind of spirit marketed as a gin but made from cane sugar, called Ginebra San Miguel, all gifts for the family.

The road to Guinaang was good as such roads go. In places, it was cemented, not the entire width of the road, but two strips of concrete set at the width of two tires to run along. The road climbed steadily through pine forests. The mountains, deeply grooved with few ridges but many drop-offs into abysses of varying degrees, shot up at formidable angles from the valley. In the distance, other villages perched on the mountains covered with rice terraces, villages that had been at war with one another off and on for a millennium. Two of the local villages used to gather across the river from one another and hurl stones—if you were hit by a stone and it raised a bruise, this would determine the size of your sweet potato crop that year.

The people of Guinaang took the heads of their enemies in the past and stored them in baskets in the back of the group houses where the unmarried men slept. But the last heads had been taken during World War II when the men of Guinaang ambushed a group of Japanese soldiers. The Japanese had come to the village and demanded provisions, but the people of Guinaang told them time would be needed to assemble everything they wanted. While the Japanese soldiers slept in the Anglican church, the men of Guinaang sent for the resistance forces in Mainit for backup. Throughout the night, whenever a Japanese soldier went outside the church to take a pee, he was quickly dispatched. By the morning, the rest of the Japanese, realizing that no one was returning once they left the church, panicked and fled down the mountain toward the town of Bontoc, first setting the church on fire. But on the way down the mountain, the Japanese were ambushed and every one of them beheaded. The only casualty the people of Guinaang suffered was an old woman lying on her sickbed. The fleeing Japanese shot her out of spite Laurie assumed. "The fellow probably figured he was going to die anyway, so he might as well take someone with him." Pakoran had been a boy then and had been evacuated with the rest of his family as the Japanese soldiers approached.

The headless bodies of the Japanese were buried in the ruins of the church. In Guinaang, there were bad deaths and good deaths, and losing your head definitely qualified as a bad death. Normally, such people were buried outside of the village, not under the church, as these men were, which caused a marked decline in attendance at church after it was rebuilt. No one wanted to sit in a place where people had died a bad death.

I wasn't sure how a group of well-armed Japanese soldiers could be killed, one and all, by spear-wielders. "Apparently, they were terrified of the people in Guinaang," Laurie told me. "They all tried to flee down the mountain, except for one fellow who, instead of running away from the village, ran into it and hid in a house. If the guy had only stayed there, he would have been all right. He would have had to be treated as a guest. But he ran out of the house and tried to hide in a pig shelter. He was easy to kill in the shelter. They simply stood over it and speared him through the thatch."

Scores were still settled in dramatic fashion in the region. Laurie pointed out a road to nowhere across the valley. The road was supposed to connect one village to the outside world, but a neighboring village didn't want the road going through their territory and so had pushed the bulldozers and other equipment over the ledges. A water dispute between Mainit and Guinaang had been resolved when the people of Mainit simply cut the pipe supplying water to Guinaang.

Before the road to Guinaang was built, Laurie used to

climb straight up the mountain from Bontoc. The trip took three hours. I didn't see how this was possible.

"Often, we'd make the climb in the pouring rain," he told me. "They used to call me mountain goat back then." Still remarkably fit, Laurie would celebrate his seventieth birthday in several weeks' time. I had never seen a picture of him from his youth, but even now, people remarked on his appearance. He's a trim man with ruddy cheeks and a well-groomed white beard and mustache. When I think of him, I see him smiling. One local man, on seeing us together, wondered jokingly (I hope) who was older, me or Laurie. Although I'm twenty-four years his junior, he's definitely got me beat on posture and weight.

When we finally arrived in Guinaang, I tried to convince myself it was beautiful, but this was a stretch. The village squatted on the mountainside, the small houses sloping down the hillside like seats in a movie theater, the pathways between houses about half as wide as a theater aisle. Certainly, it was in a beautiful setting, but the rusted metal roofs covering virtually every house did nothing to add to the beauty. Forty years ago, all the houses were thatched, but only one remained now, lived in by an old woman directly above Pakoran's.

Pakoran wasn't home when we arrived, but some of his family greeted us. His wife, Issew, grumbled when she saw Laurie's gift of Ginebra San Miguel. Pakoran, formerly the strongest man in the village and one-time barrio captain, was now known as one of the village drunks. When he wasn't drunk, he was still a great storyteller, Laurie said, but by nightfall he was invariably drunk.

Soon, we heard singing coming from outside, and Laurie said, "That's Pakoran."

"He's drunk already," his daughter Susan said cheerily.

Pakoran, dressed in a G-string and a short-sleeve shirt with a collar, plunked himself down in our midst, flush with good cheer and Ginebra San Miguel. He smiled broadly at us and spoke effusively to Laurie, often ending a sentence with the words, "Naughty, naughty."

"That's what Pakoran says when he's drunk," Laurie told me. "It's his special word—it doesn't mean anything but he always says it when he's been drinking."

That night, Pakoran was able to fill in some of the blanks in the story of the beheaded American soldiers, but spoke mostly on the subject of himself and how strong he was when he was younger. "I was the strongest man in the village," he said to Laurie, who translated. "If there was something heavy to carry, they would always say, 'Let's get Pakoran.' I could carry anything. I could carry big rocks. I could carry pigs. Anything you gave me, I could carry.

"They elected me barrio captain even though I was uneducated," he told me. "My father was the leader of the resistance in Guinaang during the war, and when they needed someone to run for barrio captain, they said let's get Pakoran because of his father."

Pakoran's monologue went on for the better part of an hour, punctuated by jarring sneezes that ended in high-pitched shouts, another effect, like the word "naughty naughty," of the alcohol. Throughout dinner, he kept up his often incoherent harangue on his prowess, his family and guests tolerant and good-natured about it.

Pakoran stood shakily to ferret along the wall for his head ax to show me. He made a half-hearted attempt to locate it and sat down again, which was fine with me. I imagined him severing my knee with it. Not that Pakoran had ever taken a head. The last man with a chest tattoo, indicating he had taken a head, had died several years ago. This was one of the men who had ambushed the Japanese. To the people of Guinaang, he had been no one special. They were much more interested in the present, in getting food and education, than in the past. The heads of the Japanese and the others kept in baskets at the back of group houses couldn't be looked at in the light or they'd cause blindness. But eventually, the people of Guinaang must have either stopped believing this or thrown out the heads at night, because the heads were long gone, tossed on one trash heap or another or perhaps over a cliff into the river. Or transformed into gong handles. The group houses, low stone structures with metal roofs (they were thatched in years past) are abandoned now.

Sometimes, you could still see old women with arm tattoos, but no one tattooed their arms anymore. The women had stopped when lowlanders made fun of them when they traveled to the city of Baguio.

The next day as we were walking back from a hike to Mainit to take a dip in the hot springs, we ran across a procession headed by a man shouldering a large black native pig trussed up on a stretcher of sorts. At first, I thought the pig was dead, it seemed so quiet. The man and the pig were followed by a line of men and boys. We fell in alongside the men and were led to a small courtyard not far from the house where we slept.

This pig started screaming as soon as it saw the knife and continued to scream long after the knife had opened a hole in its throat, its blood flowing into a bowl. It screamed and screamed, though its screams grew weaker and weaker, until it finally died, screaming. You want a pig to make a lot of noise when it's sacrificed. It's the same with killing a chicken. In Guinaang, a chicken is killed by beating it to death. The spirits like the noise.

When the men thought it was dead, they cut off its tail, but the pig was not quite dead and made one last violent and vain attempt to escape. The tail was given to a boy who played with it beside me. The men laid the dead pig across from an old man in a seat who said a prayer over it.

We were asked to contribute money for drinks if we wanted to share in the meat, but I didn't want a share of the meat. Or drinks. I wanted a nap.

I went back to our room and I slept. So did Laurie, and I awoke to a beautiful chorus of men's voices singing a chorale I didn't understand. But I knew it concerned the dead pig. I knew these were prayers offered to the spirits to accept the gift of this pig.

It sounded like a great chant to me, but it turned out to be pretty average as these things go. Laurie said they were doing the first prayer correctly, but that wasn't hard since it was completely ad lib except for the tune. When they started the second prayer, they couldn't get it going. Even Susan noticed this and said to Laurie in Bontoc, "They've forgotten the words." Well, that was a disappointment. I'd seen a pig sacrifice, but it hadn't been a particularly good pig sacrifice. In a couple of generations, after they stabbed the pig in the throat, they might be singing, "We will, we will rock you!"

Ever since attending this pig sacrifice, I've noticed ads in which a cartoon animal happily invites humans to eat members of its own species who are not cartoons: a cartoon chicken smiling over a headless frozen chicken carcass, a pig licking its chops over a line of tasty sausages. Before this, I hadn't noticed. My theory is that cartoon characters are a lot like spirits. Maybe they are spirits. In any case, not being alive, death pleases them.

The next day we took a jeepney to a village with some spectacular rice terraces, according to Laurie. The jeepney was packed with people and their goods and the only place we could fit was on top of the roof—I had never done this before, but I'd seen jeeps loaded down before in the provinces with people covering every available space except the windshield—soon I had nestled (though "nestle" is perhaps too comfortable a word) on top and between some sacks of rice and in this way, I jounced and clung on while we traversed another treacherous mountain path. After half an hour or so, Laurie yelled that we were coming into town. I nodded. And then he told me to duck and I looked ahead and saw a wire of some sort strung across the road at exactly the level of my neck. I lay flat across the bags of rice a few seconds before the wire and I met—had Laurie not warned me, the wire would undoubtedly have beheaded me.

I'd like to say that I wasn't ready to be beheaded that afternoon. But who is? You don't expect to be beheaded when you leave the church to take a piss. You don't expect to be beheaded when you get drunk and misbehave a little. You don't expect to be beheaded when you're going on a tour of the rice terraces. Such stories are much more enjoyable when they're someone else's story, not yours. Understandably, the incident spooked me a bit, and I didn't quite feel right for the rest of the afternoon.

After we'd hiked the terraces, we came upon an ancient woman, probably one of the last to have tattooed arms. Wanting to snap her photo, I asked Laurie to politely make the request. Nearly deaf and completely blind, she managed nonetheless to understand, we thought, then wrapped a cigar, lit it, and began to rant quietly. She seemed in conversation with the air, with memory as she waved her patterned arms through the billows of smoke she created. She hardly seemed to know we were there and we hardly seemed to know she was there or thought her already gone and the people around me, including Laurie, said, go on, take her picture, and I guess I needed proof that we both still existed. So I did. Everyone else at the stop laughed at her, crazy old woman with the tattooed arms. They told her she must go home, that she couldn't stay in the small store where she was resting anymore. She stood uncertainly and began her walk back home along the walls of the rice terraces, back to her distant village. If she fell the twenty or thirty feet from one of the terrace walls, she'd likely die, and perhaps it's precious and sentimental to think that she knew the path so well, like some Eudora Welty character, that she'd never lose her way. People fall and injure themselves and die sometimes in Guinaang, I can report with virtual certainty, though most often out of sight of the fortunate visitor. The fact that you know a path well does not necessarily make it less treacherous.

That night at dinner, I didn't learn anything more from Pakoran about the two beheaded soldiers. He had been drunk since breakfast but told us that friends his own age were already dead and that he wasn't going to die. He was far too drunk to relate anything in coherent fashion. Pakoran curled up and nodded off to sleep in front of us and everyone seemed relieved, not least of all his wife Issew, who smiled wearily after spending the entire day bent over in one of the rice fields, where by tradition only the women worked.

I heard something fall behind me and I thought maybe someone had dropped a cooking utensil. "What's that?" I asked.

"Oh, just a rat," said Susan with such a big smile that I thought she was kidding.

A rat jumped out onto my foot as though incensed by my doubt of its existence. Then it jumped on Laurie's foot and we all yelled and the rat scurried off to another corner of the room. Only Pakoran didn't stir.

At breakfast the next morning a toddler named Dexter was occupied with a giant beetle he had found. He experimented pulling off a couple of legs, then let it crawl on its remaining legs over his hands. Dexter held the beetle out before him, wanting the adults, including me, to share in his delight, every once in a while letting out a roar that seemed to herald his self-appointment as king of the beetles. I tried to strike a balance between good-natured approval of his find and adult reticence, not wanting to encourage too close an alliance between me and Dexter and his lone, tortured subject.

Pakoran wasn't there to say goodbye. He was in the next house, screaming his head off. I could hear Issew talking in calming tones to soothe him, but it did no good. Delirium tremens had hold of him—what poisoned version of himself he was trying to scream out of his being I couldn't know, but it alarmed even Dexter, who sat by the side of the house, saying nothing, the beetle now motionless in the dirt.

"I've never seen Pakoran like this," Laurie told me. "I've never seen him this bad."

Before we left for Manila again, Pakoran's daughter Susan handed Laurie a short essay she'd written in her native language. Laurie had asked Susan to write the essay, not because he wanted to encourage her as a budding memoirist, but because he wanted to see how much Ilocano (the language of the lowlanders) had infiltrated the local Bontoc language—many words, it turned out. But what interested me were not the changes in the language, but what Susan was trying to tell us. The story Susan had written, I learned later, concerned the problems facing the youngest child in a family. When the girl in the story was younger, she had known her father had loved her and she had loved him. Now he was drunk every night and she didn't know his feelings for her anymore. She had gone away to school in Sagada, happy to be away from the family, but then after a year, she had missed them and cried every night, and now she had returned. The old feelings were starting to come back. Sometimes she wished her father would just go ahead and die.

A few months later, that's exactly what Pakoran did—and while I didn't know this would happen so shortly, it seemed the general direction in which he was headed. As for me, I simply wanted to leave this town. It seemed somehow infested with mortality and I didn't fancy myself a connoisseur of death. I wanted to go back home to my land, where people recover, where they never die.

By the Anglican church and the never-to-be-finished recreation hall, Laurie and I caught a jeep going down to Bontoc. We were among the first passengers, and a young man who was stumbling drunk yelled some good-natured nonsense at us. He was probably thirty years Pakoran's junior, but had started young. Another man was led carefully to the front seat where he sat with his mother, his expression completely blank. He had a deep wound on top of his head and looked as though he were dead already. He stared straight ahead. Nothing moved him. He made no sound and acknowledged no sound, though first his mother tried to talk to him and then his father, standing by the window. He seemed to be looking off into the afterlife, not at the road in front of him, not at his loved ones or life in Guinaang. Would he be able to hear the pleas of the living as a spirit if he was beyond listening while yet alive? The night Taylor and his friend died, the people played gongs all night long. Much later, in Hawaii Kai, I heard the faintest echo of death's music. A little like the theme from the BBC *World Report*, but not exactly.

The jeep started up and we rumbled and jostled with a full load of passengers. I tried not to look at the man or the ghastly wound on his head, but every once in a while I stole a glance. I couldn't help it. Slowly, we descended into the valley where the world was preparing its myriad sacrifices and the spirits enjoyed all the noise.

∾ ∾ ∾

Robin Hemley is the director of the Nonfiction Writing Program at the University of Iowa, and is the author of eight books, most recently, DO-OVER!, *in which a forty-eight-year-old father of three returns to kindergarten, summer camp, the prom, and other embarrassments. His other writing includes* Turning Life Into Fiction; Extreme Fiction: Fabulists and Formalists; Invented Eden: The Elusive, Disputed History of the Tasaday; Nola: A Memoir of Faith, Art, and Madness; The Big Ear; The Last Studebaker; All You Can Eat; *and* The Mouse Town.

❧ ❧ ❧

Fruits of Childhood

The simple growth of seeds has the power to animate
memory, to unify past and present.

T HIS MORNING, PERCHED ON A WOODEN CHAIR IN
my teeming tropical garden in northern Thailand, I
am writing about Africa, the continent that still holds a firm
grip on me. The sun's warmth, after the heavy dawn shower,
has brought plants and insects to life. Brown centipedes and
gray snails are crawling towards sun-drenched places where
they can bask undisturbed. The bird-of-paradise flowers are
reaching out to the light. I recall this flower well from childhood games in Uganda—six-year-old African and Asian
boys flicking the sticky yellow pollen stems onto each other's
starched white school shirts, knowing that our mothers would
give us a verbal or physical thrashing for stains that would
take days to wash off. Today, I walk over to the Thai version
of this same flower to take a long deep smell to remind me of
the African savannah. It is still the same after all these years;

the scent beams me across the Bay of Bengal, over the Indian Ocean, and onto the red clay soil of Uganda.

Next to the flower is the *tun-tun* tree clustered into bunches of tiny, ripe yellow-green balls of fruit that pop into your mouth straight from the tree and explode with a sourness that is as sharp as raw tamarind.... On Sunday market days as a young boy, with my tiny hand wrapped around my father's middle finger, I plead with him to buy me a bagful of this very same fruit for my afternoon snack.... Today, I plop a few in my mouth to remember the taste of Kampala and my departed father's face. The tangy aftertaste takes me back to other long-lost tropical fruits from back home—or at least what was once home. That was until the madman Idi Amin kicked out all 80,000 of us Indians.

I still crave *jambura*, an inch-long black fruit with a tiny hole at the top and a green seed inside. It remains top of my list of lost fruits, especially since I haven't tasted it for more than thirty years now. I call it by its Swahili name because, having looked for it in vain during my travels through Latin America, Asia, and the English-speaking world, I have yet to find out what it is called in other languages. Like *tun-tun*, it grows in bunches on a large leafy tree. When ripe and black, it is sweet and juicy. When green or pink and still raw, it tastes sour, astringent, and leaves a purple stain on the tongue that can take days to fade away.

Second on my list of missed fruits is *kajoo*—the multicolored fruit that the cashew nut comes from. Just below this pear-shaped fruit, perched as though it were a cup-like handle, is the cashew nut, which when roasted serves as a wildly popular snack in many parts of the world. However, the fruit itself—a blend of bright reds, greens, and yellows merging on the outer skin—has chewy yellow flesh inside, and is extremely acidic and tangy with very little juice. The aftertaste leaves the tongue quite dry, almost numb with that same feeling one gets upon leaving the dentist's office after a few rounds of Novocain. As Ugandan boys, during our summer escapades—weekend picnics to Entebbe or fishing trips to Kazi—we'd bring along bagfuls of this readily available fruit to stuff ourselves with till our tongues were as dry as the Sahara, always discarding the nut as worthless. In Thailand it's easy to find raw cashew nuts, or roasted ones in vacuum-sealed bags in the supermarkets, but I have yet to come upon the actual fruit itself.

Africa, it seems, is still deep within me, despite thirty years of globetrotting.

Give me the smell of a childhood flower, the taste of a forgotten fruit, and Zap! I am back to the land of my birth, back to the patch of grass we called our soccer field, and the constant drone of cicadas in the banyan trees.

In my humid garden in the village of Mae Rim, I walk back to my laptop to resume writing. My neighbors John and Monika knock at the front door with two other friends, Eric and Ang. They want me to join them for a day trip to the Pong Khaw hot springs, about thirty kilometers into the jungles of Chiang Mai. John, built like Schwarzenegger, is a Puerto Rican ex-Marine who now thinks of Thailand as his new home. Monika is a stocky, black-haired Hungarian gypsy, madly in love with her dogs. Eric, from New Jersey, is a teacher at a Thai secondary school, which is where he met Ang, his gorgeous honey-skinned Chinese-Thai girlfriend from Lanta Island in the south. With me, the Ismaili Muslim writer, we have ourselves a veritable and eclectic group of wanderers off to trek through the Lanna jungles.

Missing Africa always depresses me, so I decide to go along with them to break free of nostalgia's black hole. Within the hour, all of us pile into John and Monika's 1950s Land Rover, along with their two dogs, Matzo and Luna.

On the bumpy dirt road, I enjoy speaking with John, Eric, and Ang, each in their own language. I don't know any

Hungarian, but Monika speaks great English in her gypsy accent. The dogs, their heads poking out of the back windows on either side, love the breeze. In the countryside we climb the lime-green terraced paddy fields that are ready for harvest. In the valleys, the clunky Land Rover weaves through scattered Hmong and Burmese villages, as startled bystanders stare at these unannounced strangers of foreign lands.

My yearning for Africa is forgotten, replaced by multilingual chatter and the green scenery rolling by.

Two hours later we arrive at the hot springs, dusty and hungry. The resort has a compound with two large open-air sulfur pools bisected by a small creek. On the hillsides, water buffaloes graze at the edge of a heavy jungle. The place is deserted except for an orchestra of jungle insects and avian sonatas. As soon as we let them out, Matzo and Luna take off to chase the buffaloes.

At the reception area we find Tong, the Thai concierge. She laments that since we didn't call ahead of our arrival, and because guests are few and far between during rainy season, she doesn't have any Thai food prepared for us. We settle for fried noodles with eggs and some pre-packaged soup to tide us over.

For the next few hours we refresh ourselves in the hot sulfur pools and the cool creek, taking turns to teach Luna and Matzo how to swim in the shallow water. It's their very first time bathing au natural in the outdoors. A hide-and-seek dance between Eric and Matzo, around a large mushroom-shaped stone umbrella with four rocks for seats, has us all in stitches. Luna tries to pull off Ang's sarong, bringing guffaws from us males that generate sneers from Monika and Ang. By the afternoon, we are ravenous again after all the swimming and running around. Tong scurries off to find fruit and fifteen minutes later returns with a bowlful of the usual seasonal offerings—lychees, mangosteens, and guavas. We wolf it all

down in minutes until there is only one pear-like green and
yellow fruit left at the bottom of the bowl that none of the
others have ever seen before. But the shape jogs my memory.

"What fruit is this?" I ask Tong.

"Himalayan mango. Very sour," she says.

I don't recognize the Thai name but ask her to cut it up for
me anyway. As soon as I see the yellow flesh inside, my heart
skips a beat. I realize this is a yet-to-ripen *kajoo*. I devour half
of it, letting the juice drip down my lips as if I was on a boys'
picnic back at Ripon Falls, the source of the river Nile. I am in
heaven. Forgetting my manners, I pass it to Monika to taste.
But she finds it way too tangy for her liking. I quickly polish
off the rest.

My nostalgia for Africa is back, stronger than before. So I
take to discussing Thai jungle fruits with Tong. She explains
that *kajoo* season in the jungle ended just days ago, which is
why she was only able to find an unripe one. For the ump-
teenth time in my life, I describe the *jambura* fruit to her,
hoping against hope. Tong has no clue what fruit I am talking
about. She says something in northern Thai to her assistant,
who disappears into the jungle. I go over to Ang, whose
English is very good, give her a vivid description of *jambura*,
and ask her to translate verbatim.

Tong keeps shaking her head, still unable to identify the
fruit. Eventually, a few minutes later, I give up on ever finding my beloved *jambura*.

Come closing time as we're about to take off in the Land
Rover, Tong's assistant, gasping for breath, stops our departure, gesturing to a bowl in his hand.

"*Haa luuk wah, re plaw khap?*" he asks. "Is *luuk wah* the
fruit you're looking for?"

My eyes light up. My mouth is agape. Inside the bowl are a
handful of *jambura*! For once I am speechless. Ecstatic, I leap
out of the car and choose a few ripe ones. I feel the texture,
smell the odor, peel off the top, and ever so slowly savor that

old, old sensation of the juice slowly slithering down as if all of Africa is now in my throat.

The assistant passes the bowl to my friends who, again, find the taste not to their liking. I couldn't care less. I am back in Uganda, on a dirt road across from my house, playing games with my childhood friends in a *jambura* tree. We are playing "tree-tag" among the high branches. One of us lets go a loud, squishy fart, causing everyone to double up in hysterics. I have a wide grin on my face.

John says it's time to go. I hug Tong's assistant, who was kind enough to climb the *luuk wah* tree in the jungle just to quench a thirst I have been carrying for thirty years. Putting the six remaining *jambura* in a plastic bag for me to eat on the road back, he *wais* to me.

"Stop at the temple in Mae Taeng on your way. There is a *luuk wah* tree there," he yells as we take off.

I convince John to look for the temple, which we eventually find after asking directions from locals three times. A solitary young monk in his saffron robe is sitting on the steps of the old, golden-spired temple. I ask him in Thai to please take me to the *luuk wah* tree so I can remember what the African tree looked like. Unfazed by this total stranger with a most unusual request, he motions me to follow him.

I don't know if he has understood me, but he leads me down to a water tank shrouded in trees. I follow him as he climbs onto a metal ladder leading to the flat top. Leaning over the tank is a huge branch covered in clusters of *jambura*. Most of them are pink and green, not yet fully ripe. He motions to me to take as many as I want. I break off a few ripe ones and share them with him as we sit on the concrete tank. I recount the childhood games I used to play in this same tree in Africa. He smiles and, talking for the first time, tells me that the English word for *luuk wah* is "mulberry." I am astonished. I begin to tell him more about Uganda, but I hear John honking his horn at the temple entrance.

As we part, the monk tells me in a soft tone, "Right behind the Mae Rim Temple, there is a big *luuk wah* tree that has many more ripe ones."

I *wai* him my thanks and get back in the Land Rover for the drive home.

The seeds of my African childhood are quietly bearing fruit in the jungles of Thailand.

✺ ✺ ✺

Mohezin Tejani is a global Muslim gypsy who has been roaming the world for over four decades now. Exiled from Uganda during Idi Amin's reign of terror in the 1970s, he was suddenly left homeless, with little sense of his own cultural identity. He spent the next forty years traveling through five continents, working with the poor. He has taught world literature in Uganda, Canada, the United States, Thailand, Guatemala, and Ecuador. The first of his three-volume travel memoirs, A Chameleon's Tale: True Stories of a Global Refugee, *was a 2007 New York P.E.N. Book Award finalist. The India edition, re-titled* Thank You, Idi Amin, *is soon to be published. Tejani has been called a "cross-cultural Kerouac," and Tim Cahill says that reading his stories "is like eating popcorn: you can't stop devouring them." Visit his website at www.motejani.com.*

AMY GREIMANN CARLSON

☙ ☙ ☙

Inside Kumano Kodo

*Isn't it time that your drifting was
consecrated into pilgrimage?*
— Alan Jones

THE ROAD FOR THIS PILGRIM HAS BEEN LEADING
nowhere but down for quite some time. I drift in
uncertainty. It has been a treacherous year full of hard edges.
Cancer has taken parts of me, chips away at my father's insides,
and threatens my brother. The family finances spiral forever
downward and worry consumes. I desperately need to recover
more than passion. I need to rediscover infinity, and scream a
Holy Yes that reverberates through my pores and pushes me
over the edge into the world of poetic traveling—longing to
see within the ordinary, everyday mud and muck, poems and
stories sacred to the core; to live awake; to recover, to reconnect, to respond, to rejoice with each breath I take…over and
over and over again…despite the depth of the darkness.

So, when I receive the call inviting me to walk the Kumano Kodo, an ancient pilgrimage route into the heart of Japan, I dash to my closet's abyss and dig for my bag. Buried in a box, I pull out my REI duffel, consecrating myself in closet dust; pilgrim I become. This journey will take me home to a culture coursing through my life since my early twenties when I taught English in Nagoya.

THE CAVE

> *we disappear in*
> *tunnels dark, through mountains deep*
> *camellias kiss sky*

All paths lead to the sacred center of the Kumano Kodo—the Hongu Taisha Shrine. We will end up there after our two-day walk through the *yamanami,* mountain waves, of the Kii Peninsula. Through cedar forest and deserted rice paddy, down intricate stone steps under dense canopy, through small villages etched into steep terraces, we will walk this vertical world full of legend and history.

My pilgrimage begins today with renewal, with a birth into the Land of the Spirits, also known as the Land of the Dead. This is the start of the Kumano Kodo. I am on the "Way," following a thousand years of pilgrims trampling toward Enlightenment. This ancient road, first walked on by emperors, embodies the heart and soul of Japan.

We enter Kumano through the torii gate of Takijiri-Oji, a place of rebirth. We climb up and over roots and stones oozing with antiquity, under giant Japanese cedars wrapped in the mystery of age, to a rock cave where many have gone before in search of this elusive Enlightenment. I am just one more seeker, spiritual in a skeptical way.

But for what am I searching? After a hellish year of cancer gymnastics, I come here for healing; for acceptance of my impermanence; to dance with my immortality. This is a perfect culture in which to immerse myself for such a journey, a culture in which impermanence and the passage of time are revered and seen as beauty in the ancient weave of generations. All is impermanent, even solid rock. Through wind and water, time leaves its mark on stone. It is here, in this seemingly forever cave, that we begin practicing refreshment, recovery, renewal, recollection, rebirth.

Brad, my traveling companion and Canadian guide who is more Japanese than the Japanese, removes his pack and heads into the cave first. He disappears. Suddenly I am alone except for the sound of scraping. I soon hear a muffled voice: "Take off your pack, come in and pass up the bags." So off goes my camera, off goes my jacket, off goes my pack, and in I crawl, dragging all of this stuff behind me through the dirt. Inside, darkness slaps me with a terrifying hand. The air ceases. Breath leaves me. "It is cancer," slams into me off the rock from all directions, echoing from months passed. Panic rises. Suddenly, light washes down over a rock above me and hits my face. The way up and out. A deep sigh escapes.

Turning within tight quarters, I scrape my hand. *Is this enlightenment? In the dark? In the dirt, groveling on my stomach? Crashing my head against rocks?* A hand reaches down from the hole above me, a small hole, a *very* small thin hole. *I'm supposed to go through that? Is this how a fetus feels on the way down the birth canal?* Stretching up as far as I can reach, I pass our bags up through the hole one at a time and then it's my turn. On my stomach, I begin my ascent, inching along the rock face smoothed by many centuries of belly wriggling. First my head pops into the light. A cold breeze takes my breath away. I'm alive! Breastless, but alive! Hallelujah.

My elation seeps back into the cave as I realize I'm not fully out yet. You're never really out yet when you have joined the cancer club. "I hope my hips will squeeze through this," I groan to Brad who perches outside, camera clicking. Using my arms, I wriggle my torso through the hole, pelvic bones rubbing on rock. I scream, triumphant. With knees dirtied, hands scraped, hips bruised, I slide upward into the Land of the Kumano Kodo Spirits, the land of welcome. The journey begins.

THE KITE

wings outstretched in blue
a kite circles overhead
deep wrinkles laughing

Up we walk through a small burg surrounded by rice pad-dies, *mikan* orange trees, and tea bushes—all on terraces. Stopping at a help-yourself roadside stand, I buy some *mi-kans* and organic *ocha* green tea, dropping 500 yen into a pay box. Frost still lines the contours of the nearby tea leaves. A denuded persimmon tree stands alone with a few withered fruit left hanging. I stand soaking in the morning sun, glad for the warmth on this wintry day. It has been snowing lightly all morning.

Good to be out of the woods for a while. Brad agrees. We meander within the gentle hum of human activity, over a hill to a pass overlooking our final destination, the first of the big three—the Hongu Taisha Shrine. Down below, Japan's largest torii shrine gate marks the original site of the famous shrine grounds, flooded out and destroyed in the late nineteenth century. Still holy land, pilgrims walk the Kumano Kodo back up the hill to the "new" site, safe from the Kumano River.

We pause at the pass to feel the *yamanami*, mountain waves, rolling off into the distance. A single stone on the pass memorializes the life of the female poet, Izumi Shikibu, who walked all this way a thousand years ago, only to see her destination unattainable as she began her monthly cycle. Now impure due to her bleeding, she was forbidden to enter the shrine. She sat right in this very spot and wrote a poem of her deep sadness. But a Kumano deity came to her in a vision and told her that all are welcome in the Kumano Kodo, the heart of Japan, no matter in what condition. She was invited to complete her journey. Rejoicing, she rose and descended into the valley.

Since my ovaries got yanked prematurely, thanks to the cancer, I don't have the blood obstacle, but I definitely have a condition that warrants a sad poem if I let self-pity in. But today I only let in a bit of disbelief over my last year, and feel quite skeptical and unspiritual about these legends swirling 'round.

I take my skeptical self and join Brad for our walk down into the shrine. Two old farmers, lounging in the sun in their *mikan* orchard, corral us, just waiting for walkers like us to tarry at the rest stop nearby. Seeing my need to wash my hands, sticky from the *mikan* I just devoured, one of the farmers offers his well water. A wizened gent, skin darkened and wrinkled from years outside, he turns on the tap. He insists on my drinking some as well—fresh mountain well water, cool and delicious. I splash some on my face and squeal with the cold. He's delighted. I'm refreshed.

Anxious to keep moving, I thank him and begin putting on my pack. But again, he insists that we see the view from above his orchard on the hill. Brad and I exchange a "we need to get going" glance. But with a raised eyebrow or two, we silently agree to leave *chronos* time behind again, for is this not what pilgrimage is all about? We drop our bags and our anxiety about achieving our goal for the day and follow him. Rewarded by a nearly 360-degree view of the disappearing *yamanami*, we share a sweet juicy *mikan* freshly picked off a nearby tree. Suddenly, a large bird, a "kite" *tonbi*, soars over our heads. The old farmer laughs, the wrinkles around his eyes crinkling as he says, "Even if you have no money, you can always have a bit of fun." He grabs onto an imaginary kite string attached to the bird and begins to fly the bird. Out over his orchard it flies, then he pulls his string back around over his head, and here comes the *tonbi*, circling back above our heads. Did he know the play on the word "kite?" Did he know how much I worry about money? He knows no English and he certainly doesn't know me and yet, mysteriously, the moment gives me a gift, a message of grace, internalized forever.

I begin to realize that this pilgrimage in Kumano Kodo, designated as a World Heritage Site, classified as a cultural landscape—where people and nature meet—truly mixes the power of people and the power of nature into a mysterious, potent elixir of health. I am refreshed from the mountain water. I am refreshed by the mountain farmer. I am refreshed by the kite that flies above my head. I am thankful.

THE TREE

> *from inside the trunk*
> *deep tree energy rises*
> *breathing in cedar*

It is cold and snowy today. We huddle behind a shelter high up on a ridge watching the snow zoom uphill on gusts of air as we eat our sushi *obento* in haste! I want mittens, NOW! Chopsticks in cold fingers don't work well. It is freezing up here! Pilgrims of old used to purify themselves in the cold Kumano River during an enlightenment process. Brad muses that perhaps the snow and the cold act as our purification for the day. We are more than prepared—wind pants, heater packs, hiking boots, thermos—no straw sandals like pilgrims of old. Actually, the blasts revitalize my pink-cheeked Scandinavian soul and get my blood moving.

Back down into the trees we walk, relief for a time. Slippery footing slows us down, but it feels timeless here. We float in *kairos*, a Greek notion of being outside time. Goals become phantoms. Worries evaporate. There is only wind and snow and tree and path. We both breathe from our toes. Our shoulders drift down like cats puddling in the sun.

But once again, into human activity we trudge, a bit tired from the verticalness of it all. This time we pass an old tea house that, tomorrow, will be rewarded with a new thatched roof and will once again invite pilgrims to rest their weary feet and revive their flagging spirits with a cup of steaming *ocha* green tea. But today, its roof needs repair and its paper doors have holes, so we pass on by to another shrine along the way—Tsugizakura Oji—where we suddenly descend *up* a long stone staircase into the holy presence of deep tree energy. Hobbits would be happy here. I am happy here.

I look up and up and up into the branches of an 800-year-old Japanese cedar with thick branches reaching south, all of them. Oddly wonderful, this particular species is called *ippo sugi* and grow arms only on its side facing another holy shrine of the big three, Nachi Taisha, the shrine of the holy waterfall. Is this coincidence or divine design or the cunning technique of a good arborist?

I put my ear to its rough bark and listen for sap rising. Is it my imagination or can I feel the energy of this alive entity emanating, touching me? I close my eyes and commune. Clock time stops and again I float into *kairos*. My heart beats strong. My palms feel enlivened under the bark. I can now believe Tolkien's talking trees. I slowly back away, craning my neck to see if I can see the top—out of sight. Suddenly, to my delight, I spy a hole in its trunk down alongside the stairs. Without hesitation and to Brad's dismay and delight, I take off my pack and climb down and in.

Unlike the cave's cold rock, the tree's insides calm me, warm and quiet. The hole leads me into a cavern where I can stand. I look up and see a bit of sky. I am standing inside this 800-year-old tree and feel protected, safe. I am in its heart. Closing my eyes, I breathe cedar, reaching out with palms, touching wood, touching old, feeling the power of nature;

the power of a living being who will be here long after I am
gone and who was here long before—the passage of time per-
sonified in living matter. It calms. It gives perspective. It gives
infinity. Rooted, I long to stay here, but like all of life, impermanence crashes in and the moment is over. Brad coaxes me
back out into the light and the cold—rebirthed again. Back
to journey ever onward, I sigh in the moment and walk back
down the stone steps to the path.

THE BATH

> *morning light bathes as*
> *steam rises through chilly air*
> *yellow plum blossom*

Steam rises like wraiths off the river rushing beside us. Our
tired feet bring us into the town of Yunomine Onsen just as
the shadows begin to gobble the light. Arriving at Adumaya,
an inn or *ryokan* which has been in the family for sixteen
generations, we are greeted by a graceful kimono-wrapped
woman who gently bids us follow her into the land of hospitality.

> Make a delicious bowl of tea, lay the charcoal so that it
> heats the water; arrange the flowers as they are in the
> field; in summer suggest coolness; in winter, warmth;
> do everything ahead of time; prepare for rain; and give
> those with whom you find yourself every consideration.
> —Soshitsu Sen, Master of Tea Ceremony

Living by this essence of Japanese codes, our hostess gathers us up and sweeps us quietly into our rooms. The slippers
come off in honor and care of the tatami floor. Our sock
feet sigh with relief as we step onto the luxurious spring of
the grass mat. Sitting on *zabuton* cushions on the floor, I am
close to the mat and get a waft of freshly mown field, a fresh,
natural dried grass smell that calms the spirit. My eyes close

and I breathe in deeply. Let me live in the smell of tatami, out of time, in peace and tranquility, away from the march of my culture's crazy-making demands of busyness.

A knock, a slide of a paper door, and our hostess arrives kneeling with some steaming green tea. The hot liquid warms not only the weary body, but the restless spirit. Sipping, I smile as I know what comes next—the bath before dinner.

With no central heating in a drafty antiquated building with paper doors, the bath becomes ever more necessary and inviting. I change into a *yukata* cotton robe and slip into the padded jacket that accompanies it. Stepping off the tatami back into my slippers, I reach for a towel and head back down the stairs and down the hall to the *onsen* bath where Brad waits pointing to the women's side.

A warmly lit entrance with a red door hanging invites me in. I slide another door, this time wooden with glass, and step into a changing room. Off go the clothes into a locker. It is cold in here and I feel shy of my scars for the first time, so I hold a small hand towel to my chest. I don't want to freak anyone out. Already to be bathing with a foreigner is novel enough. I slide yet another door and step into another world, a steamy sensory paradise—the sound of running water; the faint smell of sulfur and wet wood; the feel of steam beading on the face; the clunk of shampoo bottles being set down. I sit on a small bamboo stool on the floor. Here, I am to thoroughly scrub myself from top to bottom. I watch what others do and follow their lead. They smile and gently instruct when I fumble. Which is the shampoo? How do I turn on the hot water? Where do I put the bucket after I'm done?

After this complicated matter of cleaning, it is time to immerse; the moment I have been waiting for since the last few miles. I walk out into the outdoor sanctuary of this hot spring bath. I sit on the side and dare a toe before risking my whole body. These baths are known to be hot on this volcanic island. It is dark now, and steam rises from the pool up through the light of a lantern. An arm of an asymmetrical pine, held up by a thick bamboo pole, reaches out and over my head. I slide into dark, wet warmth, a "hush profound" swirls into my body. A sigh escapes. The tension in my sore calves from thirteen miles of walking begins to melt away. I close my eyes and remember, reconnect with the 800-year-old tree energy—the sap coursing through my veins. I am the tree. I am the water.

I am hungry. My rumbling stomach snaps me out of my oneness with nature. I suddenly realize that my awareness of time has once again returned and dinner beckons. Reluctantly, I ease my bright pink body out of the pool, the towel still to my chest, and head for the changing room. I dry quickly and don the *yukata* for my trip back to the room. As I slide the door open, a blast of cold air urges me to hastily shuffle back to my quarters where Brad, my now-pink, *yukata*-clad companion, downs an Asahi beer.

We sit on *zabuton*, our feet under a warm *kotatsu*, a low-blanketed table with heat underneath. Soon dinner arrives in waves of small courses artistically placed in small dishes—an infinite variety of fish, and fish parts, prepared in every form imaginable—filleted, whole, diced, raw, boiled, raw, wrapped, raw, fried, raw...I stop asking and just revel in the subtlety of flavors and colors passing by my tongue. Our hostess proudly announces that everything that is cooked is done so in the hot spring water of this famous *onsen* town known for its healing waters. Emperors and peasants alike have stayed here to gain rejuvenation from the water.

Tomorrow morning at 7:00, I have reservations to get purified in the most special of baths—Tsuboyu—a bath with so much history and legend that it has made the World Heritage roster as one of the only baths in the world of its kind. Seven hundred and fifty yen buys a half-hour of solo bathing in these healing waters.

My watch alarm gently jingles me awake at 6:30 A.M. I sleepily dress and head out into the early morning sun just touching the tops of the surrounding vertical hills. Frost still clings white to the tile roofs. Crossing the river to the old wooden pay booth, the bubbling steam wraps me in its blanket of moisture. I breathe deeply the sulfured air. The old gentleman in the warmly lit booth knows I am coming, the *gaijin* writer. He bows. I bow. We exchange morning pleasantries, a bit of yen, and off I descend into the legend of Tsuboyu and the story of Ogurihangan and Terute, the Romeo and Juliet of Japan.

Ogurihangan and Terute married against their families' wishes. Her family sent a spirited horse as a "gift" to Ogurihangan, hoping it would throw and kill him, but he tamed it. Foiled, they invited him to dinner and poisoned him. He died and descended to the land of the dead. A powerful judge reviewed Ogurihangan's misdeed of marrying against the family wish and decided that the family's misdeed of murdering him was a far greater offense, and sent him back to the land of the living, but with a slap on the wrist. The judge returned Oguri deformed and blind. Around his neck, the judge placed a sign that read, "If you help this man to get to Yunomine Onsen, he will be healed." A monk found Oguri by the side of the road and added a sign that read, "Anyone who helps this man along his journey to Yunomine Onsen will gain a thousand karmic prayers of power." People began carrying him across Japan to Kumano's Yunomine Onsen. His beloved wife, having been thrown into the river by her family and sold downstream into slavery, even helped to carry him, though they did not recognize each other. He finally arrived at the *onsen* and bathed in a pool, now known as Tsuboyu, and was completely healed. He returned to his aristocratic family who gave him land to oversee. And, of course, that happened to be where Terute lived as a slave. They saw each other, reunited, and lived happily ever after.

It is into this stone bath I go swirling with Kumano Kodo themes—healing; traveling arduously, gaining merit along the way; accepting everyone no matter their condition; connecting to the underworld, the power of nature, rebirth. This is quite the responsibility I am given in this next half-hour! I walk down cold stone steps to an old weathered door which creaks as I open it and descend even more steps into a womb-like rock-surround.

Steam rises from cloudy, thick water bubbling in a small pool in the corner. Warned that it would be scalding from the hot spring waters rising up right there beneath the stones under foot, I open the cold tap wide while I undress. I tiptoe across the cold rock to the one-person pool trying to wrap my imagination around the long healing history of this water. God knows I need the healing after the year that I've had. Gingerly, the toes go in, the calves, the hips. I sink up to my shoulders in the thick mineral water. A sigh of the hush profound yet again escapes my lips. The eyes close as I wave warm water toward my chest. It feels like silk being drawn across my body ever so slowly, caressing, fluttering over my scars. Deeply the breath draws in. I am alive. Hallelujah! *Ichi go ichi e*—once in a lifetime chance—beauty lies in a fleeting moment which passes quickly. Live fully. Melancholy beauty seeps into my pores. I sink deeper into the pool, wanting to stay, but in thinking so, the moment leaves as I try to hold on to it. My eyes pop open, almost on cue, and focus directly on the big clock on the wall—back in *chronos*. Damn. It is already time to get out.

Am I healed? Time will tell. Am I relaxed? Definitely! Back into the cold and light, I have once again experienced the gift of Japan—restored and revitalized to continue the journey.

THE PRIEST

> *a secret smile spreads*
> *on a kneeling green-robed priest*
> *a camellia blooms*

Through this vertical world we walk—

Up through primeval forest, monkeys hiding in the trees,

Down through reforested rice paddies where wild boars dig in the earth,

Up and over roots of ancient stands,

Down stone paths beneath dense canopies of farmed trees, a red pheasant explodes out of the woods,

Down through deserted remnants of villages long gone,

Up by a woodworking shop whose owner feeds us sweet dried persimmons,

Down past a woodcarver who sells cedar walking sticks to pilgrims on their way by,

Up into a bamboo grove on the way to the top of a blustery ridge where we huddle behind a shelter to eat our *onigiri* rice balls,

Down we plunge into an *onsen* hot spring town and walk the street.

The variety of terrain and experience given to us on this ancient path is pure gift; the stories, rich—a *fukai* deep place full of *shinpiteki* mystical beginnings.

It's almost dark. Snow has slowed us down, the footing treacherous on wet mossy stones. The *hiza warau* knees laugh and the feet cry from all-day maneuvering in a vertical landscape. We agree that it is time to bail and hitch a ride into town with a maintenance man going home for the night. There's a feeling of sadness that pervades, like the female poet who was almost there and wrote a poem about her disappointment. But this journey is not about completion, it is about the Way, the process, the refilling of the heart, and we certainly have done that today. So I let go and enjoy the chance to sit in a warm van as we snake down the hill to our inn, arriving in hospitality's embrace.

The morning brings sun, a new chance, and a ride back up the mountain to the point where we stopped last night.

With refreshed knees and spirits, Brad and I head down into this holy center of Japan. A young Shinto priest greets us as we walk into the grounds filled with sculpted trees, plain wooden buildings, statues of three-legged crows and lion-type growlers, praying pilgrims dressed in white, amulet booths, giant rice-straw braids, and torii gates with their inverted arches, stones under foot, moss immaculately kept even in January, and an office full of quiet people dressed in robes busily taking care of the business of running a shrine. The priest has been waiting for our arrival and leads us into the office to register us for purification.

Today we get purified, for we have been walking in the land of the dead, and it is here that we will be reborn. I thought we already had done rebirthing through the cave, but more than once can't hurt. Do I believe this? Not really, but does that matter? I feel American today, from a young country unable to fathom the depth of antiquity surrounding this place. Thousand-year-old paths. Ancient ritual passed down through generations beyond count.

Who am I to be standing here, from a Lutheran Protestant weave, about to enter this place of Shinto worship? Far too simply put, Shintoism, translated, "the way of the Gods," is used in the everyday to pray for good grades, healthy kids, a prosperous fishing season…used for life cycle events such as marriages, coming-of-age celebrations, harvests…. And deifies the power of nature, worshiped in waterfalls, rocks, trees…. And here I am a believer of Christ's Way, full of grace and forgiveness.

I squirm a bit while waiting for Brad to register us. I resonate with the power of nature, that I understand, but a shrine for toothaches, a shrine for heartaches, a shrine for headaches—this I do not understand. It feels superstitious. The young priest, in a hushed calm, begins to explain to us the process. He stands there, dark eyes, soft lilting voice like *seseragi*, the sound of a creek, dressed in an immaculate white robe over which lies a poncho of bright green gauze. On his head sits a coffee bean, a strangely stiff, black-woven vertical hat that has a chinstrap that moves as he speaks softly. It seems I need to choose from a laminated vertical menu of prayers written in *kanji*, Chinese characters—a prayer specifically for me for which he will pray for 5,000 yen. I choose "family health." He bows, accepts the money, and leads us into the sanctuary of the main worship building.

Two Japanese pilgrims accompany us on this journey. Handing us white cotton jackets, he asks us to put them on to become clean and pure. We sit on *zabuton* cushions on the cold, red-carpeted floor. Brad hangs back to take pictures. The priest steps up to the altar area to a large *taiko* drum, kneels, and begins a chant in a deep melodic voice. He then begins a drumming sequence that fills our bodies with vibration, especially in the chest cavity. With crescendos, we wake. With decrescendos, our hearts grow still. He captures all of us with the rhythm. I could live in the beat all day. This I can do. This I understand.

Suddenly, he stops, bows, stands, and lifts a *gohei* from a holder, a stick on which hang bright-white lightning bolts of paper that represent the gods. He moves toward us and shakes this paper over our heads, chanting all the while. He asks us to bow twice and clap twice. I half-heartedly bow my head and skip the clapping as I still feel uncomfortable, though wanting to be respectful.

With precise sliding steps, as in tea ceremony, he moves to the plain wooden altar in the center of the room where he sits on a square of tatami facing the offerings of salt, rice, water, and fish. This time, he begins to chant not by heart, but from a scroll with specifics—our names, the date, the time, and the prayer we requested from the menu. He periodically asks us to bow. I bow my head thinking of Jesus.

The waft of fresh tatami greets my senses and brings instant calm. I love that smell. It transports me back to my first time living in this country. A cold breeze passes through the room as there is only a curtain of white gauze hanging behind the altar between us and the outside to obscure the objects of worship—three buildings in which the Kumano Deities reside. Down the step behind us is also wide open to the outside where other pilgrims come to pray, pulling on a large rope with a bell attached then bowing and clapping twice. It's distracting.

But the priest is on the move again to yet another pole to the right of the altar. This time, hanging, are long lines of golden metal tabs with bells attached to the bottom of each. He once again rattles this holy contraption over our heads, chanting all the while. It rattles me. I prefer the quiet swoosh of the paper gods. We bow. It is over.

And here comes the hospitality. Brad and I are immediately invited to a side table behind which sits a robed woman offering shallow bowls of *ume* plum wine to sip after our long journey to rebirth. The young priest comes over to speak with us. I, for some reason, tell him of my need to bring Jesus in with me for my comfort. He responds, "Shintoism is open and free. Be what you are. Christian? Be Christian. Muslim? Be Muslim. All are welcome." This is the spirit of Kumano. Banners flutter in the icy wind with a vertical word, *yomigaeru*, which means, "return from the mythical land of the dead."

Now, do I feel purified and reborn? Perhaps many times over on this trip so far. I'm reborn every day for that matter. Why so cynical?

It's a synchronistic place. After we are purified in the Shinto ceremony, we head to the Buddhist Temple at Nachi Taisha, the third of the big three, to spend the night at the temple's lodging house overlooking the holy Shinto waterfall of Nachi. We are met in the parking lot by a smiling Buddhist priest with mischief twinkling in his eyes and a Dalai Lama calm. We are late for our appointment. He lets Brad know and walks us to our lodging. Tomorrow morning we will wake at 4:30 A.M. to attend a sutra chanting service the priests perform twice daily.

Over yet another elegant meal of *sakananami*, my term for "waves of fish," knowledgeable Brad tries to explain the difference between Shintoism and Buddhism, so intermingled here in this land that it is hard to separate them, although it has certainly been tried. I'm going to try, again, oversimplified. Unlike Shintoism, which deals with the everyday of the living, Buddhism, Japanese-style, takes care of the dead ancestors, the afterworld, and stores up karmic power to aid the dying and dead on their journey across the river to the other side.

Within Japanese Buddhism, there are many schools, one of which is called Shugendo that believes in the power of nature to reach enlightenment. Shinto fusion swirls. Through a ten-step process, these special *yamabushi*, mountain ascetics, move to enlightenment from the base to Buddha by training arduously in the rugged mountains, chanting, *"sange sange rokon shojo"*—look back upon yourself, repent, confess, be one with nature and feel its power, get rid of past lives and go deeply into the purity of all six senses.

A practicing *yamabushi*, the smiling priest who met us in the parking lot last night, sits in a frigid waterfall every January to meditate for forty minutes before he continues his maniacal mountain training in straw sandals. Does he leave his body for a zone beyond? Beyond my comprehension, certainly! And *I* wince at getting up at 4:30 to sit in a freezing cold temple to hear chanting I don't understand. But I do understand a couple of things—the power of a chanting voice, regardless of the words, to reach deep down and bring the listener to her knees, and the sense that this Cheshire Cat ascetic smiles with light shining from his lips and a secret teasing in his eyes. He knows something. He has been in touch with a force I cannot even imagine. He tells me that to become an enlightened person, *hokote ni naru*, we must lose our egos. "Humans," he continues, "have huge egos and impurities caused by desires and needs. The whole idea of the enlighten-ment process is to erase the needs and desires, hence the ego. When we are born, we all are the same, but as we grow, the chains of ego pull us down. We need to train ourselves to turn in the right direction away from the ego. We are all of one mind in this universal longing to turn." He smiles, bows, bids us bring peace to the world, and walks briskly away to attend to his priestly duties for the day.

I turn to look off into the hills beyond. What to make of all this? Kumano. Pilgrimage. What did I come here for, besides responding to an invitation? How does all this relate to my Western spirit's yearnings for Emerson's notion of an *under-song*, Basho's idea of an *underglimmer*, Anne Lamott's *rhythm and blues*, and William Stafford's belief in a river running beneath all of life, a river full of something much larger than all of us that we *can* access? Must we sit under waterfalls and deny our physical body to do so? I wonder if the *yamabushi* rises above it all and truly turns away from his ego? Does he do so only in the extreme of the frigid water? Is that accepting self or trying to eradicate self?

I hope to embrace Kumano, to come to terms with my mortality, to become more heart and less head, to move be-yond the stuckness of me, to be turned in the right direction away from the ego, to head towards the light, to become more enlightened, at least a millimeter closer...but I still feel like the woman who has had cancer and who worries about money until she's paralyzed; still the woman who agonizes, who feels tired and disappointed. Is this the lesson? We are who we are. Accept and transcend. All are welcome in Kumano no matter the condition of body or spirit. There's neither Jew nor Greek, male nor female. I came with yearn-ings. I leave with yearnings unanswered, ever-present. By the grace of God, may I have the wisdom to let it be as it is and move beyond, accepting the now and the here with more than just resignation. In the Kumano spirit, let me turn in the right direction toward mythical rebirth and move down into the river of renewed life, celebrating in the flow.

~≈ ~≈ ~≈

Amy Greimann Carlson wears a silver ear cuff with a dangly and eats grilled Hummel's hotdogs from New Haven. When she's not reading Basho or pilgrimaging in Japan, she is teaching children the power of words—Avra Kedavra. On occasion, she dabbles with the adult right brain in writing workshops around the Pacific Northwest. She is coeditor of Travelers Tales' Japan *and has also written for or edited other anthologies in the award-winning series:* A Woman's Path, The Gift of Birds, Travelers' Tales Australia, *and* A Woman's Asia. *Her writing has also appeared in the online magazine,* Perceptive Travel. *She lives in the Cascade Mountains with her husband and rabbit.*

MARIANNE ROGOFF

～ ～ ～

12 Hours in Barcelona

A little time is more than you think.

THE FLIGHT FROM PALMA, MALLORCA, SPAIN, TO San Francisco, California, included a long layover in the city of Gaudi. I landed in Barcelona at 6 P.M. and would be on another plane from the same airport at dawn. I could easily have killed time at the huge airport: shopped, ate, read, slept in uncomfortable chairs. I considered dropping some euros on a hotel in town. But why kill time, when time is all I have? I place my luggage in a large airport locker and get on a bus to the center of the city. No plan, except to see where in the world I am tonight.

I've been to big cities: New York, Los Angeles, London, Paris, Mexico DF. Barcelona, too, is huge, a sprawl, with miles of concrete and uncountable numbers of people. Twelve hours seemed like a really long time and now I see it is a single half-moon on the face of the ever-cycling clock of eternity. No amount of time could be enough to absorb what is here: true of any lifetime, in any place: never enough time.

But I try.

I see right away that I will not be able to cover much ground on foot. The blocks are long, the buildings loom, imposing shadows and blocked views. The double-decker red city tour bus pulls into line at the downtown square and I become exactly what I am: a tourist here.

I step up with the others and pay the price for a guided drive through the city on the open-air upper level of the bus. Three beautiful young British men help me with the headphones and point out where we are on the map: a dot inside interlocking circles. They have tour-bus passes that allow them to step on and off buses for three full days: stay, linger, view, walk, hop back on elsewhere, return each day for more. I will not be here long enough to make full use of my one-day pass, just long enough to take full advantage during this fortuitous, out-of-time interlude in Spain.

Dusk in Barcelona. September. The air is perfect. I am dressed just right with a light sweater. And I am alone in the world.

Mallorca, too, was an interlude. Yachting around the island, six of us, three couples. I was part of that, coupled for a week. I kept the captain happy, I smiled, was pretty; we bantered, took off our clothes, got drunk, made love in the V berth. Separate people, together at times, otherwise on our own. A loose arrangement, desirable for those who've been burned by love, still paying for the last arrangement, smarting, on guard; meeting new mates, we proceed without commitments, with caution, so the heart won't break again if this, too, should end. Don't all relationships end? All lives end. We pass through, touch down, connect for a moment, move on, leave so much behind. And it matters so little? Our little cracked hearts, in the grand scope of things. Big Barcelona makes that obvious. Hundreds of couples, fighting and kissing, children now teenagers, all the lonely people (like the Beatles said), where do we all come from?

The coupling was good (they have all been good while they lasted), but I had to get back to California, to teaching. I'd already played enough hooky at the start of the new school year. My guy was staying on, renting a Ducati and motorcycling through the Pyrenees for another week. I was invited to join him for that as well. But there was school. And I also knew he'd be happier alone on his bike in the landscape. He is happiest alone. I understood that; it's not something about him that could be changed. I had my week, we kissed goodbye at the yacht harbor, and I left any feelings of wanting more from him there. Is this true about myself as well? Am I happiest alone?

The dusky light gives way to streetlights on the gaudy Gaudi structures erected incomprehensibly in the middle of, next to, juxtaposed with, the surrounding architecture that looks nothing alike. Where were the city planners when this city was built? Barcelona is a wild amalgamation of architectural styles, shapes, heights, and colors. I breathe it in, adjust my eyes to the shifting twilight, move the tiny headphone buds deeper into my ears to learn the history, where to focus my eyes and thoughts, as we pass along through this chaos of sights-to-see.

I hear bits and pieces:

The Olympics were here in _____.

There is the Jewish Hill....

The _____ Museum, _____ Library, _____ Theatre.

In the giant downtown gazebo, are those Russian ballerinas pirouetting?

A series of color-lighted fountains are spewing in sequence to a Bartok symphony!

Now, fireworks explode into skies between buildings.

Hundreds, no *thousands*, of people are out walking the streets.

Wow, Barcelona! It is ALIVE! Is every night like this?

No, of course not. I happen to have a twelve-hour layover in Barcelona on a festival occasion, a night when free ballets and symphonies and theatrical performances are taking place all over town, lending a glow, heightening our pleasure, focusing the eye out of the chaos of so-much-to-see into the framework of the arts: dance, music, language. Over there, young spoken-word poets are rapping hip-hop beats; here, it's Shakespeare in Spanish; now, a celebratory speech; in my ear, the stories of Barcelona's past and future. I see it all from my perch atop this slow-moving red bus.

Having circled one loop of city highlights, I step off the bus and enter the strolling crowd of pedestrians on La Rambla. On any night of the year, I had heard, what you do most especially in Barcelona is walk La Rambla with its outdoor cafés, restaurants, shops, and galleries. It is nighttime now and I am alone in the teeming city, fearless. *What makes me have no fear?* I believe that the worst things I could have imagined when I was a young and fearful woman have already happened: rape, robberies, death of my baby girl, death of my marriage to Dearly Beloved, death of myths of how life is supposed to be. There's no such thing as supposed-to-be! I know this now. There is only HOW IT IS and (like Barcelona) life is like this: chaotic, unpredictable, dynamic. And, it is also orderly (like symphonies and ballets), predictable (there will always be hundreds of pedestrians walking La Rambla), and energized (life is forceful, changeable). I have changed. Never thought I'd feel this kind of free joy again, this loose/liberated ability to couple and part, this independent willingness to enter the stream of strangers, one of them.

Near midnight I find a pleasing restaurant—a clean, well-lighted place, with soft lighting and more people than you'd think would be still out dining at midnight (unlike at home, in the bedroom community of early commuters and high achievers, where everyone is ready for bed by 10 P.M. or earlier).

I ask for red wine and a bowl of soup. The bread arrives with the wine and I serve myself Holy Communion, redeemed of sins, penance over, at the center of heaven. I am the mother of a happy, healthy grown son; I love my job; I am a free spirit.

I chat with a Dutch man dining alone at the next table. He's living here for a month, studying Spanish and art.

"How long are you here for?" he asks.

"Twelve hours. And it's half-over."

Half over, like life? Not over yet!

❧ ❧ ❧

Marianne Rogoff's "Alive in Lisbon" appeared in The Best Women's Travel Writing 2008. *Her story "Raven" was selected for* The Best Travel Writing 2006. *She has published the memoir* Silvie's Life, *along with numerous stories, essays, and book reviews, and teaches Writing and Literature at California College of the Arts.*

❦ ❦ ❦

Frenzy and Ecstasy

On a Greek island, the author explores
the legacy of Dionysus.

Through the forests that overhang the sea, the
Maenads madly rushed. Maskale of the fiery
breasts, howling, brandished the sycamore phallos,
smeared with red.
All leaped and ran and cried aloud beneath
their robes and crowns of twisted vine, crotals
clacking in their hands, and thyrses splitting the
bursting skins of echoing dulcimers.
With sopping hair and agile limbs, breasts
reddened and tossed about, sweat of cheeks and
foam of lips, oh, Dionysus! they offered in return
the love that you had poured in them.
And the sea-wind tossed Heliokomis' russet
hair unto the sky, and whipped it into a furious
flame on her body's white-wax torch.

—from "The Maenads" by Pierre Louys

F ROM THE BUS DEPOT ON SKYROS, I COULD HEAR THE
din of bells, hundreds of them clanging and clashing,
echoing through the narrow streets. The old woman, my
hostess for the week, recognized me by the green rucksack
I had said I would be carrying. She grabbed my arm tightly
as I disembarked and led me up the hillside into the thick of
it. Lights blazed in the night along the main section of town
where a crowd pressed in a thick circle around the source of
the noise and excitement—the Geri, the Geri were out, and
dancing! I pushed through to a group of great hulking beasts,
upright, humpbacked, black hooded, their coats shaggy and
dark. Their mottled faces seemed to stretch and dangle down
to their chests with nothing but black holes for eyes—a mask
made with the fresh hide of an aborted goat fetus. You could
smell the stink of them. Their waists bristled with rings of
brass goat bells, some as big as tea kettles, with twenty, thirty,
forty bells on cords wound round each dancer. As the Geri
thrashed their hips back and forth, the bells rang out like
three hundred fire alarms gone berserk, deafening, and yet the
swinging of the hips gave the bells a certain hypnotic rhythm,
catching the Geri and the spectators in a trance. The brass
flashed in the bright streetlights, black against the night, as if
the dancers themselves were throwing off sparks.

I stood transfixed. After sifting through so many ancient
artifacts and ruins, so many myths and books, here was something older than I could possibly imagine, yet alive, powerful,
dancing in the streets. I had read that this festival was a relic
of Dionysus's rites, the ecstasy of his followers, the man-beast
satyrs and the wild maenads, when the god possessed them
and filled them with divine madness. Was this it, the spirit
of something so old it had all but passed from the world?
One of Dionysus's many names was Melanaigis, "he with the
black goatskin," and in the myth about him, he appeared to
the daughters of Eleuther as an apparition dressed in a black

goatskin. I shivered. It was cold outside. I saw my breath. Steam rose from the backs of the man-beasts. I wanted to lose myself in those bells, wanted to step into that black circle and dissolve.

Suddenly the circle broke apart, the dancers stormed round the ring of onlookers, some breaking free and clanging up side streets at a full run, one or two raising their great shepherd staffs and whacking spectators on their heads and arms, eliciting cries of surprise and foolish smiles. It was a blessing, I was told, to be struck by a Geros: if you were a man it meant riches, if you were a woman, strong babies. The clamor of the bells receded. My grandmotherly escort pulled me by the arm, leading the way through crisscrossing narrow streets lined by whitewashed plaster houses. I looked down one alleyway and saw a lone Geros sitting on a low stone wall, a glass of ouzo in his hand. His posture was erect and dignified, though his chest heaved from recent exertion. A woman stood in front of him, dressed in gay colors—a bright red embroidered vest, long white skirt, some sort of translucent veil, and a frilly black eye mask that disguised her identity. She was singing a trilling, high-pitched song to the Geros, her audience of one, waving an embroidered handkerchief and taking small steps in a refined, reserved dance of her own.

"Korella," the old woman said, and pulled me on up the hillside.

Brides of the Geri, the masked Korella dressed in traditional Skyros wedding costume. Until recently, they were cross-dressing males, not real women like the one I had seen, whose curves could not possibly have been padded. It was for them that I had come as much as for the Geri, for if the beast-men enacted the rites of Dionysus, then could the Korella be the descendants of the women who danced attendance on the god across the hills of ancient Greece? The old woman led me to her guest room, and as I lay under the covers that cold February night, every now and then I would wake to a sudden burst of bells clanging in the distance, past midnight, past 2 A.M. They were out there still, these wild creatures, these great grandchildren of Dionysus, racing through the streets. I smiled, thinking of them, thinking of him, still alive after so many centuries.

Wherever I traveled in search of the Goddess, Dionysus was there, haunting her myths, appearing again and again as son, lover, priest, and sacrifice. He was born in Elias, near Olympia, and the sixteen Elian priestesses of Hera were his priestesses as well. As bastard child of Zeus, jealous Hera tried to kill him twice—by dismemberment and immolation. But each time he was resurrected. As an adult, Hera drove him mad, and he wandered though Asia until the goddess Cybele cured him with her sacred rites. He married Cretan Adriane, and as Zagreus, a horned god from Crete, he was torn apart in the shape of a bull, and then resurrected. As Zagreus, Plouton, Brimos, Iacchus, or Bacchus, Dionysus was the son of either Demeter or Persephone, and in Athens his rites of new wine became meshed with the lesser mysteries of Eleusis—a merging of his cult with that of the twin goddesses of fertility. Below Athena's Parthenon, the great amphitheater of Dionysus was the center of Greek drama, and he became the god of theater, with all its masks. And at Delphi, it was his tomb that lay beneath the navel of the Earth, and in the winter months, when Apollo left for places north, Dionysus rose again and ruled. His frenzied female followers there filled the slopes of Parnassus with their wild song.

Called the "women's god," by German scholar W. Otto, Dionysus led his maenads into thick forests and the snowy mountains to enact his passionate and bloody rites. God of intoxication, he was not merely worshiped by his devotees, he possessed them. Depictions of these women, hair wild, arms and legs askew as if contorted and writhing reminded me of the seal rings from Crete of ecstatic women dancing before a goddess. Greek myths tell how male authorities resisted the advance of the mad god's cult, but how women threw themselves into it with disturbing abandon—disturbing to husbands who saw their obedient wives turn into savage creatures, untamed, suffused with ecstacy, their limbs and teeth unnaturally strong, strong enough to tear a bull to pieces and devour it raw—a frenzied eucharist in which the blood and body they consumed was the god himself, for Dionysus, as I recalled from Crete, was a bull god, a god of sacrifice and rebirth, death and resurrection.

The followers of Dionysus drank deep. Intoxicated by the vine, they left their lives of circumscribed propriety, took up the wild drumming that accompanied the dithyramb: verses "full of passion and change, of confusion and swaying." They lost themselves in orgiastic revels, and carried giant phalluses in their processions. God of sex and drugs and rock and roll, he was their Elvis, their Jim Morrison. The screaming madness which made droves of young women dangerous at Stones and Beatles concerts—dangerous because if they got their hands on them, they would literally have torn them to pieces in order to possess a shred of what they loved—this was the primordial power Dionysus could unleash.

Yet his followers were also his nursemaids, and at times the god was a young boy who needed to be protected, nurtured. To hide him from wrathful Hera they dressed him like a girl. As a youth, he was tender and beautiful, depicted with flowing locks and curls, crowned with ivy and grape leaves, and wearing effeminate robes. The maenads who would tear a fawn to pieces with their teeth would be just as inclined to place the creature to their breast and, imagining it to be their god, would let it suckle there. This crazy, animalistic power, this fury that needs such tender care— Dionysus reached something in women that the other gods (and perhaps their male inventors) surely could not fathom. We men, we naively think that women want a dashing hero: a John Wayne, a James Bond. It's hard for us to understand the attraction of someone Dionysian, someone like Prince or David Bowie, someone who crosses boundaries: phallic yet effeminate; wild yet refined; powerful yet vulnerable; immortal, yet dying.

The early Greeks tried to keep him at arm's length. They labeled him a foreigner, an interloper from some faraway land—Asia, or perhaps the barbaric north. The myths tell how he had to fight his way into Greece and win a place for his rites by force and the fury of his women followers, until eventually he was awarded a seat at Olympus among the divine twelve. Imagine how poorly he fit in with the other gods: Zeus: God of Thunder; Aries: God of War; Hephastos: God of the Forge; Poseidon: God of the Sea. They all seem like two-dimensional, cutout figures next to Dionysus. To call him God of Wine is a parody. It's ecstasy, liberation, union with the swirling chaos of the universe that Dionysus represents, a spiritual state, not a technology or piece of turf. So the Greeks kept him an outsider, even while his rites were celebrated across the land. Today, the story of his late arrival doesn't wash. Recently translated Linear B texts turned up his name both in Crete and in Pylos, southern Greece, back in fourteenth century B.C. Also, on the island of Keos, just south of Attica, a Mycenaen-era shrine to him contained a group of life-sized terra cotta statues of dancing women all in flouncing Cretan dress. This places the "god of women" among the oldest named of the divinities of Greece. How old is beyond guessing; some scholars trace the dance at Skyros back to the rites of paleolithic shamans.

In the course of my research I joined a Dionysus newsgroup on the internet, and through it met an articulate scholar who was also a self-professed member of a modern maenad sect. I asked her what it meant for her to worship Dionysus, both spiritually, and in terms of specific rites and practices. Assured I would keep her name confidential, she wrote me this reply:

I begin writing this with some trepidation. Publicly, I tend towards silence on the topic of religious ecstasy of any kind. States of mind are so subjective, the topic is so broad, and beyond that I just feel that some things should be talked of sparingly.... However, I do think that something can be gained from a brief foray into this strange and often frightening realm.

Socrates said "our greatest blessings come to us by way of madness," but qualified this with "provided the madness is given to us by divine gift." This is an important distinction. I am not advocating random insanity with no goal and no guidance; that is rarely productive. Rather, I am thinking of the many traditions which embrace altered states of consciousness, within a magical and/or religious context, for the benefits they bring....

Dionysus is a god of extremes, the "god of ecstasy and terror, of wildness and of the most blessed deliverance" (Walter Otto). Thus he is reached through extreme actions—in the myths, these include wild dancing, excessive drinking, and the tearing apart and eating of live animals. Many people might cringe at these accounts, but there is no middle road for the wary, there is no way to tiptoe up to Dionysus and nudge him on the shoulder. Nor should there be...

On a personal level, divine madness can bring life-changing results. But it can also bring ruin, sending a person over the edge, which is why this is not for everyone. We don't have a system in this culture to prepare us for such experiences, we think only in terms of "sane" and "insane," which is why going over to the other side can easily destroy the sensibilities of anyone. But for those who wish to go Beyond, to see the outer realms, to touch the gods, which is an incredibly dangerous but exhilarating path, there is no choice but to surrender part of oneself, which becomes a sacrifice of sorts. It cannot be done lightly, nor without purpose. However, although you may work within a ritual context, and act responsibly and carefully, you can never truly control what happens. If you choose to open yourself to the "madness of God" you must accept the consequences, for good or ill....

I will say that (in my experience) it can bring communion with the god, of a quality and intensity that usually cannot be reached through other religious actions.... And it frees you, as Dionysus freed the maenads, Dionysus the Liberator, the Looser of Bonds. It releases you into a state both outside yourself and extraordinarily within yourself, where you can catch a glimpse of your own soul, and the soul of the world.

How do you enter into this madness? I cannot recommend any specific methods, for many are dangerous and/or illegal. With Dionysus, the way must usually begin with his gift, the vine. For other gods, or other paths, it will be different.... If you are committed to the task, you will find a way. And you will never be prepared for what will come, and you will never exhaust the possibilities. But it will change you. Surrendering to madness even once leaves a mark. Gripped by Dionysus, you may find yourself suddenly attracted to the smell of the hunt, and the cries of the maenads will be music, as it is music to his ears. If you think you are ready for this, then he is waiting for you.

I have felt Dionysus draw me, too, and recognize in this modern maenad's description the force that tore through my life ten years ago like a whirlwind, crushing everything in its path. But even the whirlwind can bring deliverance. For me there was the sexual barrenness of my married life, but just as my wife and I were talking of divorce, in a brief moment of passion, we conceived a child. I have never felt so twisted and confused in all my life: so happy over the child soon to be born, so desolate, bound by that child to a woman who recoiled at my touch. Something in me snapped then, broke like the shell of an egg, releasing something frightening inside of me, alive and stirring. It was as if a split personality emerged, a Hyde to my Jekyll, a werewolf in my clothing. A shadow side of my being suddenly found its voice, its will, and before that will I surrendered. That was all it took—surrender. It said to me, *I will take what I need; now get out of my way.* I began to live a double life. It shocked me that this ferocious thing in me proved so adept at seducing women. The ones who agreed to go with me, they seemed to like the beast, and this made me laugh bitterly. All my life, I had believed the way to win a woman was to be good to her, tender, thoughtful, a gentleman, a snag. But now I discovered I could be direct, blunt even—this was about sex, not a relationship. And so I would abandon myself to the dark space, feel its desire for female flesh come alive, and lose myself completely.

By all that I believed, I knew what I was doing was wrong, yet in those days I felt so keenly alive, just out walking along a road at night, feeling my body move through the evening air, smelling cut grass and honeysuckle, gulping it in, intoxicated, thrilled just to be a body, to feel lust and hunger like a violin string thrumming in my veins. Such ecstasy I had never known, and in those several months, I was a child of Dionysus, frenzied, living on the edge of a lie that was bound to explode, as it finally did. One pays for this. One must. So when the sordid mess was all revealed, my wife took our son and left the country, and I endured the well-earned public shame for all my private deeds. For a year and a half I tried to reconcile with her, contrite and celibate, the beast locked back in the cage. She made it clear that she could never, ever trust me again, and in the end, we agreed to divorce and share custody of our son. I have lived in the United States for a decade now, away from my friends and a modest career as an author in my native land—small payment, to be honest, for being with my son. And yet, the destruction of my whole false life, a death of a kind, it freed this dark thing in me that still survives. In my first glance at the Geri I felt such strong kinship, such recognition. These shaggy man-beasts, to see them dance round and around the streets, it was as if someone had taken a picture of my insides and thrown it out in front of me.

"Geros—ha, it's just for blowing off steam." That's what a young Albanian mechanic who worked at the air force base on the island told me on the ferry ride to Skyros. "These people are crude, rude, rough, even the dialect is rough. Shepherds, fishermen. No spirit of hospitality. They hate outsiders, even through we bring lots of money to the island. They always think we are out to sleep with their women."

The Albanian then allowed that he did have to meet his Skyros girlfriend in secret, because if her parents found out they were sleeping together, there would be the Greek equivalent of a shotgun wedding.

In the morning I got a different opinion from one of the organizers of the festival events. Her name was Soula, one of the few native Skyrians who spoke English. She worked as a town administrator, and I had spoken with her by phone before my arrival. Polite and articulate, Soula had curly hair and a smile of genuine happiness. She had lived in Athens many years she told me, but recently came back to Skyros with her Athenian husband and two kids, because, she said, life was so much better here.

"In Athens, I was always running, always in a hurry. You always have to jump across the road because a car is coming. Here, there are no cars. The streets are too narrow. So no rush. Life is more simple, yet you depend on the community."

We went to a café for coffee and she told me her first memory of the Geros.

"As first I was so scared—the black color, the masks, the noise! But after that, I learned that if you dress this way, others will be afraid of you, and I liked it very much. I have costumes for my boys now. My oldest, he's fifteen, and he was dancing last night, and I was so proud of him. It's very difficult, you see, with the bells, the whole costume weighs over fifty kilograms. They have to run up and down the steep streets for hours and hours, and to swing the bells so that they ring just right—it takes skill, strength, endurance."

An old man at a table next to us was arguing loudly and jovially with the café owner. Both looked as if they had been up all night, and indeed they had. Soula told me the man had been a Geros the previous night, so I asked him what he experienced when he danced.

"You don't just decide, 'tonight I put on the bells,'" Soula translated for him. "Only when you feel it like a necessity. Otherwise, you can't do it. When I put the mask on, no one knows who I am underneath, and this gives me the courage to make the bells ring strong."

"How do you dance for so long?"

"For the first one, two hours, it's difficult. All that weight, you can't imagine. You can't keep it up for four, five, six hours. So you have to run hard, very hard at first, straight up the hill. After that, something goes out of your body. You don't feel the weight of the bells. There was a time the dancing went on ten hours, sometimes all night and all day, the Geros would piss in their pants and just keep on dancing. They don't eat, only drink ouzo. Ouzo and water, lots of it, otherwise you'd faint. It's not possible for a human being to act like this, but when you're a Geros, you think that you're not a human being!"

He told me that in the old days, the Geros used to run full tilt at each other, like charging rams, and that the cover of the mask would be used to settle old scores, sometimes resulting in serious injuries. At times, the spectators and Geros would turn on one another and full-scale war would take place between them in the streets, with the crowd throwing handfuls of bran or ashes at the Geros to try and blind them. But things had settled down for many years now, he assured me. Soula told me that the dance went on for three consecutive weekends during which the whole village drank and feasted. On the last day, they would perform satirical plays and have a great banquet—and then the next morning, Clean Monday, everyone would dress in their best linens, and go to church for the start of Lent.

Soula told me more about the Korella too. She said she had danced the Korella part many times herself, and that her role is to help the Geros, to look out for what he needs. "You know what he is doing is too heavy, too hard, but you can't tell him you're tired. No, you must say that you want to give him a song, and ask him to sit. That gives him the chance to rest, to gather his strength. Then you sing, and when you stop, he stands and rings his bells in a special way, just for you."

"If you don't have a Korella, you don't feel the same," added the man. "You get tired, lonely. It's a sad thing that there's fewer and fewer of them these days."

Soula translated part of a Korella's song for me:

Big lad, young man, because time passes,
Who knows if next year we are still alive or still here...
You look like an angel to my eyes,
And you are dancing like an angel,
My flower that used to open in the cold wind
Your steps are like lemon branches, blown by the wind
My gold eagle, I am under your feet
Fly with your wings, and I wish to fly with your wings
And I will be glad if you are happy....

To my surprise, I found my eyes welling with tears. To the Korella, the Geros was no wild monster. That she could see in his shaggy, lumbering strength such grace reminded me of the capacity that women have to see beauty in the beast, to love it, to want to care for it—the capacity my wife Teresa has to love the beast in me.

Soula invited me to her home for lunch, where I found her son Karefillis surrounded by bells and the paraphernalia of a Geros. He was packing up for a trip he and twenty-eight other dancers were to make to Thessaloniki, where they would perform that coming weekend. He was a tall, athletic, and polite young man, his English good enough that he and his mother made a game out of correcting each other's occasional mispronunciations. He showed me the various parts of his costume, going into some detail about the goatskin mask, which had to be selected with care for its dark coloring and the quality of the tanning. A poorly cured goat hide pressed all night against a hot, sweaty face could be suffocating. He handed it over for me to sniff—a sour bouquet reminiscent of feta cheese and urine. He was still working on his own collection of bells, which in the old days were borrowed from the local shepherds. Now, each family buys their own, which run to $50 each for the big ones. The Geros coats were originally the fleeces worn by shepherds in the winter, turned shaggy side out, but these too had been replaced in modern times, and would-be Geri had to have their coats custom made. The whole outfit cost over $1,000, Soula explained, a huge expense for the average Skyros family, but one they were willing to pay to keep the tradition alive. The fact that teenagers like Karefillis are keen to dance bodes well for its survival.

"It's joy, great joy," he told me. "I no longer know what I am. I don't know what's inside of me. You can hardly see out the eyeholes, and the smell of goat is so strong. One year, it was raining, and I didn't even notice until I stepped in a puddle and soaked my foot."

I asked what he knew about the roots of the dance, and he replied, "It's an ancient thing, from Dionysus. One of the tasks the Geros must perform at least once every night is to run from the bottom of the town all the way to the monastery at the hilltop, and ring the church bells. You see, it was built on the site of a temple to Dionysus. He was always the special god of the island, and one of the pillars holding up the chapel, it is from the original temple."

I climbed to St. George's a few days later to see that pillar, together with a local teacher named Mimis who spoke English, and offered to interpret for the lonely young monk at the top. Father Gerondious had studied for fifteen years at one of the famous monasteries of Mt. Athos before taking up his solitary post on Skyros. He was pleased to have a visitor, and gave us the tour: the miraculous well from which new wine was dispensed at an annual festival, the silver crusted miraculous icon of St. George, and in the chapel itself, the one worn, ancient pillar, standing among the rest, draped with a purple banner embroidered with grape clusters on the vine, and in Greek the words of Jesus: "I am the vine, you are the branches…"

We stayed for a special service, a ceremony dedicating candles and cakes for the dead. It all seemed so familiar, after my recent visit to Eleusis. The rites of Dionysus and Demeter survive, but instead of eating raw flesh, ecstatic dance, drunkenness, orgies, feasts, torchlight processions, in the church there is a little wafer, a little sip of wine, a few hymns—a meager gift from an absent god.

A shopkeeper in the village told me that when the current priest arrived on Skyros, he knew nothing about the Geros, and on the first night of the festival, he was terrified when the beast-men charged in through the gate to ring the bells. At first he thought that they were demons, then that they were village men mad with drink, and when they swung the hips at him so that their bells would sound, he thought they were making lascivious advances towards him, and that terrified him even more. Father Gerondious himself told me nothing of this, only that, well, Skyros people at times were very difficult to understand. He was quite clear that the Geros dance had nothing to do with Christianity, that it was from Dionysus. But as long as the dancers respected the monastery, he did not object, and they could come and ring the bells.

He was interested in my research, however, and told me that Mt. Athos had been sacred to the goddess before the time of Christ, and covered with her temples. The mountain itself was shaped like a giant breast, he said. When Mary, Mother of God, set sail for Cyprus after the crucifixion, she was blown off course, and landed on the shores of Athos instead.

"The priestesses all gathered to see Jesus's mother," Father Gerondious said, "and when she started to teach the new religion, the pagan statues of marble all crashed to the ground! A voice from heaven spoke, saying 'This entire area is a present from God to Maria!' After that, they began to build small monasteries on the ruins of the old temples, until in the tenth century, they built Magistra Lavra, the first great monastery, which is still standing today!"

Father Gerondious told me that to honor Mary, no females were allowed to set foot anywhere on Mount Athos—not even female dogs or cows.

"Before Christ, the Holy Mountain was for women *only,*" he told me vehemently. "But after Mary's visit, there is only *one woman* honored at Athos, forevermore."

For his first five years on Mount Athos, George did not see his mother. In fact, even mentioning the name of another woman was forbidden. Then, when he went home for a visit, his mother was so proud of him, she kissed his hand every night before she went to bed, and since then has only ever called him "Father." There was something Oedipal here to ponder, something peculiar in the smile he gave as he told this story, the triumph of a celibate over the one who gave him birth: the son becoming father to the mother.

Every evening, hundreds of people lined the town square, the deafening sound of the bells, *kachung, kachung, kachung,* bouncing back and forth off the buildings like the clang of a thousand ricocheting pinballs. Sitting at an outdoor café, the drinks vibrating on my table, it was like being buried in sound. People sat and stood around for hours, watching, the kids plugging their ears. It's not like a parade, not like anything new happens. There's no drama that will unfold, just immersion in the event. Saturday night I stood for three hours before I took a seat, unable to drag myself away. TV crews arrived from Athens with their cameras, but how could they hope to capture this? The deafening noise would just sound tinny on television. Reduced to screen size, how could the Geri surround you, dance on your insides? How could the ringing fill you up if it came from a little box?

When Karefillis and Soula returned from Thessaloniki they told me they would never take dancers off the island again. On a stage, they said, the bells are not the same, that when people look at the Geri as an act, a folk dance, there's something missing and it doesn't work. From now on, they vowed to try and keep the dance on Skyros, where it was meant to be. The Geros has his home here, in these winding streets, but in the modern world, he can't breathe, he can't be heard.

I wondered if this is how the people of Skyros feel too, as the world closes in on them? The men hate change, so I had been told, and the presence of the air force base, the largest in all of Greece, merely makes them pull their world and their women in so much tighter. Looking round the café-bar, I saw lots of groups of young married couples, and they didn't look as happy, not nearly as happy, as the old folks out dining in the restaurant across the way.

I met an Australian woman, married to a Skyrian, who runs a restaurant in town. She told me with dismay that marriages on the island are still arranged with girls as young as thirteen, and that weddings at fourteen or fifteen are not uncommon. Any sign of romantic interest results in parental meetings and family alliances being drawn, and in such a small town, that means pretty much everyone gets married young. The girls want it too, she said; they want to escape the discipline of their parents, and like the thought of setting up their own house, dropping out of school and having babies. The problem is, young wives are bored stiff by the time they are in their early twenties. The men get engrossed in the world of boats and goats…and the women, well, the air force base and its 300 men becomes a source of great interest.

Late that night I moved indoors and stood at the crowded bar. After about an hour, suddenly, the man to my right turned and introduced himself. Iohannes spoke virtually no English, yet we could communicate well enough with just a few shouted words and gestures. He was tall, rugged, a man who spent his life outdoors, with big weathered hands that clapped me on the shoulder. He bought me a drink, I bought him a drink. We talked about the festival. Crazy, but good crazy. He liked Canada, he said, but not Europeans. And Athens? Disgusting, no life at all. But here in Skyros, one could rest, fill the lungs, breathe easy. Unfortunately, his wife of fifteen years went nuts and left him. His eyes were sad. He reminded me of the island itself, solitary, something wild, yet straightforward, welcoming on his own timing, when no one's trying to push him around or take advantage. When a pop song blared though the speakers about the anguish of a broken love, he touched his own heart and looked at me morosely.

A Geros broke into the bar late that night, leapt up on a table, the dark god suddenly among us, swung his hips, the bells drowning out the music, all conversation ceased, all eyes turned on the epiphany. The waitress rushed to bring him a glass of ouzo and water which he downed in a gulp, then staggered on. A blessing, sure—yet I could not help but feel his solitude, with no Korella by his side to sing for him, care for him through the wild night. Soula tells me it's hard for young girls to learn to be Korella, because if they dance for a Geros, anyone other than a father or a brother, they will find themselves engaged. But the Geros alone is only half the dance. It's not a solo act. Without the Korella, how can he survive?

My last day on the island, Soula invited me for dinner at her house. She asked how my research was going, what discoveries I had made. I told her that while the dance was fantastic, what I had seen on Skyros left me perturbed that one of my hypotheses had been disproved. I said I'd thought that by visiting places that kept to ancient traditions, I might get an idea of how relations between men and women might have been different. But from what I'd seen of Skyros, relations between the sexes were even worse than in other parts of Greece.

Soula sat quietly for a while, mulling this over. After all, what could she say? Though she loved the island, she herself had left Skyros as a young woman, and came back with an Athenian husband.

"Well, maybe I can say tell you something from my own experience about how things are unique on Skyros," she offered. "I can tell you three things that make us different from the rest of Greece. Thirty years ago, it was the woman's role to manage the household. Sure, the husband provided income from his job, brought firewood, and he was head of the house. But the woman would advise him, and he would listen. A university professor who studies folk culture told me Skyros is unique in all of Greece because it's the only place where the women's traditional dress doesn't have an apron. In Skyros folk songs, it is the woman who sings songs that flirt with the man and she calls him an angel. Everywhere else on Greece, songs are by men who do the flirting.

"Now let me show you something in my own home," Soula pointed to a large elaborate embroidery framed on her living room wall. "This is the embroidery which I did when I got married. You see on the large ship in the center, everyone is working on an oar except the man sitting at the bow who is twice as big as the others. He's playing a guitar. That's the husband, and the meaning is, that I am going to make his life like this. Up in the corner is a bad man in a cage, a jail.

That means I am keeping all the bad things away from my husband. Surrounding him, you see only good things, sweet things. Birds, flowers and so on. So I think these three things from our folk history can tell you something special about our island."

"But what about in the past thirty years?"

Soula sighed. "These days only two in ten marriages are between Skyrians. A lot of outsiders have come in. Then there's the base…"

She told me the islanders had protested, but the government told them they didn't have a choice. Skyros is the best location for an air force base. Halfway between Athens and Turkey, the best site to intercept an air attack. But, they have survived invasions before, and she hopes they'll survive this one too. Maybe Greece and Turkey will call a truce, then there's no need for the base at all. In the meantime, as long as the Geri dance, Soula said, the unique spirit of Skyros will stay alive. The dance has endured much worse than this. What's most important is that boys like Karfillis still want to become a Geros, and it's a good sign that girls again are dressing as Korella, even if in small numbers. Families are spending lots of money on costumes and bells, so it's a huge commitment of the community. But it's natural, and everyone who does it, does it for the right reason.

I asked Soula if she could do me one favor. I remembered Karefillis had said they were still scraping money together to buy a few more bells each season. I asked, could I give some money so she could buy a bell for him, so that in the midwinter festival, in years to come, there could be a bell from me, that swings from a Geros's belt.

On the boat ride back to mainland Greece I tried to sort out what I had seen. The refined Korella in her bridal garb was clearly a far cry from the maenads of the past. Could one imagine each Geros surrounded by a group of them, like the ring of flounce-skirt dancers from the Dionysian shrine of Keos? Perhaps she too is recovering from centuries of suppression. It is only with this generation that women are allowed to dance the Korella's part at all. But in her songs, in her attraction to the Geros, I saw the resemblance to her sisters who once raged upon the hills. It's not the man inside the coat, but the spirit that comes over him, when the bells are swung just right, and the sound crashes through the narrow village streets. That's where Dionysus lives, and when the boor who is her husband puts on that black coat and mask, something comes alive in her, something that has survived three thousand years of Orthodoxy and Olympianism with its soul intact.

I think that we men get so caught up in reasons why we are important to women, as providers, protectors, progenitors, priests, and politicians, we become convinced by our own propaganda that it's our hard work that keeps civilization on its track. But how much of this is bluster, masking an underlying fear that if not for these practical matters, women would have no use for us at all? Perhaps that's why so many men resist the participation of women in the working world, and like the men of Skyros resent the changes that make it easier for a woman to lose her dependence on a man. What Dionysus holds out for us is a different vision of the male, something as inexplicable as that great shaggy beast wrapped round with bells. It evokes in her a hunger, a nurturing, an ecstasy, a touch of madness, a song. And if we could trust in that, and let the rest go, what a different world men and women would share.

Can any man be Dionysus? It's not like that exactly; Dionysus is an archetype, or perhaps a presence that may inhabit man just now and then, at least in the eyes of a particular woman. It is not essentially personal, not a bond of love. Erotic, yet not romantic, easier, in fact, to put on the cloak with a stranger, and let her be maenad in the dance. In our culture, aside from the rock concert, we've lost all the

Dionysian rituals that could unite us thus. We have no May Days, no Lupercalia festivals when respectable women had license to break taboos and choose any man as Dionysian consort for the day. Familiarity with one's spouse makes it difficult to clear the street for the arrival of the god in domestic life, while for many singles, there's such casualness to sex, so much ego in seduction, that the god, though often hoped for, is painfully absent. Perhaps the closest a North American woman comes (outside of the rare maenad clubs) to a framework that offers her the chance to encounter Dionysus is in adultery, where taboos are broken, there is a sense of danger, and the focus is exclusively on the erotic act without personal bonds surrounding it. But there are no ritual structures in our society that redeem or support this act or make it sacred. I have played Dionysus here, and while in the moment it may transport a couple into ecstasy, afterwards one wakes to real life, and feels like shit.

Is there any hope then, for men to let Dionysus into our lives? Is that even a good thing for us to contemplate? If we knew that women loved us not for the security we provide (perhaps the biggest lie ever told), but rather, for what we are, for the god within, then we might find it easier to relax our grip on power, and instead of trying to force women to depend on us, let them be free. Maybe if we do that, Dionysus will find a way to breathe through us again, and perhaps we will find an erotic way to create a dance with the one we love. It may even be—and this is idle speculation—that the reason Dionysian rites of women were not typically directed towards a husband was precisely because the social bonds of marriage so constricted her, she needed anonymity to be free.

In my own relationship with Teresa, I sometimes fear that the Dionysian role I sometimes play for her will diminish, become domesticated, that sex will be reduced to a perfunctory release of tension, and that the shaggy beast she sometimes sees in me will become the household pet. I picture

Dionysus, no more intoxicated by the vine, but sitting on a La-Z-Boy, drinking lite beer and watching reruns on T.V. That specter of complacency scares me more than death or baldness, and I don't know what I would do if it happened to me. My only plan to forestall it is to give Dionysus that clear street in which to dance, a place of ritual and taboo within our marriage vows. In short, Teresa and I have agreed to initiate a secret love affair—with each other.

Tim Ward spent several years roaming around prehistoric temples and sacred sites across southern Europe while researching his book on the sacred feminine: Savage Breast: One Man's Search for the Goddess. *His experience in Skyros was part of that larger journey to understand life before "God" went mono. He has also written* Arousing the Goddess: Sex and Love in the Buddhist Ruins of India, What the Buddha Never Taught: A Behind-the-Robes Account of Life in a Thai Buddhist Monastery, *and most recently the all-too-practical* Author's Guide to Publishing and Marketing. *Find him on the web at www.timwardsbooks.com and www.savagebreastbook.com.*

～ゃ ～ゃ ～ゃ

French Dolls

A troubled father inspires a life-long love
of the faraway.

TO THE END OF HIS DAYS, MY FATHER INSISTED that my travels were nothing more than "escapism." Whenever I said I was going somewhere alone, he accused me of running away, of being "avoidant." It didn't matter whether it was Europe or the movies.

"What is wrong with you?" he once snarled at me on the eve of a trip. It must have been the long one to South America, when I expected to be gone a year. A year without income! He was appalled. "What makes you want to do this?"

The answer was so obvious, I almost laughed. My longing for the world began before his rages did, when things were good between us, when I first knew him. He was the person who gave me the wanderlust he claimed to despise.

I'd been born while he was away in the war—stationed in England before the invasion of Europe and in France afterward, where he lived with other medical officers in a chateau near Paris, playing gin rummy between shifts and keeping track of the score on the elegant, abandoned walls.

I knew about France before I knew about him, because the person that everyone else called "Daddy" had sent me a present from there: three French dolls that came in the mail. They were, I know now, what Frenchmen called Apache dancers or, more likely, Parisian whores—strange gifts for a child, but he was new to fatherhood.

I don't remember playing with them, but I remember how they looked in their red, white, and blue clothes—striped t-shirts, side-slit skirts, little neckerchiefs and berets. They had flouncy hair and long eyelashes, curvy lips and dangling cigarettes; the tallest had a little black spot painted on her cheek.

The last time I saw them, they were wrapped in tissue in a drawer in my grandmother's guest room, the same special drawer where she kept something else I coveted—the white lace fan she had carried when she married my grandfather, the fan I pretended I'd carry at my own wedding someday.

I was nearly three by the time my father followed the French dolls home. He spent the next year getting acquainted with his little girl and, whether he meant to or not, acquainting me with the world.

That year, the year before my brother was born, we had a daily ritual—what he called a "tête-à-tête," my first French words. We would sit at my red play table in the basement and divide a single, green-glass bottle of Coca-Cola into tiny mugs the size of shot glasses. He poured, we clinked mugs, we drank. And he told me war stories.

During one tête-à-tête, my mother and grandmother were upstairs baking sugar cookies—the big, plump, chewy kind my father had longed for during the war. My grandmother cut them out the way she cut baking-powder biscuits, with a drinking glass whose edge she dipped in flour; the results were always round.

My father told me to stay put and disappeared upstairs. He came back a long time later, bringing still-warm sugar cookies he had cut out himself. They weren't round. If I could guess what the shapes were, he promised, I could eat them.

The first was easy: a butterfly. The next was harder, but I knew that one too: the Foshay Tower, the first skyscraper in Minneapolis; my grandfather had taken me to see it. The last cookie was another tower, the curvy one that *Life* magazine showed nearly every week, the one where Daddy was.

"Paris," I said. "Eiffel Tower!" I remember feeling proud because I knew it and because he was pleased.

That is how it should have gone on—a daughter growing up happy, the pride and joy of her wise, funny, interesting, doting father. But that is not what happened. Our family illness is depression, and it began to claim him while I was still in childhood. There were no good drugs then, and he wouldn't have admitted that he needed them, even if there had been.

Instead, he medicated himself the old-fashioned way, with three six-packs of beer a night, while he sat at the kitchen table and worked on his stamp collection. "You can't be an alcoholic," he told us often, "if all you drink is beer."

My younger siblings learned quickly not to walk through the kitchen after supper. I never caught on. Most nights, I'd drop by, hoping to talk. And most nights, from the time I was twelve or thirteen until I moved away, we fought. Or rather he fought, and I stood, backed up against the refrigerator, and took it. He used words exquisitely, and late at night, when he turned them on me, he used them like switchblades. I have thought often that if I had to choose a form of victimization, I would have preferred to be beaten with sticks.

These are a few of the knives my father threw at me. "You're a fake. Someday they'll all find out you're a fake." "You're mentally lazy." "Neurotic." "Freak." "I don't care if I sacrifice my entire relationship with you, as long as it makes you a better person."

And finally this one, "You are unloving, unlovely, and unloved." He said that one night when I was in high school. Ah, how the man could carve a phrase. That line alone would have earned my father an A in my rhetoric class. Shakespeare couldn't have said it better.

What appalls me now is not what my father said, or the fact that he said such things over and over and over, night after night after night. What appalls me is that I believed him. He had always been my hero—the man I thought knew everything, so I believed that he knew the truth about me.

Why did I keep trying? Why did I keep going to him, keep asking for his help with algebra, with German, with English themes? Denial is too easy an answer. It felt more like hope—that maybe the next time it would be different.

Once, years after I'd left home, I was crossing a plaza in a Mexican town when I saw a man punch his dog so hard in the ribs that I thought its chest would cave in. I expected the dog to collapse in pain, to die or at least run. But instead it crept closer to him, cringing, wagging its tail, trying to lick his hand, apologizing, seeking comfort from the very man that hurt it—as if it had deserved the blow. I understood that dog.

Four decades after our last tête-à-tête, I sat by my father's hospital bed, knowing he was never going to leave it, and struggled to find something safe to talk about. By then, I was a professional traveler who had been all over the world—and in Paris so often that I no longer kept count. Writing about trips was how I earned my living, and I'd heard from others that my father was proud of my work. But that still didn't mean trips were safe topics.

What I wanted to talk about was even less safe. I wanted to ask him why I had made him so angry, so often, for so long. Why he had criticized everything I did, everything I said or wrote, how I walked, even how I breathed. It was too late, of course. Even if he had known the answers, he couldn't have given them now. He lay inert, his eyes shut. I didn't know whether he would even hear me.

I reached farther back and hit an old, sweet memory. "Do you remember the French dolls?" I asked, not expecting an answer.

My father startled me. "Yes," he murmured, his voice coarse and distant, as if he hadn't intended to use it again. "Do you still have them?"

"No," I said, amazed that he thought I might. "I think they got played with"—the family euphemism for what happened when younger kids got hold of older kids' things.

But what had become of them didn't matter. Merely mentioning the dolls had conjured them up. They reappeared like sparkling ghosts in that sterile gray room—fresh as perfume, brand-new and brightly painted.

I knew my father was seeing them again too, as clearly as he had when he wrapped them in brown paper and addressed the package to the daughter he had never met. That was back when his own war was over, and before our war began.

~⁂~ ~⁂~ ~⁂~

Catherine Watson is travel editor for MinnPost.com and a former travel editor of the Minneapolis Star Tribune. *An award-winning travel writer and photographer, she is the author of two books of travel essays,* Home on the Road *and* Roads Less Traveled. *She teaches travel writing and memoir in university-level workshops in the U.S. and abroad.*

JEN PERCY

❧ ❧ ❧

Training Ground

She studies life and death on an island still being born.

MORNINGS, WE SLEPT IN MILITARY TENTS.
Evenings, we sat on faded, pink-striped lawn
chairs and watched the sun die. We were surrounded by lava
fields and black dunes, plants I didn't know existed, the hum
of a military chopper. Everywhere palm trees curved and
rotted. I was working in Volcanoes National Park, Hawaii,
getting paid forty dollars a week to tag and monitor endan-
gered sea turtles along the Big Island's southern coast.

To prepare for the field our boss gave us a walkie-talkie, a
waterproof field notebook, a flashlight, a burn kit, an emergency cell phone. We had a truck check, a pack check, a boot
check. He gave us all camo pants and army hats and we wore
heavy packs and we were dropped off at the bottom of a road
that fell two thousand feet from the jungle to the coast. We
formed a line and hiked along the black sand.

Our boss, Will Cody, ran the program out of a house in the

jungle with funds from the National Park Service. He usually wore short-shorts and ripped shirts and his socks were always pulled up past his calves. The house had two rooms, five desks, a Mac from the late '80s. The walls were covered in topographic maps, anatomical sketches of turtles and their shells. There was a dead turtle by the computer, trapped in a bottle of formaldehyde, and every time I came in the office it faced a different direction.

We were in the field for two weeks at a time, in groups of three or four, sometimes in pairs. On our days off, we stayed at the Kilauea Military Camp—just a mile walk from Will's office. I lived with two girls in a house outside the military camp.

The Kilauea Military Camp is a sixty-acre plot of grass and trailer homes and bad restaurants, full of American flags and picnics and men sitting on benches. It used to be a training ground for the National Guard but now it's a resort, a vacation destination for soldiers. For a while, on my days off, I just wandered around the camp eating macadamia nuts or going to the Volcano Museum. Sometimes I took walks around the rim of a nearby crater, watching the tourists crawl around its yellow insides. At night, I went to the Lava Lounge with its electric signs and wilting flowers and little tubs of fake lava made from curled plastic and red bulbs, and I would find the retired military officers drinking and wearing camo and slapping each other on the back, talking about AK-47s and Vietnam and how sometimes they wished they were back there, in the dark, wrapped in creeper vines, sinking into the mud. It's where the boys who wanted to be soldiers came to drink; the boys who were soldiers were here too—the boys who might have just returned from Iraq or Afghanistan— who might be shipping off in a C-17 tomorrow, in a month, a year.

I would go to the Lava Lounge and find them drinking Miller High Life with their heads down. I'd walk by them, between them, going to the bathroom or to get a drink, and though sometimes I would put a hand on one of their shoulders to excuse myself, getting close enough to smell something like wet wood, they remained where they stood, absorbed by their own voices. Dreams still clung to them—I could see it in the way they shaved every morning, how they crossed their legs like folds of paper.

The Lava Lounge is where I'd find my boss dancing alone, his long, greasy hair let loose in the fluorescent light. The first time I saw him at the Lava Lounge he was sitting in a cloud of smoke with a group of soldiers, a woman with tattooed eyebrows, and a park ranger named Kelly. He wore a military uniform and had his hair tied back in a neon scrunchie.

"So what was it like? What was it like when you got shot in the face?" Will asked one of the soldiers wearing a gold earring. The soldier smiled, and the scar, looking like a wad of chewed gum, pulsed like it was alive. He told everyone it was like dying but not in that way, another way, like something that you didn't know was there had died inside you, and you miss it even though you aren't really sure what it was or if it was there at all.

Tattooed eyebrows said "bullshit." She took a drag, went to piss.

A soldier at the table with crow-colored hair sat quietly and drank his beer, looking into his bottle before each sip. He asked what I was doing, and then we drank together and three songs played, and then I fell in love and we decided to climb Mauna Loa. That night I imagined our bodies together on the top of the volcano, my feet facing the ocean, his facing the sky.

His name was Luke and he was twenty-three years old and a soldier at the Pohakuloa Training Area just outside of Volcanoes National Park.

There are 45,000 military personnel in Hawaii. Most of the military bases used during WWII have been converted into training grounds. The Pohakuloa Training Area (PTA) is the largest in Hawaii and it's used year-round for aircraft and ground-troop training by all branches of the U.S. military. They use rifles, mortars, and howitzers in what the local paper terms "the closest approximation to combat short of war." Near the PTA, on the slopes of Mauna Kea, is the Bradshaw Army Airfield Facility, which supports the 25th Infantry Division and its associate units: Wheeler and Schofield Barracks, the Hawaiian Army National Guard Hilo, and the 45th Support Group.

While I was on the beach running sunscreen up my leg, people died around me. I read the articles in the *Hawaiian Tribune*: Soldier killed, three injured when a hand grenade exploded during a night training accident at Schofield. A soldier with the 65th Battalion killed and four injured when a mistake was made rigging two bangalore torpedoes at the PTA. Six soldiers killed and eleven injured when two Black Hawk helicopters collided during a night training exercise. Etc.

They died before they even went to war. Some of them dying in ways no one knew you could die. Maybe that was the whole point.

When I was in the field, sitting in my pink-striped lawn chair or crouched in the bushes counting turtle eggs, I thought about Luke, the soldier. I'd often imagine that I was with him on the training ground, that my cot was a real military cot, and that at night I would lift my headlamp not to illuminate a turtle but a face, pale in the dark. I wondered if he was also awake night after night in the darkness, not knowing why he was here.

When I was a kid my family lived in Kaneohe Bay, Oahu, and our neighbor was a retired military officer. He was a muscular old man but for a heavy, swollen gut. Sometimes I would see him standing in his lawn following the glint of distant planes landing at the Kaneohe Bay Marine Air Station.

One summer he had a garage sale and he sold me a knife, a box of war movies, and a wristband that said ROCK. I wore the wristband around my bicep and started telling people my name was ROCK. Sometimes at night, from my bedroom window, I would spy on him. If I was lucky I would see him moving from each yolk-colored room to the other, lifting things, kicking the air, dancing as if in combat. I watched him as I would watch an adult film I did not understand.

To save the turtles we had to kill mongooses: packs of them that lived in the dunes. The first time I killed a mongoose I was at a beach called Apua Point. The beach was all black sand and black water. A volcano in the distance seeped and glowed red at night. I was with Will and two girls: Cam, short and butch, and Jess, just the opposite. Cam said she once saw a mongoose eating a baby turtle: it was red and soft like a piece of cherry pie.

We set up twenty cages on the dune and baited them with tuna fish and cat food. At night I heard the cages falling one by one, a metallic clank followed by quiet screams. In the morning, when the sky was pink and the ocean looked solid and hard we put on our boots and climbed the rocky dunes. Will was wearing one of his Desert Storm hats and an un-shaven beard that went all the way down his neck.

He found the first mongoose and called us all over to look at it. He stood over the animal with his leg bent, his back straight.

He showed me how to kill it properly. I needed to put on the special leather gloves and keep a finger on the metal re-lease switch as I lifted the cage into a white garbage bag. He showed me which way to turn the orange knob on the carbon dioxide tank, where to place the long black tube that fed the gas into the bag.

I turned on the tank and the mongoose reached a hand against the bag as if to remind me of its form. The bag grew and I wanted to sympathize with the mongoose, imagining my lungs filling with the stale gas, but Will paced around me, checked his watch, and when I looked into the bag five minutes later the mongoose was curled and taken by gravity.

I killed ten mongooses before I saw my first turtle. It was as big as me and completely black. Colonies of other creatures lived in its shell. When I found the turtle I waited until it was halfway up the beach and then got down on my stomach and crawled over the black sand, following it into the bushes where it nested. I watched by the light of my headlamp as she buried hundreds of plum-sized eggs beneath the earth. When she finished, taking care to cover each egg with sand, I wrapped her small head in a towel and held her jaw closed as I pushed myself onto her wet back. She dragged me towards the ocean while I punctured each flipper, leaving her with a metal tracking number.

Sometimes people would appear in the middle of the night and find us on lawn chairs watching the ocean. I imagined that for some time they waited and observed us from the shadows: the way the metal legs of our chairs sank heavily into the sand, how through the faded pink stripes of the lawn chair they might have been able to discern the silhouette of our torsos, the bend of our legs. They must have watched how we spoke, how we moved, what we ate and drank, how we dealt with boredom. Eventually they emerged and walked onto the sand and said something casual.

Once a group of soldiers came to our camp in the morning when we were still sleeping. I woke up and they were sitting among us. They wanted some of our water and we gave it to them. As a way of saying thank you, one of the soldiers climbed a palm tree, cut down a coconut with a machete and carried it to us. He rolled up his sleeves. He made lunging motions. Then he smashed the coconut with a machete, and when it opened, white and clean like a bloodless wound, he poured rum inside each half and passed it around the camp.

One soldier named Edwin didn't really say anything when he came to our camp at night. Sometimes we would wake up and he would be sleeping among us, tangled in a hammock between two palms like an insect caught in a gossamer of thread. He was tall, corpse-thin, and wore delicate glasses that he was always cleaning. He said he was just checking on things, monitoring the beaches. Every once in a while we would be hiking, sweating among the black rocks and bleak sky, feeling our bones dry and our muscles eat themselves, and he would lap us, walk right by us whistling a tune, and then disappear back into the heat from which he came.

Everything became monotonous. The flies that covered our bodies, the ants in the water jugs. Usually I just tried not to pass out from the heat. I started to forget about the turtles and why I was there and I remember one time I killed a mongoose and I was surprised at the thrill I felt looking inside the cage. I buried it in the ground and put a rock on top of it.

I didn't hear from the soldier for weeks and then he called me on the emergency cell phone. He said the Mauna Loa plans were still on. We met at the Lava Lounge on an empty night when the sky was clear and the air was even a little bit cold. At the bar, insects swarmed the ceiling. They left their oily casings piled in the corners, in the ashtrays, the curved rims of plastic lamps.

Will was with the military guys on the red leather couches whispering things to the Lava Lounge girls. They were dark-skinned girls: Filipino, Indonesian, African, Chinese. I watched their mouths open, their heads fall back. There was a young Japanese girl wearing a muumuu made of purple-and-white fabric, her lashes matted from humidity and laughter. I watched my boss watch her take a shot, thinking about her delicate brown neck. Her body defined and damp. Later that night, I found the white petals of her lei pressed in seat cushions, floating on the wet bathroom floor.

The only time I met Luke outside the Lava Lounge was when we went swimming at a pool that was about 200 degrees and tucked into a swampy area right next to the ocean. It steamed and made everyone swimming inside look ghostly and old. The pool was surrounded by mango trees that left their yellow fruit to stain and rot the cement. I hoped that when we jumped in we would disappear into the steam and then into the sky so he wouldn't have to go to war but we didn't because when we stepped into the water we just looked pale and human.

When he arrived, the bartender sat atop her bamboo stool and stared at us, eating small pieces of pineapple. I could see the yellow pulp in her teeth. He ordered bourbon. I flattened a napkin across my lap and ordered the same. But we didn't talk about Mauna Loa because last night his friend was shot by a machine gun. He's fine, he told me. It got him in the arm.

We held each other in the red light of the Lava Lounge and I pressed my nose into his shoulder, smelling the fabric of his uniform. For a time, I let him touch me, let his hand work up my thigh. I knew we wouldn't climb Mauna Loa. He knew he might not be back, and he told me this, and I realized that it didn't matter because he was already somewhere else.

When the eggs hatched in late summer, Will led us to a nest marked by white coral. He showed us a turtle, just born, wilted and brown like a dishrag, half-buried in the sand. It took hours to push itself out. Hundreds followed. We counted them, we took notes. They were covered in mucus, eyes shut. Some died on the way to the ocean, some died when they dived into the water breaking their necks in the waves. A mongoose came and took the smallest ones away. I got up to help the stranded turtles but Will told me that wasn't protocol so I just sat on the beach and watched them die and began to understand why Will was here, why he always wore a uniform and said things like "over and out," and made us sleep on the black beaches along the Kilauea lava flow for nights and days waiting for the turtles. I thought about the uniform heavy on his back, how it must have seeped into his skin, molded his face, his eyes, the way he spoke. I thought about the soldiers and how the uniform gives them a sense of moment, of being. How it let them look someone in the eye with blood all over his face and smile and say *it will be O.K.*

✺ ✺ ✺

Jen Percy grew up in the high desert of central Oregon where much of her childhood was spent listening to Garth Brooks and eating T-bone steaks. Her most recent adventure took her to Serbia and Bosnia-Herzegovina where she wrote about the influence of aphorisms on post-war identity. Currently, she is an MFA candidate at the University of Iowa's Nonfiction Writing Program. Her essays have appeared in such magazines as The Atlantic, The Indiana Review, The Literary Review, *and* Brevity, *among others. She has received scholarships from the Bread Loaf Writers' Conference, the Iowa Arts Foundation, the Stanley Foundation, and the University of Iowa Museum of Art.*

Acknowledgments

Introduction by William Dalrymple published with permission from the author. Adapted from an essay which originally appeared in the *Guardian* on September 19, 2009. Copyright © 2010 by William Dalrymple.

"Saigon Trio" by Richard Sterling published with permission from the author. Copyright © 2010 by Richard Sterling.

"Stuck in Bulawayo" by Laura Lee P. Huttenbach published with permission from the author. Copyright © 2010 by Laura Lee P. Huttenbach.

"A Dugout Canoe in the Darien Gap" by Martin Douglas Mitchinson was first published as four stories—"A Dugout Canoe in Darien," "Carajo!," "Butterflies," and "Afraid of the Dark"—in *The Darien Gap: Travels in the Rainforest of Panama* by Martin Mitchinson, Harbour Publishing, 2008, www.harbourpublishing.com. Published with permission from the author and Harbour Publishing. Copyright © 2008 by Martin Douglas Mitchinson.

"Epiphany of a Middle-Aged Pilgrim in Tea-Stained Pajamas" by Peter Wortsman first appeared in *The Brooklyn Rail: Critical Perspectives on Arts, Politics, and Culture* in October 2006. Published with permission from the author. Copyright © 2006 by Peter Wortsman.

"A Viking Repast" by Cameron M. Smith published with permission from the author. Copyright © 2010 by Cameron M. Smith.

"Bored Japanese Housewives" by Phil Goldman previously appeared in a different form on Nerve.com in October 2009. Published with permission from the author. Copyright © 2009 by Phil Goldman.

"*Kaptein, Span die Seile*" by Brian Eckert published with permission from the author. Copyright © 2010 by Brian Eckert.